THE CLEVE

WRITING SPORTS SERIES
Richard "Pete" Peterson, Editor

THE
CLEVELAND
INDIANS

FRANKLIN LEWIS

The Kent State University Press

KENT, OHIO

© 2006 by The Kent State University Press, Kent, Ohio 44242
All rights reserved.
Library of Congress Catalog Card Number 2006002387
ISBN-13: 978-0-87338-885-6
ISBN-10: 0-87338-885-2
Manufactured in the United States of America
10 09 08 07 06   5 4 3 2 1

Library of Congress Cataloging-in-Publication Data

Lewis, Franklin A.
The Cleveland Indians / Franklin Lewis.
p. cm. — (Writing sports series)
Originally published: New York: G. P. Putnam's Sons, 1949,
with a new foreword by Russell Schneider.
Includes index.
ISBN-13: 978-0-87338-885-6 (pbk. : alk. paper) ∞
ISBN-10: 0-87338-885-2 (pbk. : alk. paper) ∞
1. Cleveland Indians (Baseball team)—History. I. Title. II. Series.
GV875.C7L48   2006
796.357'64'0977132—dc22   2006002387

British Library Cataloging-in-Publication data are available.

TO VIRGINIA

COAUTHOR IN TRIBULATIONS AND INSPIRATION
IF NOT IN NAME

CONTENTS

FOREWORD

FRANKLIN "WHITEY" LEWIS, WHO AUTHORED this first history of the Cleveland Indians, was something of an enigma; that is, "He was the team's best friend and its severest critic," as was written in his obituary upon his death in 1958.

Lewis "mercilessly panned the booboos and boners of managers, players and the front office, always demanding better baseball for the 'Joes and Josephines,'" the typical fans of Cleveland who read his columns—and they clung to every word he wrote.

Whitey, so nicknamed because of his shock of blond hair, was the sports editor and columnist of the *Cleveland Press,* which in the 1940s and '50s was the city's dominant newspaper, in no small part due to the presence of Lewis in its sports pages.

But unrelenting critic that he was when the situation demanded, Lewis also was thrilled with, and doted on, those same Indians—as did his Joes and Josephines—when the team did well, especially in 1948.

That was two years after the arrival of dynamic owner Bill Veeck, when he, with the outstanding play of manager-shortstop Lou Boudreau, fashioned what was thought to be the start of a "Golden Era" of baseball in Cleveland. It was in 1948 that the Indians won their first pennant and World Series in twenty-eight years, only their second in the forty-eight-year history of the franchise, which had been a charter member of the American League.

It was Veeck himself who best identified Whitey's Joes and Josephines. "They were the guys and the gals who went to baseball games, who bought tickets one at a time and worked hard for a living, not the people who buy season tickets," Veeck was quoted. "Whitey wrote in a language the cab driver could understand, his own language. And because of it, he was a friend to people who had never met him—and I'm delighted to say he was my friend, too."

The late Frank Gibbons, who replaced Lewis as the sports columnist of the *Press,* wrote, "If Whitey could be called back, he would admit that he was a Joe many times himself. A Joe Fan. The kind who had such affection for sports he couldn't help yelling out loud when things weren't right."

Lewis was fifty-four when he died of a heart attack on March 12, 1958, while covering the Indians in spring training in Tucson, Arizona.

He'd been an athlete himself—a very good athlete as a young man—which undoubtedly provided him with rare insight as a sportswriter. Growing up in Cleveland, Lewis attended Glenville High School, where he played basketball and was an all-league halfback in football. One of his football teammates was a sophomore named Bennie Friedman, the same Bennie Friedman who went on to become a three-time All-America tailback at the University of Michigan and later a star for several teams in the National Football League and then a college and NFL coach. "And to think," Lewis often quipped, slightly stretching the truth, "that in high school Bennie Friedman was my substitute."

Whitey also was a catcher for teams in Cleveland's top sandlot baseball leagues, a competitive swimmer and lifeguard, and an amateur boxer. As a high school youth in Cleveland, Whitey peddled ice during his summer vacations. One of his pool-playing pals who also grew up on Cleveland's East Side was movie star–comedian Bob Hope, with whom he shared a lifetime of genial wise-cracking. It was his football ability that won Lewis a scholarship to Purdue University, though he dropped out of college and became a professional acrobat for a brief period.

But it wasn't only sports in which Whitey was proficient; he also wrote and had published several songs (including "My Virginia Rose," 1932; "My Baby's Comin' Home," 1933; and "Sweetest Hour of All," 1935) and perceived himself as a singer and actor, though he never did so professionally.

Lewis dropped out of Purdue after his freshman year (freshmen were not eligible for intercollegiate athletics then) and went to Florida in 1925, where he used his swimming ability to get a job as the chief lifeguard at Daytona Beach. He also decided to try his hand at writing about athletes, instead of trying to be one, and worked for newspapers in Daytona Beach, Miami, and Orlando before returning to Cleveland in 1929.

He was hired by the *Press* as its boxing writer, wrote a column called "Knockout," and also covered the Indians, college football, and hockey. Eventually he became the newspaper's assistant sports editor.

Eight years later Lewis left the *Press,* tired of what he then called "the newsprint racket," and became a sportscaster on Cleveland's then-premier radio station, WGAR. But the "newsprint racket" beckoned again, and Whitey returned to the *Press* as its sports columnist in 1939 and held that position for the next nineteen years, until his untimely death.

It was Lewis's ability to relate to sports fans that established him as a great columnist. To Lewis, baseball existed primarily for the public and his constant column cry was to "give the game back to the fans—the Joes and Josephines."

The late Larry Atkins, a sport promoter in Cleveland and longtime friend of Lewis and often his target of criticism, recalled, "Whitey used to say that an umpire calls a strike the way he sees it. And while the batter and the fans might not like it, Whitey said he wanted to write the same way, and he did. Cleveland was his town. I grew up with him and I know how he felt about it. When the Indians won the playoff game for the pennant in 1948, Whitey was in the middle of the celebration and somebody asked him if it wasn't great. 'I'd rather be back in Cleveland, celebrating with the Joes and Josephines.'"

It was always Lewis's intention to do everything he could to right what he considered to be wrong. It was that determination that resulted in a major change at the *old* Municipal Stadium in Cleveland and also with the city's beaches and recreational area alongside Lake Erie.

It was Lewis's proposal to construct an inner fence at the Stadium, which had been built in 1932 and whose outfield dimensions were so extreme that Babe Ruth once declared in desperation that "you need a damn horse to play the outfield in this place." Whitey said he wanted an "honest ball park," and though it took three baseball seasons, he—and his Joes and Josephines—finally got it. On April 17, 1947, Veeck had what he called "the Lewis Fence" installed. It remained until the Indians moved out of the Stadium and into their new ballpark, Jacobs Field, in 1994.

It was also Lewis's tireless crusade to "clean up the lakefront" so that his Joes and Josephines could use it for swimming and other recreation that finally resulted in it being done. He also battled for "an even break for horse bettors." He teed off on "unfair pari-mutuel odds" and eventually won an adjustment. "If a sucker's gonna be a sucker," he wrote in his inimitable style in his "Mutterings by the Monday Muse" column, "at least he ought to get an even break."

Athletes, even those he criticized on occasion, had great respect for Whitey, as the late Bob Lemon, a Hall of Fame pitcher, said at the time of Lewis's demise: "He was our kind of fellow. He got around among players and found out what they really thought."

One of Lewis's peers, Hal Lebovitz, a 2000 recipient of the Baseball Hall of Fame's J. G. Taylor Spink Award, remembers Lewis as "a wordsmith and a real puncher . . . a hard-hitting guy who was always interesting and very colorful. He was a Cleveland version of Damon Runyon. Whitey not only wrote about characters, he was a character himself."

And Bob August, who was executive sports editor of the *Press* under Lewis, called him "a dynamic guy who was well known around the country and well-respected in the [writers] fraternity for his toughness, and his integrity." August related a humorous anecdote about Lewis, which portrays another side of the columnist's confrontational and colorful nature:

[In the 1940s] Whitey was very close to Nate Dolin, who was a minority partner of Veeck's in the ownership of the Indians. The two of them, Lewis and Dolin, hatched an idea to buy the San Francisco 49ers [then a member of the All-America Football Conference] from Tony Morabito. The plan was that Dolin would buy the team and Whitey would run it.

Before any of us [at the *Press*] heard anything about it, a wire service broke the story, but we couldn't locate Whitey for confirmation because he was out of town. There we were, beaten on a story in which our own sports editor was one of the principals. You can imagine how embarrassing that was.

When we finally found out when Whitey was going to return to Cleveland, we sent a reporter to the airport to meet him. When he got off the plane and was confronted with the question, he said, "No comment." Can you believe it? The sports editor of the *Press* stiffing us a no comment!

But that's the way Whitey was. You never knew what to expect.

Another time, according to August,

One of our writers was in one of the downtown restaurants where all the sports figures hung out. He went into the men's room and never saw what hit him . . . but somebody did. And hard. The poor guy was knocked cold.

When he finally came to, a mob-type guy told him, "The guy who hit you made a mistake. He thought you were Whitey Lewis and didn't like something [Lewis] wrote."

If it had been Whitey, you can be sure he wouldn't have backed off. He was tough as hell, and when he saw something that he thought was wrong, he said it and didn't care who didn't like it. And stood up to anybody who didn't like it.

There were no ivory towers for Lewis. He was everywhere —in the dugouts, in the clubhouses, in the bleachers, at ringside, in the front offices—and after he soaked it all up he had his opinion and wrote it, pulling no punches. He was aggressive and tough, and nobody pushed him around. But he also was fair. And when he was critical of anybody, he always made himself available the next day to defend his opinion.

Among the tributes paid Lewis upon his death was the following by Veeck, who'd often been a target of Whitey's criticism as well as the recipient of his praise: "He was a good friend of mine, an awfully good friend. But when he thought I was playing cute or getting off base, he rapped my knuckles good—

then we went out to dinner together." Louie B. Seltzer, the late editor of the *Press,* who brought Lewis back to Cleveland in 1929, said, "Whitey loved life, and people, and events, and wanted always to be a part of everything that was happening. And he was. He was not only one of the best of the sports editors in the business, he was one of the best by a standard any of us ever applies to any man."

Read and enjoy this first history of the Cleveland Indians, by Franklin "Whitey" Lewis, who told it better than anyone could.

And, Lewis said so well on the final page, "Baseball in Cleveland started in 1946 when the common people's beloved burr head—William Louis Veeck, Jr.—arrived. It may have started earlier, but it never really got going good until then."

RUSSELL SCHNEIDER

ACKNOWLEDGMENTS

ONE OF THE RICHER REWARDS in being a newspaperman is the opportunity to meet other newspapermen. No amount of research *solus* could turn up the facts, anecdotes, and delicate intimacies vital to a narration of eighty years in baseball.

My fellow scribes leaned far back from their own typewriters to lend a thought in this compilation of diamond lore. To them—Ed Bang, Gordon Cobbledick, Ed McAuley, and Frank Gibbons—I give them the highest accolade of our craft, "Nice going." The late Henry P. Edwards provided, in countless conversations and in treasured written recollections, much of the humanness I have attempted to depict between batting averages and final standings.

To Bob Godley and his sharp knowledge of old-time baseball, to Gordon Thayer of the Cleveland Public Library and his intense interest in baseball history, to Marshall Samuel and others of the Cleveland Indians' current staff who dispense news and figures so willingly, and to numberless giants of the national sport including Lou Boudreau, Tris Speaker, Alva Bradley, Steve O'Neill, Bill Veeck, Roger Peckinpaugh, Cy Young, Jack Graney, Mel Harder, and Bob Feller, I bow in gratefulness.

From side whiskers to side shows, nameless fans have determined the course of baseball. This book is for them, and may they enjoy the reading as much as I have enjoyed the writing.

FRANKLIN LEWIS

ILLUSTRATIONS

THE CLEVELAND INDIANS

C H A P T E R   I

TALE OF TWO MISSIONARIES

It was a long time between missionaries along the banks of the Cuyahoga River, a stream that crawls circuitously southward from Lake Erie, yet millions of Ohio's baseball-happy citizens are convinced the 150-year interval must have been the handiwork of fate.

The Rev. John Heckewelder, a Moravian come to soothe the primitive instincts of Indians of half a dozen tribes, put foot on the glittering lake sand in 1796 and addressed his few, faithful, and fearful followers:

"Bless us, Cuyahoga will be a place of great importance."

The reverend was only guessing, because there was no Cleveland spreading upward from the junction of the Cuyahoga and the lake, and there were no steel monsters carrying iron ore passing in the harbor with the frequency of waiters shuttling about during the evening dinner hour.

But he was an expert prophet, as it turned out, because in 1946 a modernized missionary named Bill Veeck arrived to bring an unprecedented importance and popularity to the water-front area.

Veeck began immediately, in his new role as president of the Cleveland Indians of the American League, to arrest the economic crumbling of the world's biggest baseball arena. He went forth to woo a recalcitrant baseball public. Within a matter of weeks, he had gained assurance from frequent assemblages of seventy-five thousand fascinated fans that they approved of his efforts to make the mouth of the Cuyahoga a community of tremendous importance in sport as well as in the industries that serve as vertebrae for Cleveland's spine.

Only a few rods to the east, not much farther away than the distance of a Babe Ruth home run from Rev. Heckewelder's beach encampment, there was built the twin-tiered horseshoe

3

of concrete known formally as Cleveland Stadium. To this mecca pilgrims now travel by air, land, water, and foot to comprise the grand army of fans of the Indians, field champions of baseball for 1948 and turnstile champions of baseball for all years.

There are numerous fractures in the historical line that connects these relative occurrences on the southernmost tip of the Great Lakes. Baseball in Cleveland did not have its beginning on the packed sands of the beach, for example. The game itself rolled around the city's spreading saucer of humanity for almost eighty years before arriving back on the rim of Lake Erie.

Various parks were established on the East Side, some of them not much more than scraped surfaces previously dedicated to such basic exercises as grazing and gardening. But the trail of dollars, ballplayers, fans, disappointments, dismissed managers, and championships led back to the lake front, known as the rumpus room of Cleveland's mammoth industrial house.

As president of the Indians, as ringmaster of a show without equal in sports, Bill Veeck preaches a doctrine of entertainment. He tries to reach the largest total of people with his evangelism, which is innately only a love for the game he has followed from the more wondrous inner sanctum of the official baseball family since boyhood, his father having been in turn a sports writer and later president of the Chicago Cubs of the National League.

What the younger Veeck would have done to lure a monstrous audience in 1869 is subject to conjecture, but he probably would have thought then that the two thousand curious residents of Cleveland who fringed a makeshift baseball diamond comprised a tremendous and excitable congregation.

Those 2,000 were assembled on what was known as Case Commons, the first of five parks in which Cleveland's professional baseball teams were to perform. Around Case Commons, an unfenced expanse located on Putnam Avenue (now East 38th Street) between Scovil and Central Avenues, were ringed the gentlemen and ladies drawn by the prospect of watching the already nationally famous Cincinnati Red Stockings play.

Their opponents were the Cleveland Forest Citys who, on this bright June 2, 1869, were forsaking the ranks of the ama-

4

teurs to speculate in the market of professionalized baseball. It was a gamble because play-for-pay was not accepted in the better social circles without the lifting of cultured eyebrows.

The Forest Citys were not, as it happened, a 100-per-cent professional team. They had been, in their formation the year previous—1868—a gentleman's varsity. Various forms of baseball had been played in Cleveland, but the concentrated brand was still restricted to comparatively few localities. Such teams as Hoboken, Washington, and Cincinnati got a head start on Cleveland prior to 1869, though in that year the National Association repealed a clause that prohibited play for money.

Even so, four members of the Forest Citys decided to remain sportingly pure; third baseman A. R. "Pikey" Smith, shortstop Eben Smith, center fielder Art Burt, and second baseman L. C. Hanna preferred to play without compensation. They had performed with the amateur Forest Citys of 1868. When the switch to a pro team was made in the ensuing winter, most of the amateur team was dropped and replaced by out-and-out pros.

Perhaps the most famous of these was the catcher, Jim White, one of the first of the .300 batters. Later Jim moved on to Boston to become the personal catcher of the immortal A. G. Spalding. Richest of the Forest Citys in social graces and rank was Hanna, brother of United States Senator Marcus A Hanna. The infielder, a strapping, handsome man, was the father of Leonard C. Hanna, currently one of Cleveland's leaders in society and commerce.

The other Forest City regulars—in fact, the roster included only nine players—were pitcher Art Pratt, first baseman Art Allison, center fielder John Reiley, and left fielder Johnny Ward. These and the amateurs previously mentioned had accepted a challenge by the Red Stockings, who, themselves, had just turned professional and had embarked on a nationwide tour.

They were the ruthless, powerful, crunching Dempseys of their period. A Cincinnati rival, the Buckeyes, dared to oppose the Red Stockings who had imported such noted stars as George Wright, Harry Wright, and the fabulous John Hatfield, owner of the strongest throwing arm known. The Red Stockings out-

5

classed the Buckeyes and the losers were so discouraged they moved out of town en masse.

The Forest Citys had an inkling of their fate in the reports of the early games on the Red Stockings' tour. The Great Westerns were beaten 45 to 9, the strong Kekiongas of Fort Wayne 86 to 8. The Red Stockings swamped the Antiochs at Yellow Springs, 41 to 7, and followed with two similarly discouraging defeats of Kekionga, this time 41 to 7, and Mansfield, 48-14. Then it was time for the Red Stockings to visit Cleveland. The team arrived at 10:30 on the morning of the game and the players were hauled in special rigs through lines of gaping fans to the Weddell House, then the Ritz-Carlton of Ohio. The Forest Citys were not only opponents of the Red Stockings, they were hosts to the downstate players, and in style worthy of the social standing of several members of the Cleveland team, the visitors were accorded courtesies fit for kings.

"If this is what professional baseball will be like every place, I'm certainly glad I'm in it," declared the Cincinnati first baseman, Charles Gould, an extremely agile and pleasant young fellow.

The Red Stockings arrived at the park in their private and spacious horse-drawn bus and looked upon a carnival scene. There was a covered stand that extended in a small quarter circle around the home-plate portion of the field. But most of the two thousand fans were in rigs or standing behind ropes.

Admission to the grounds was twenty-five cents for pedestrians and fifty cents for rigs. However, members of the Cleveland Baseball Association, sponsor of the Forest Citys, were admitted without charge. Whether they paid or were franked in, the spectators revealed universal interest in the uniforms of the Red Stockings.

For the first time, players had adopted the knickerbocker type of trouser. Expanses of cardinal-red stockings showed between knee and shoetop. The Forest Citys were a close second in the sartorial race in their white pantaloons and bright blue stockings.

But, alas, any competition by the Cleveland team ended on a fashion note. Only a smashing home run by Burt, the center

6

fielder, offered a bright ray in the gloom on Cleveland's near East Side that sunny afternoon. The final score was 25 to 6. Incidentally, the Forest Citys did much better with the Red Stockings later that summer, a second game ending with the Cincinnati team on top by the football score of 43 to 20.

By way of proving that they were an offense-minded aggregation, the Forest Citys played a couple of other high-score contests in 1869, losing to the Eckfords of Brooklyn, 41 to 27, but splitting with the Haymakers of Troy, New York, in a pair of games in which the total of four scores was 109 runs!

Perhaps such scores provided the impelling force for an editorial in *DeWitt's Baseball Guide for 1869,* edited by M. J. Kelly of the *New York Herald Tribune.* Preached baseball reporter Kelly: "Any man now desirous of using his physical and mental powers to their utmost advantage must ignore first, intemperance in eating, and second, refuse to allow a drop of alcoholic liquor whether in the form of spirits, wine, beer, or cider, to pass down his throat."

The shoe, or the bottle, went on the other foot the next year when the Atlantic Club of Brooklyn dropped into Cleveland for a game. It was on May 17, 1870, and their only excuse must have been that the Atlantics had had a rough overland journey.

At the close of the fifth inning, the Forest Citys were leading, 132 to 1. In the first inning, Cleveland scored fifty-two runs and beat that total with fifty-four in the third. The Forest Citys' total of 101 safe hits good for 180 bases never has been equaled. Whether that game went the scheduled nine innings has not been established. It is presumed the scorekeeper swooned from exhaustion in the sixth inning, because there is no record of play thereafter.

IN THE BIG LEAGUE

EARLY IN MARCH 1871 Cleveland joined with Boston, Brooklyn, New York, Philadelphia, Washington, Troy, Chicago, Fort Wayne, and Rockford to form the National Association of Baseball Players, the first out-and-out professional league in history. The Cleveland team still was known as the Forest Citys, but there was no monopoly on the nickname. The Rockford, Illinois, club also was known as the Forest Citys and there was considerable confusion in the limited editorial space the press of that era allotted to the newfangled game of baseball.

Even so, two years of the sport had whetted the appetite of Cleveland fans and there was tremendous excitement in the rapidly expanding lake shipping center upon announcement that Cleveland finally was in the big league. There was considerable rain that spring, and much difficulty was experienced in assembling the team to practice.

Too, the star catcher, Jim White, was busy being the star of his own wedding in Indiana that April. He wrote J. F. Evans, the new manager of the Forest Citys, that he would be unable to report for spring practice on time. Jim's brother, Elmer, an outfielder, was best man and he, too, was late in reporting.

However, a team was finally assembled for the opening game on May 4 at Fort Wayne. After seven scoreless innings, both teams broke out in a rash of base hits with the Forest Citys finally winning, 14 to 12. The Clevelands moved on to Chicago, but the fire of 1871 had destroyed a new baseball park there, so the Cleveland and Chicago teams traveled to Cleveland to open the home season on May 11.

That day probably was the most important in the history of Cleveland baseball. As a starter, the Forest Citys had been provided a new park, the city's second for professional purposes, located at Willson and Garden Streets, only a few blocks

8

removed from the first playground. For the first time a sale of season reserved seats, now accepted as an adjunct to operation of a big-league franchise, was put into practice, and many fans flocked to the store of Rawson and Pratts on the Public Square to get choice locations.

Purchasers were advised of two plans for the newfangled season tickets.

"If only for yourself, the cost will be six dollars for the season," the store clerks informed an eager populace. "But if you wish to bring a lady, there is a special deal available ... only ten dollars for you, your lady, and your carriage." The carriage or rig could be pulled up to a specified location behind first or third base and there would be no necessity for stepping down to the turf at any time.

There was considerable skepticism apparent among the sporting bloods of the year, however, not toward the purchase of tickets but in regard to the new league itself. Hence, only about a thousand persons put in an appearance for the game with the Chicago squad. Yet that thousand received one of the treats of all time in Cleveland baseball.

First, the Forest Citys appeared in what might be described best as musical-comedy raiment. They wore white shirts with blue trimming, blue hose, and blue belt, russet leather shoes, laced tightly to the ankles, of course, and on each shirt was a huge monogram of the Cleveland Forest Citys.

Second, the game was destined to end in a riot. One of the rules of the new professional league dealt with the selection of umpires. The league had not been in operation long enough to provide for trained arbiters, and, besides, the day of the first professional umpire was still far distant.

Under the rules of the National Association, the umpires were selected in this manner: the visiting team submitted a list of five men to the home team. The home team was thus entitled to select the umpire from the first nominees.

The Chicago team did not come unprepared. They had brought along a sports writer of the *Chicago Times* named James L. Haynie. It just so happened that Mr. Haynie had had experience in umpiring and it so happened, also, that his name was one of the five submitted to the Forest Citys.

"Why not let Haynie umpire?" asked the Chicago captain. The Forest Citys, new in baseball and naïve, agreed immediately and in the greatest of innocence. When the Cleveland team awoke to the rooking they were getting, it was too late.

The climax came in the eighth inning, after a wild time in the sixth. The teams were tied, 6 to 6, after five innings. In the top of the sixth, the Forest Citys engineered a double play on a grounder to the third baseman Sutton, who stepped on the third-base bag to force one runner before throwing the ball to the first baseman, Carleton, for what seemed to be a simple out. But Umpire Haynie, running toward first, ruled the base runner safe, and before the third out could be posted the visitors had scored five runs.

In the eighth inning, Haynie ruled against the Forest Citys for the sixth time in the afternoon, or so they thought. Haynie picked on the Cleveland left fielder and captain, Jim Pabor, to call out at third base. Pabor protested strenuously to Haynie, but the hand-picked umpire stood his ground. Then Pabor walked over to the Cleveland bench to talk to Manager Evans.

"We're taking our team off the field," Evans and Pabor advised Haynie. "We'll appeal your decisions and the final score to the National Association."

And with that fast speech, the Forest Citys withdrew to leave the White Stockings from Chicago with an 18 to 10 verdict in an eight-inning game.

A historian describes the final scene, shortly after the eighth inning, in the following quaint and probably careful language: "After the Forest Citys had quit the game, everybody swarmed on the field and talked to their heart's content."

So was established, at least, a pattern for the many league games to be played in Cleveland in the next seventy-eight years. A few of those did conclude in riotous scenes and disorder, but no such situation was again created by the importation of a partisan umpire or, at least, one who confessed his allegiance in advance.

Whether this event was a harbinger of failure for organized baseball in Cleveland is a matter of opinion, but there was no professional or amateur team representing the city in national competition from 1873 through 1875, though the Forest Citys had struggled through the 1871 and 1872 seasons, even playing mixed schedules in the professional and amateur circuits.

The instability of the sport in several cities was reflected in a general unrest in the league and so the Forest Citys were disbanded, but not without first serving a very useful purpose to the sports-writing fraternity.

Prior to 1871, the box scores of games were divided into two parts, one for batting and one for fielding. No averages were used in either category, though total chances at the bat and in the field were listed. The scoring of runs was much more important to the authors of the day than base hits.

Then Henry Chadwick, a noted baseball writer of the era, originated a condensed system of totaling and detailing the batting and fielding deeds of both teams in any one game. So far as is known, the Chadwick system was introduced in a game played at Fort Wayne between the home Kekiongas and the Cleveland Forest Citys.

Following is the copy of the first box score of its kind, one that is easy to follow because it is, to all intents and purposes, the box score as reproduced in today's daily newspapers:

Forest Citys	R.	1b.	PO.	A.	Kekiongas	R.	1b.	PO.	A.
J. White, c	0	3	9	0	Williams, 3db	0	2	2	0
Kimball, 2db	0	0	4	0	Mathrews, p	0	0	1	0
Pabor, lf	0	0	0	0	Foran, 1b	0	1	2	0
Allison, cf	0	1	2	0	Goldsmith, ss	0	0	3	1
E. White, rf	0	0	1	0	Lennon, c	1	1	9	1
Pratt, p	0	0	1	0	Carey, 2db	0	0	4	0
Sutton, 3db	0	1	0	1	Mincher, lf	0	0	4	0
Carleton, 1b	0	0	6	0	McDermott, cf	0	1	0	1
Bass, ss	0	0	1	4	Kelly, rf	1	1	2	0
Totals	0	5	24	5	Totals	2	6	27	3

Runs scored
Kekiongas   010 010 000—2
Forest Citys   000 000 000—0

Runs earned
Kekiongas   010 000 000—1
Forest Citys   000 000 000—0

First base by errors: Kekiongas 1, Forest Citys 4. Double play: by Carey 1. Umpire: Mr. J. L. Boake of the Live Oak, Cincinnati Club. Time of game: two hours.

C H A P T E R   I I I

STREETCAR MAGNATE

FIVE YEARS OF sand-lot baseball, with games played on unfenced corner lots, got under the skin of William Hollinger, a
young businessman who himself enjoyed playing the game. So
in 1878 Hollinger began the task of inducing good ballplayers,
most of them professionals at the time, to come to Cleveland.

He completed the organization of his team that summer and
in the autumn appeared at the postseason meeting of the
National League and asked for a franchise that would become
active in the spring of 1879.

There was much wrangling in the inner council of the league.
Finally, the club owners and representatives got into open war-
fare with the result there were two professional leagues formed,
one called the National League and one to be known simply as
the League.

Hollinger's franchise was granted by the latter, along with
Buffalo, so that the circuit could be expanded to eight teams.
The six that were held over from 1878 were Providence, Boston,
Syracuse, and Troy, all in the so-called Eastern division, and
Chicago and Cincinnati in the West. The latter two were
joined by Cleveland and Buffalo.

The other pro loop, the National League, went ahead with
operations based on ten teams: Albany, Rochester, Holyoke,
Manchester, Washington, New Bedford, Springfield, Utica,
Worcester, and Jersey City. Because of transportation problems, it was not always possible to move a team from city to
city according to league schedules, so several interleague games
were played, though these did not count in the final standings
of the individual organizations.

The Clevelands—once more known as the Forest Citys—
might have been better off in an amateur league, judging from
the final standings. Manager Joe Mack, who started the 1879

season with a squad of 10 men, soon encountered difficulties and ran into a string of "Chicagos," or shutout games. When a shutout was recorded, a team was considered to have "Chicagoed" the opposition. The hapless Forest Citys were geographically beaten much of the time.

The team finally wound up sixth in the field of eight with a record of twenty-four victories and fifty-three defeats, a compilation that cost Manager Mack his job. However, he was not to blame altogether if the batting averages for the year are to be considered. The leading Cleveland batter was first baseman Bill Phillips, who batted .281 and was twenty-second in the League's individual hitting list.

Still, the Clevelands might have done better except for an injury to catcher Doc Kennedy, who had two fingers broken in an early game. Manager Mack, desperate, shifted Phillips behind the plate and moved Charley Eden from right field to first. Both Phillips and Eden were outstanding for the Forest Citys, but the team lacked a spark.

Then owner Hollinger made a deal with a new pro team in Clinton, Massachusetts, for a catcher named Barney Gilligan. When Barney reported to Cleveland, the other players looked at him and agreed, "He's a catcher? Humph, he doesn't look big enough."

Gilligan was small and slender. But he was wiry, Irish, and determined. He went behind the plate for the first time in Cleveland in a game with the Chicago White Stockings to catch for Jim McCormick, a giant right-hander who was Cleveland's only pitcher. The *Cleveland Leader,* in its sparse account of the game, remarked, "The wiry, agile, little Gilligan caught the swift shoots of the big McCormick with an ease that made him a hero with the fans right from the start."

About the only other memorable feature of the season was the Forest Citys' appearance in Cleveland's third ball park, this one on Kennard (now East 46th) at Cedar. Baseball was edging to the east, following a line of commercial houses. The west sector with its expanding residential area, and the south with its sprawling factories, mills, smelters, and foundries were not considered as sites for baseball fields.

The Forest Citys played a heavier and more profitable

schedule in 1880, finishing third in the League with a mark of forty-seven victories and thirty-seven defeats, but these cold facts were dwarfed by the recording of the first perfect game pitched in organized baseball. Sadly, the Forest Citys were on the short end.

John Lee Richmond, a right-hander pitching for the Worcester team, faced the Forest Citys in the Massachusetts city the afternoon of June 12, 1880. While the Forest Citys were not the best team in the League, being topped by Chicago and Providence, certainly they were not the worst. A new manager, J. F. Evans, had taken the wreckage of the 1879 team and used it as the foundation for a new squad with a bright spirit.

But on that day Richmond was too superb even for a team as improved as the Forest Citys. When it is remembered that only six perfect games have been pitched in the history of professional baseball, Richmond's achievement takes on added stature. However, there is a question concerning the game that probably never can be answered satisfactorily. It deals with the authenticity of the retirement of twenty-seven batters consecutively.

The *New York Clipper Annual,* referring to this game, offers this account: "A contest without a base being run was unprecedented until June 12, 1880, when the Worcesters retired the Clevelands in one-two-three order nine successive times, a wild throw being the only error in this exceptional contest."

In the *Little Red Book of Major League Baseball,* a compilation of all the imaginable averages and records in the sport, Richmond's "perfect game" is the first of the six recognized. Hence, it is probably safe to assume that the wild throw was made by a Cleveland player. The score, incidentally, was 1 to 0, and it is likely that the wild throw led to the only run of the classic.

Two other incidents that occurred during the play of the 1880 Forest Citys are noteworthy. At season's end, the Clevelands were invited to New York's already famous Polo Grounds to play the New York Metropolitans, that city's first representative in organized, professional baseball. The Metropolitans were formed in September of that year, yet they beat the

Clevelands, 4 to 3, after losing the opener of a two-game series, 9 to 3. Both games were played in late October.

A tragedy, the first of many in Cleveland's baseball history, threw a pall over the Forest Citys early in the season. Al Hall, the shortstop, collided with another fielder in making a catch during a game with Cincinnati. Hall broke his leg and was forced out of baseball permanently. His continuous brooding over his retirement resulted in intense melancholia and finally in insanity. Hall died in an asylum in Warren, Pennsylvania, in 1885.

The League, as it was operated in 1880, provided a very acceptable model for later-day organizations. The eight teams for the first time went through the entire season without a club being disbanded.

Every club except Chicago lost money because of a fifty-cent tariff imposed by the league officials. Perhaps the most notable achievement of the summer was the failure of any team to be pulled off the field in protest at an umpire's decision. Prior to 1880, a disgruntled manager was apt to take his players away in their omnibus, leaving the spectators with only arguments among themselves as a source of amusement. The umpires were approved by all clubs that year; a complete schedule, including time for travel, was adopted; and it might be said literally that big-league baseball as it is known to moderns was born in 1880.

Cleveland tried eighteen different players and a new manager, J. E. Clapp, in 1881, and owner Hollinger even went so far as to hire a second pitcher to assist big Jim McCormick, he of the famous "drop ball" and the flaming red mustache. But the Forest Citys couldn't hit and finished seventh, though McCormick pitched in 59 games and allowed only 4.72 runs per game. This was not an earned-run average as are today's computations but a representation of actual runs scored, including those attributable to errors, etc.

Clapp, a part-time catcher, was succeeded by Herman Doscher in 1882. Then Cleveland baseball felt its first breath of scandal. Just what Doscher, who had umpired the previous year, did to bring him into the bad graces of the League was never revealed, but he was fired at the end of the 1882 season "for alleged dishonorable conduct."

The Forest Citys were fifth that season, a circumstance that might have had some bearing on the situation. Too, the League began to take on the bearing of a more important circuit. Troy and Worcester, finishing seventh and eighth, quit and were replaced by New York and Philadelphia.

Nothing of importance except a pair of no-hit games occurred to the Forest Citys in 1883, though there were indications that the team was disintegrating. In the first of these no-hitters, the redoubtable Charles "Hoss" Radbourne of the Providence team hung an 8-to-0 shiner on the Clevelands, but the latter gained a measure of credit in the late stages of the campaign when Hugh Dailey, who had come along to become McCormick's number-one replacement, pitched a 1-to-0 triumph over the Philadelphias without permitting the weak Easterners a hit.

If the Clevelands were in a state of confusion in 1883, they were merely reflecting the national baseball scene. For that was the first year of baseball daffiness. In Philadelphia alone, a dozen freak stunts were introduced, such as games between Chinese nines, Negro male and female teams, squads of amputees, sides composed of sixteen girls, and many other ludicrous conditions and situations.

A game was played in Chillicothe, Ohio, between combinations of old men over sixty and boys under twenty, the first all-Indian nine was formed, and six teams claimed the world Negro championship—Philadelphia, Washington, Pittsburgh, St. Louis, Cincinnati, and Cleveland.

In view of these quaint twists to the sport rage of the period, it was not surprising to the "veterans" in charge of the professional teams that an outlaw movement should take form. A Union Association came into being. It had no connection with the League or the National League, the two operating bodies in professional baseball. But its backers had money.

They lured two Cleveland players to the new St. Louis team in the Union before the 1884 season started. Second baseman Fred Dunlap and outfielder George Shaffer jumped first. In the midst of the Forest Citys' schedule, with things going from bad to worse, pitcher McCormick, shortstop J. W. Glasscock, and utility infielder Briody, ignoring their contracts with Cleveland, left the team one day and signed on with Cincinnati in the new league. The Clevelands lost heart, faded to seventh in the League, and finally submitted a resignation from the organization early in 1885. It was accepted and Cleveland was replaced by St. Louis.

"I'm going to put Cleveland back in baseball," promised Frank DeHaas Robison in the summer of 1886, "if I have to buy a team myself, sell the tickets, and haul it around in my own streetcars."

Robison, a forceful man, was not without a touch of the theater himself and the treasurer of his proposed venture was a flamboyant citizen named George W. Howe. Robison wasted little time after his inaugural speech. He sent Howe to represent him at a meeting of the American Association in December 1886. The directors of the association voted Cleveland into their fold, first dropping Pittsburgh.

Robison owned two streetcar lines, the Payne and Superior Avenue branches. Thus it was only natural for the new president of the Forest Citys to build a ball park on one of his car lines. He did, at Payne Avenue and East 39th Street, and so a Cleveland professional baseball team had a new home grounds for the fourth time.

As events of the next two years were unfolded, it seemed that Robison might have been happier running his streetcars than assembling a baseball team. His first manager was Jim Williams, who, rightfully or otherwise, was blamed for the distress of a team that finished a very cold eighth and last in the association's 1887 race, winning only 39 out of the 130 games. The Forest Citys trailed, in this order, St. Louis, Cincinnati, Baltimore, Louisville, the Athletics, Brooklyn, and the New York Metropolitans.

Yet the competitive collapses of the club in 1887 and also the next summer were not without compensation to owner Robison. For one thing, he had discovered a young catcher, slim and agile, who bore the unmistakable marks of a great performer despite, or perhaps because of, the handicap of catching day after day with no more protection than a finger mitt on his left hand, a skintight, fingerless glove on the right and a shout of encouragement on his lips.

He was Charles L. Zimmer, born in Marietta, Ohio, in 1860, educated in baseball on the corner lots in Ironton, and graduated to the major leagues by the Poughkeepsie Indians of the Hudson River League. Zimmer batted .409 for the Indians in 1887 and Davis Hawley, the Cleveland secretary, bought the twenty-seven-year-old star for five hundred dollars. The Forest Citys wasted no time assigning the nickname "Chief" to the new backstop in recognition of his servitude with the Poughkeepsie tribe.

The Chief enjoyed a remarkable baptism in the American Association. He was the featured star, even as a rookie, of the thirteen players comprising the Cleveland team. These were H. L. Oberlander, C. N. Snyder, John Stricker, Augie Alberts, J. S. Faatz, Bill Crowell, Bob Gilks, P. J. Hotaling, Enoch Bakely, Bill Stemmeyer, Ed Hogan, M. J. Goodfellow, and Zimmer. They were recruited mostly from amateur and semi-pro teams and their over-the-season percentage was a paltry .298.

But they helped establish three records that are to be found in the "before 1900" archives of baseball. These rather amateurish batsmen were struck out seventeen times in one game by Pitcher Claude Ramsey of the Louisville team, but they achieved a measure of revenge later by working two Louisville pitchers for a total of nineteen bases on balls in one game. This latter record, not recognized in today's histories, has never been matched. Then, in a postseason game, the Pittsburgh team of the National League and the Forest Citys finished nine innings in sixty minutes.

At the close of the 1888 season, the National League elected Cleveland to replace Detroit, a move eagerly sought by Robison, Hawley, and Howe, who controlled the stock of the Forest Citys. When the Cleveland players reported to the city in the spring of 1889, Howe took one look at the aggregation and moaned.

"They look awful," he complained. "All skinny and spindly. They're nothing more than spiders."

Howe dolled up the players in white and dark blue uniforms, a garb that only accentuated their skinny appearance.

"Might as well call this team the Spiders and be done with it," Howe said in resignation. And so the Forest Citys became known officially, with the assistance of the local sports editors, as the Spiders.

The change in identification didn't help much on the field, however. The Spiders finished sixth, beating out Indianapolis and Washington but being topped by New York's Giants, Boston, Chicago, Philadelphia, and Pittsburgh.

If the Spiders couldn't win games, they could and did win most of the year's fights. They became known as the National League's toughest and roughest bunch. In the month of June, the Spiders had no time for scrapping. They won seventeen out of twenty-four games and were getting the headlines of newspapers in every city in the league.

But the Spiders weren't actually that good and they hit the skids in August when they won only seven games while losing nineteen. These defeats did more than send them down in the standings. They infuriated the players and made them so pugnacious that the league governors were considering legislation to curb the Cleveland tempers.

The roughhouse antics of the Spiders reached a peak on August 14, 1889, as the team was in the worst depth of its slump. The Spiders were playing the Giants at the Payne and 35th Street grounds in Cleveland. Jimmy McAleer, the Spiders' great outfielder who was regarded by contemporaries as the surest judge of a fly ball in the game, lined a hit to the outfield and slid into second base just as the ball arrived at the bag.

"He's safe," ruled Umpire John "Jack" Powers.

There was a scream from the vicinity of home plate and Buck Ewing, the Giants' peerless catcher, stormed across the diamond and rushed up to Powers.

"You blind so-and-so!" hollered Ewing. "The man was out. Anybody could see that."

Powers, excited by the protest, reversed his decision and called McAleer out.

Then the Spiders descended upon Powers in a body. Led by Pat Tebeau, Eddie McKean, and Cub Stricker, all men with free fists and fiery tongues, the home players pushed and jostled Powers.

The umpire did the human thing. He turned and ran for the clubhouse. He beat the enraged Spiders to the door, barricaded it, and waited nervously for the arrival of police. Finally, a squadron of cops ordered Powers to unbolt the door on the promise they would see that no harm befell him.

There were just over four hundred fans in the stands, and as Powers returned to the field, flanked by a dozen officers, they hooted their complaints.

"Robber, thief, no-good!" they howled. As one of the Cleveland writers mentioned in a report of the fracas, "For just a minute, I thought Powers was being unjustly accused. Then I thought again of his decision at second base and I knew the fans were correct."

The game was finished with the police lined up along the first and third base lines, and as the teams changed fields, the guardians would converge upon the arbiter and wait until most of the players were a comparatively safe distance away.

Whether by design or by coincidence, the Spiders played the most important role possible in the selection of the 1889 pennant winner. Not only were they a wild lot themselves, they represented a city in which visiting players contrived to get themselves in the company of well-meaning, well-heeled, and strong-drinking "sports."

The Boston Beaneaters and New York Giants were locked in one of those flag races we would describe today as a "photo finish." First the Beaneaters led, then the Giants. As October began, the Beaneaters moved into Cleveland for an important series with the Spiders. The visitors won the opener while New York was losing in Pittsburgh. That put Boston a full game ahead.

But the Spiders were honest, if inclined to be hoodlums. Beatin, the Cleveland pitching star who worked in more games than any other flinger, held the Beaneaters to four hits and defeated them, 7 to 1, as the Giants were beating Pittsburgh. Beatin had his task lightened because the catcher-outfielder captain of the Boston team, the mighty Michael "King" Kelly, arrived at the park in no condition to play.

Kelly had imbibed much too freely with friends the previous night and Manager Jim Hart refused to permit him in uniform, though he did allow his slugging star to sit on the bench. But he couldn't keep Kelly quiet. There was an argument over a play at the plate and Kelly accused the umpire of being unfair. Kelly was ordered removed from the park and the cops removed him, not gently.

A Boston reporter, traveling with the team, telegraphed his paper, "Cleveland is Kelly's bad town. However, he is not the only Boston player who has enjoyed life in Cleveland."

Yet the Beaneaters retained a chance for the pennant and on the last day of the season they were playing in Pittsburgh. New York was in Cleveland and leading Boston by percentage points.

A Boston publisher promised the Beaneaters a thousand dollars if they won the pennant, which probably is what prompted the team management to send this telegram to the Spiders: "We will give your team $1,000 if Boston wins the pennant, $500 to the battery in today's game, and the like amount to the rest of the team."

To the disappointment of the Beaneaters, the Spiders muffed the chance to earn extra money by losing to New York.

There was sufficient dissatisfaction with the salaries paid to National League and American Association players to spur a number of stars in both circuits to "go outlaw" in 1890. The Brotherhood was formed with teams in Cleveland, Chicago, Pittsburgh, Buffalo, New York, Boston, Brooklyn, and Philadelphia.

Cleveland retained teams in both the Brotherhood and the National League. Cleveland teams lost money and a peace pact was signed at the finish of the season. The Cleveland teams did right well in individual statistics, however. Larry Twitchell, a fine outfielder, led the Brotherhood in batting with a sterling .417 mark. The National League Spiders had one pitcher who stood out from the rest in the league, a young fellow named Young.

C H A P T E R I V

THE BIG FARMER

THERE IS NO RECORD of the first man to misjudge a piece of baseball flesh and thousands of other mistakes have been made in appraisals of young players over an eighty-year span. But what was an unlucky flip of fortune for one team was eternally beneficial to Cleveland. This was the "boner" pulled by one of the sharpest baseball players of all time, Adrian Anson of the Chicago Colts.

Anse, peerless genius of late-nineteenth-century diamond lore muffed Denton True Young for his greatest error!

Another major leaguer, whose name is not to be found, went deep into Ohio in 1889 to scout a twenty-two-year-old third baseman playing with the Tuscarawas County team. He reported back to his club that the third baseman was destined for a career of high shoes, awkward hands, and punishment behind the plow. One thing was certain. The boy was not major-league infield material.

A year later, this rough-hewn infielder had become a pitcher with the Canton team in the Ohio and Pennsylvania League. He was now twenty-three, big, strong, and with a "shoot" that could terrify batters if it was thrown in the general vicinity of home plate. Dent Young's trouble was in firing the sphere the required fifty feet in an attempt to conform to the newly adopted regulation of three strikes and four balls to each batter.

George Moreland, manager of the Canton team, found Dent Young and his pioneer father, McKenzie Young, on their farm in the spring of 1890.

"How much is the boy making in the fields?" Moreland asked McKenzie Young.

The answer was ten dollars a month and keep.

"I'll give him forty dollars a month to pitch for us," Moreland offered. Dent Young eagerly awaited his father's decision.

The boy's face went ashen as McKenzie Young said nay. He wanted Dent on the farm and felt he needed the help of his strapping offspring.

However, baseball was in Dent Young's blood by now, and he persuaded his father that there might be a future in the sport. So Dent Young reported to the Canton team. In one eye-opening pitching practice, the raw farm boy fired the ball with such speed that Moreland was extremely pleased with his acumen in acquiring such a future star for only forty dollars per month.

But Dent Young was no raw farm boy when it came to a dollar. He recognized the enthusiasm in the voices and actions of the Canton owners and players. Promptly, Dent became a holdout. He demanded a contract for sixty dollars a month and got it!

It took more than blinding speed to win ball games, even in the Ohio and Pennsylvania League, and Young had choppy sailing in his first couple of months. Yet stories of his fireball were getting national circulation and one of these reached the ear of Anson.

The great figure personally went to Canton to scout the "phenom."

Anson looked him over carefully, then voiced his verdict.

"No good," ruled Anson. "Just another big farmer."

Davis Hawley of the Cleveland Spiders didn't think so. He kept careful watch on Dent Young in the next month and noticed great improvement in the youth's control. Young won five straight games.

"I'll give you two hundred and fifty dollars for Young's contract," Hawley approached Moreland. The Canton owner accepted the offer and in July of 1890 Dent Young packed his cardboard suitcase, pulled on his best high shoes, and embarked for the big city.

A commonly quoted story of Young's arrival in Cleveland deals with his "purchase" from Canton the day before he pitched his first game for Cleveland. However, this tale has been distorted through the years.

The historian of Dent Young's life and career with the fullest knowledge of facts is Bob Godley, former sports writer for the *Cleveland Press* and currently a Cleveland radio sports announcer. Godley wrote Young's life story after spending many weeks in constant association with the grand old man on his farm and sharing in his activities in the town of Peoli, Ohio.

"Young went up to Cleveland on a promise of seventy-five dollars per month," Godley reported. "They—the Spiders—told him to work out around the park for a few weeks while the team was on the road. The Spiders came home from a disastrous trip around the first of August and Manager Gus Schmelz advised Dent he would pitch the second game of the series with Anson's Colts."

The young pitcher did not become nervous, scared, or excited at the prospect of pitching against the famous Cap Anson. Anson was a remarkable batter, National League champion in 1887 and 1888 with averages of .421 and .343.

But he was also the man who had called Dent Young "just another big farmer." So instead of undergoing mental torture at the prospect of his first big-league start, Dent Young was plain country mad.

He fired his best fast ball at the Colts all that afternoon of August 6. He struck out the side in the fourth inning and the third victim was Anson himself.

"I just threw the ball past Anse," Young recalls, "right where he liked it, high and close."

After Young had restricted the Colts to three singles, exhibited perfect control, and won his game, 3 to 1, treasurer George Howe of the Spiders bumped into Anson in a hotel.

"Does he still look like just another big farmer?" Howe chided.

Cap answered with a grumble and moved along.

Anson wasn't the only man with a complaint. Strangely, Young was very unhappy about his pitching.

"I didn't have my usual speed today," Dent beefed to Hawley.

"We thought you did," Hawley replied. "What happened?"

"Well, down in Canton the catchers couldn't hold me, I was so fast," explained Young. "But Chief Zimmer had no trouble today, so I guess I didn't have much speed."

Hawley laughed heartily.

"That's a left-handed compliment to Zimmer," he informed Dent. "The Chief is the best catcher in the league, not one of those fellows who couldn't hold you in Canton."

Young grunted.

"We'll see," he finally conceded. He saw and was convinced. The battery of Young and Zimmer became the most famous of the times.

It was Zimmer, incidentally, who smashed the custom of catchers working with their special pet pitchers, a practice accepted in all baseball circles prior to 1890.

"I'll work every game," Zimmer informed Schmelz. And he did until his wife's illness forced the Chief to break the string. He caught in 126 games consecutively, a mark that stood for many years and one that was all the more remarkable because the Chief wore only the barest minimum of protection.

At that time Young was still known as Dent Young. It was not until his second start for the Spiders that a sports writer coined the name "Cyclone" in reference to Dent's fast shoots. The Cyclone soon became Cy, and to this day the name Cy Young represents the acme of pitching skill.

Starting with the Spiders in August, after having pitched thirty-six games for Canton, the sensational rookie won ten games and lost seven. The Spiders won a total of only forty-four games all that season.

The Brotherhood folded in 1891, leaving the National League Spiders as the sole representatives of professional baseball in the city. Several players who had jumped to the outlaw league the year before now sought their old jobs in the National. In spite of Cy Young's twenty-seven victories against twenty-two defeats, the Spiders were fifth, largely due to a policy of argument instituted by the team captain and shortstop, Ed McKean. The Spiders gained a sour reputation in the league because of their constant squawking to the umpires, but finally McKean's tongue was curbed and the team settled down.

The Spiders were beginning to take on the manners and appearance of a big-league team. Robison, Hawley, and Howe added Kid Cupid Childs, a second baseman who led the team in batting with .295, Jake Virtue, Jesse Burkett, Jack Doyle, George Davis, and half a dozen others.

"We'll have a truly good team next year," Robison promised. "And we'll have a new park for them to play in."

The grounds on Payne Avenue had been thrown into considerable disarray in June of 1890 during a visit by the Chicago Colts. Shortly after the game started, a thunderstorm broke. Lightning struck the grandstand and it splintered to bits with pieces falling in flames to the ground. The park was used for the rest of that season but was abandoned the next spring.

Robison's streetcar lines also ran farther to the east and so he selected a site at Lexington Avenue and East 66th Street on which to build the new grandstand. Hence, on May 1, 1891, League Park was formally opened as ten thousand spectators jammed each inch of the green wooden structure for a game between the Spiders and the Cincinnati Redlegs. The new park —still standing and used by the modern Indians as late as 1946 though currently restricted to football—was declared "fit for kings and fans" in the daily press. Robison's streetcars deposited and loaded passengers twenty feet from the entrances, which was dandy for the fans, even as the kings approached in private vehicles.

Robison's promise of a winner was fulfilled the next year though the Spiders did not win a clear title. The collapse of the American Association threw hundreds of players on the open market and the eight-club National League was expanded.

Four additional clubs were admitted and the only twelve-team National League race in history was under way. To ease the awkwardness of a packed schedule, the season was divided into spring and fall series. The Red Sox won the first-half championship, the spring series, with Brooklyn, Philadelphia, Cincinnati, Cleveland, Pittsburgh, Washington, Chicago, St. Louis, New York, Louisville, and Baltimore, finishing in that order.

The Spiders' first-half race, during which they won forty while losing thirty-three, did not please Robison, and so when the second half was started, he elevated Pat Tebeau from captain to team manager, replacing Bob Leadley. Tebeau continued at third and his inspirational play and scrappiness in dealing with umpires was a force strong enough to lift his teammates to the second-half championship.

"The Spiders are the best team that ever represented the

Forest Citys in baseball," acclaimed the *Cleveland Leader*. "Mr. Robison is to be highly commended for installing Tebeau as manager. He will gain national recognition for not only the Spiders but for Cleveland."

Winning fifty-three games while losing only twenty-three, the Spiders made owner Robison and the Cleveland sports writers seem accurate and legitimate in their praise. Tebeau played out the string with Jake Virtue on first, Cupid Childs on second, and Ed McKean at short. Jesse Burkett, Jimmy McAleer, and Jimmy O'Connor comprised the outfield while the reliable Zimmer handled the three Cleveland pitchers, Young, John G. Clarkson, and George Cuppy.

Young was "in a jovial mood all that summer." And well he might have been. Then twenty-five years old, the massive right-hander won thirty-six games and lost only ten for an astounding percentage of .783. Childs batted a neat .335 to lead the team for the second straight year.

The Spiders were a confident and happy lot as they battled their way into the first World Series, as the press of the day designated the playoff set. The Boston Beaneaters were far from the most popular team in the league. They were outstandingly the best team, which accounted for a share of the jealousy, but they were not above tricks that were regarded as slightly more dirty than sly.

The Series was scheduled for nine games, three in Cleveland, three in Boston, and in case of a tie after these six, three more to be played on neutral grounds. But the latter provision never was exercised. The Spiders were outclassed as a team though Young managed to come up with the outstanding Cleveland pitching performance.

This was in the opening game on October 17. Cy and Happy Jack Stivetts, ace of the Boston staff, locked gloves before six thousand spectators at League Park. They wrangled for eleven innings, with the Beaneaters getting six hits off Young while Cleveland could tag Stivetts for only four.

Not an error marred the game, and the fielding was as spectacular as it was clean. But "the sportsmanship" of Mike "King" Kelly, Boston's pugnacious catcher-outfielder was not quite either. Kelly was the most hated player of the period, a man with such an intense desire to win (and also to win bets he placed on his own team) that he would resort to any methods.

In this classical first game, the tension mounted going into the ninth inning. The Beaneaters, first at bat, got one of the few breaks of the game. Stivetts popped one of Young's fast pitches high into the air in foul territory between the plate and first base. The Spiders called for Zimmer to take the ball.

Then Kelly yelled to Virtue, the Cleveland first baseman, to try for the catch. Virtue crashed into Zimmer and the Chief dropped the ball. The Spiders swarmed onto the field and charged the umpire, demanding that Kelly be removed from the field.

"It did not benefit the Bostons, however, as they scored a blank, despite Kelly's dirty work," reports the *Spalding Baseball Guide* for 1893. "He was fined 10 dollars for the call."

That scoreless deadlock got the Spiders off to at least an even start with the Beaneaters, but their luck from then on wasn't very good. Clarkson, released by Boston to Cleveland in midseason, was a loyal, nervous pitcher who had endangered his arm by overwork in the Hub. Even so, he was Manager Tebeau's nominee for the second game. Clarkson bowed to Harry Staley in the second game, 4 to 3, partly because of the batting of Hugh Duffy, the small hitsmith who had gone over to the Beaneaters from the Boston Association team.

Stivetts and Young returned to the battle lines in the third game with Happy Jack edging the great Cy, 3 to 2, this time in nine innings. The following day, October 20, the teams transferred their series to Boston, where the Beaneaters won three straight. Kid Nichols beat Cuppy, 4 to 0; Stivetts outlasted Clarkson, 12 to 7; and in the final game, after a two-day delay, Nichols had no trouble defeating Young and a band of discouraged Spiders, 8 to 3.

The Spiders of the next few years were a formidable team under the management of Tebeau, but they lacked a spark. Not even the masterful pitching of Young could keep the Spiders on or near the top of the National League, close enough to participate in the Temple Cup Series. A Pittsburgher named William

Chase Temple had donated a trophy to be played for at the close of the season by the League's top two teams.

Then, in 1895, the Spiders were endowed with the needed spark by, of all people, a fine hitter with a testy disposition. He was Jesse Burkett, the team's lead-off batter and left fielder. Burkett was known throughout the league as "the Crab," so sullen was he. But there was no sulking at the plate for Jesse. He batted .423 in 1895, and .410 the next year. His influence may be measured by the fact the Spiders finished second each time and earned the right to challenge the famous Baltimore Orioles for the Temple Cup.

The Orioles included some of the all-time stars of the sport, men whose names are far more revered today than they were fifty years ago. Muggsy McGraw played third and Willie Keeler was in right. Hughey Jennings was the shortstop, Steve Brodie the center fielder, Kid Gleason the second baseman, and Wilbert Robinson the catcher.

But if the Orioles had names, the Spiders had Cy Young, Chief Zimmer, and Jesse Burkett. These men were respected in baseball. The Orioles were hoodlums, troublemakers, and in patent disgrace in the affections of all other teams in the National League. In fact, when the Spiders beat the Orioles in the 1895 Series, Connie Mack, then managing the Pittsburgh team, "spoke in dignified praise. . . . I am happy that gentlemen have won the Temple Cup!"

They won in 1895 because Young beat the Baltimore team three times. They won despite threats by rowdies in Baltimore. Burkett had a great time in the five-game series. He batted an even .500 and grumbled at the Orioles through every game. It was Burkett's double in the ninth inning of the first game in Cleveland that set off a winning rally.

Young was being bested by John "Sadie" McMahon, the Baltimore star pitcher, when the Spiders batted in the ninth. Burkett's hit was followed by singles by McKean and Childs. A pair of infield outs accounted for one more run and the victory, 5 to 4. The Spiders won the second game, 7 to 2, on Burkett's four hits and Nig Cuppy's steady hurling. Old Tuscarawas Young came right back in the third game and thrilled a "giant crowd" of 12,500 with a 7-to-1 triumph. Not until the ninth inning could a Baltimore batter drive a ball to the out-field.

The Spiders moved on to Baltimore for the fourth game. As they left their hotel to go to the park, a group of citizens pelted the Cleveland players with vegetables and eggs, neither especially fresh, and a few rocks and stones. Baltimore sports writers who had been in Cleveland stirred up the Maryland fans until they were ready to use any kind of physical force to beat the Spiders. Upon leaving the park, even after losing the fourth game 5 to 0, the Spiders were assaulted in their high-sided omnibus.

"The Cleveland players had to sprawl flat on the floor of the bus to escape serious injury," reported the *Cleveland Plain Dealer* correspondent on the scene. "Childs was beaned by a piece of rock while many players later showed their souvenirs of stones and pieces of steel they had picked up from the floor of the bus."

The Spiders were bruised but not scared. Young turned back the Orioles the next afternoon, 5 to 2, to win the Temple Cup, four games to one. Cleveland sports writers gloated in their dispatches to their home newspapers.

"The Champions' pennant is all smeared with mud," chortled the *Plain Dealer*. "The Orioles kept up the clip for a while, but then the streaks of 'yellow' showed and it was all over."

There was only moderate singing by the Cleveland authors the next autumn when, for the second straight time, the Spiders finished in second place and went into the Temple Cup Series with the Baltimores once more. But Young had gone through a strenuous summer while winning twenty-nine games and was pretty well pitched out by the time the series was started. The Orioles beat Young in the first game, 7 to 1, and walked through the next three to sweep the Series.

This was a much sadder series financially for players of both teams. The Spiders received 528 dollars per player in the 1895 series while the Orioles won shares of 316 dollars. But in 1896, due to a declining interest in the Temple Cup, the winning Orioles received only 200 dollars while each Cleveland player was given about 115 dollars.

Though Cleveland was growing rapidly as a city, thanks to the oil, coal, and iron-ore interests, there was such a general decline in baseball that owner Robison decided upon some drastic changes following the 1898 season.

He bought the St. Louis franchise in the National League and instituted a shuttle operation for his ballplayers. The wealthy Robison installed his brother Stanley as chief of the Spiders and sent Tebeau down to St. Louis as manager of the club there.

Too, he transferred most of the Cleveland stars to St. Louis. In the winter of 1898–99, Young, Cuppy, Zimmer, Crieger, O'Connor, Childs, McKean, Wallace, Powell, Burkett, Blake, Hendrick, and others were moved to St. Louis by Robison. Any players that Tebeau tried out at St. Louis and found short of big-league requirements were shipped up to Cleveland.

Clevelanders wasted no time in deriding Robison and his baseball maneuvers. "The Misfits" became the accepted name for the erstwhile Spiders. If one of them showed up well in a game, there was a better than 75-to-25 chance that he would be on a train bound for St. Louis that night.

A hapless baseball figure by the name of Lave Cross was burdened with the management of the leftovers. One day he called on Robison to present a plea for assistance.

"I need about five players to have a pretty good team, Mr. Robison," Cross began. "A couple of pitchers and a shortstop would help. Give me those and even with the other misfits we'll win some games."

Robison fixed Cross with a stare.

"I'm not interested in winning games here," reported the owner. "Play out the schedule. That's your job."

He played it out—on the road. The fans, scorching because Robison had removed from League Park all the old favorites, stayed away from the grounds in such large numbers that, after twenty-seven games there, the team became a road troupe exclusively. It probably was the worst professional team of all time. Its record of 134 defeats and only 20 victories stands out like a festered lip on baseball's strong face.

CHAPTER V

YOUNG'S HEYDAY

DAVIS HAWLEY was a banker, but he was a dreamer, too. As secretary of the old Spiders he had bought Chief Zimmer, Cy Young, and many other men who placed their indelible imprint on Cleveland's diamond history. For more than a decade, he had been not only a baseball executive but a loyal fan.

But now—in the dead of the 1900 winter—Davis Hawley had to be content with his position as president of the Cuyahoga Savings and Loan Association. The Spiders were gone. All baseball was gone from Cleveland. Hawley sat in his office, looking toward the snowy streets, his mind on Burkett, the Temple Cup Series, League Park. . . .

Four men stepped into Hawley's office. One was known to the banker, M. E. Gaul, passenger agent for the old Lake Shore Railroad.

"I want you to meet these gentlemen from Chicago," Gaul began. Two were railroad men. The third was a full-faced, stocky man with sandy hair and a bristling air.

"This is Mr. Ban Johnson, president of the Western Baseball League."

Johnson spoke immediately.

"It used to be the Western League, but we're going to call it the American League," he corrected. Then, using the direct approach for which he was to become famous and frequently disliked, Johnson went to the point.

"Mr. Hawley, we'd like to put a ball team in Cleveland. We're sure there is room for another major league in this country. Cleveland should be in it."

Johnson went on to point out that his plans called for the Grand Rapids franchise in the Western League to be moved to Cleveland. A man named Charles Comiskey had owned the St. Paul team, but he was planning to move it to Chicago. There would be clubs in Milwaukee, Chicago, Kansas City, Minneapolis, Cleveland, Indianapolis, Detroit, and Buffalo.

"Very frankly, Mr. Hawley," Johnson declared, "we need some money. We'd like you to become president of the Cleveland team. We can beat this National League if you'll join us."

Hawley shook his head.

"A few years ago I might," he said somewhat sorrowfully. "But now you need some younger blood. I have the men for you. Meet me at the Hollenden Hotel in an hour."

When Hawley arrived for the meeting, he was accompanied by two young men with a thirst for adventure. They were Charles W. Somers and John F. Kilfoyl.

Charley Somers was in the coal business with his father. The family fortune had been increased over the years and Somers had ready cash, much of it. Kilfoyl owned a men's furnishings store on Public Square. With less money than Somers, but with more business acumen and an equal amount of enthusiasm for baseball, Jack Kilfoyl fitted into the picture very well.

Kilfoyl became president and treasurer of the Cleveland organization while Somers, though destined to play a more active role in all phases of baseball, was contented with the title of vice president.

There were two major weaknesses in the setup. Kilfoyl and Somers lacked (1) a baseball team and (2) a baseball park. The Robisons still owned League Park and refused to lease it to the American League.

But they did have one big advantage and that was Somers' bank account. Charley was a handsome young man who was willing to take almost any kind of a gamble, in business or in sports. The National League, which had been watching closely the rearing of Johnson's new circuit, adopted an attitude of smugness and superiority and practically dared the newcomers to fight. That was all Ban Johnson needed, a challenge and Charley Somers' money.

"We'll make all the stars of the National League jump to us by paying them bigger salaries," threatened Johnson. "We'll go right into Boston, Philadelphia, Washington, and Baltimore and install teams. You want a fight, you'll get it."

An outright battle was circumvented when the directors of the National League met in the Hollenden in March. They agreed to allow Comiskey to move into Chicago, to recognize Kilfoyl and Somers in Cleveland, thereby granting them a lease on League Park. As his part of the bargain, Johnson agreed to keep the American League, or Western League, a minor organization for one year with its players subject to draft by the National League.

Shortly after this peace pact, Somers loaned Charley Comiskey, later to be known as "the Old Roman," enough money to finish construction of his new park on Chicago's South Side. Today Comiskey Park stands as a monument to the family ownership of the White Sox though an inscription in honor of Charley Somers would be appropriate.

Somers' financial lifts to the new league did not end in Chicago. He and Ben Shibe, who manufactured sporting goods, financed Connie Mack in Philadelphia. Charley also loaned money to the St. Louis team and when the league decided to put a team in Boston and buck the entrenched Braves, or Bean-eaters, Somers came through again. He financed the Boston team for two years before a purchaser could be found.

In fact, during the first three years of existence of the American League, Somers called upon his coal and commercial resources for close to a million dollars, which he invested in baseball or loaned to various clubs and individuals. His faith in Ban Johnson and his open checkbook were the legs upon which the American League learned to walk. Without them, there would be no American League today.

Somers was a rabid fan, as well as a generous owner, but he did not match his partner, Kilfoyl, in intensity of interest in each individual game played by the team. There is a marked similarity between Kilfoyl and the late Harry Grabiner, a White Sox "career" executive who became vice president of the Indians in 1946.

Neither Kilfoyl nor Grabiner could stand to watch his team lose. Kilfoyl became so wrapped up in the Cleveland Naps of 1908, when they were fighting bitterly for their first championship, that the team's loss in the final moments of the race forced Jack to the side lines. He took the reversal so hard he retired from baseball in ill health. Grabiner likewise brooded over defeats, and the excitement of the Cleveland team's bid for the flag in 1948 was a contributing factor to his breakdown and ultimate demise.

For want of any more recognizable name and because they clung to the traditional blue uniforms of the old National League Spiders, the new Cleveland club came to be known as the Blues. Many times during the 1900 season others connected with the Blues had that old sunken feeling. One of these was Jim McAleer, perhaps the most graceful outfielder known to the game with the exception of Tris Speaker.

McAleer, after stardom in the National League, had retired to his home in Youngstown. Kilfoyl and Somers induced Jim to return to baseball as their manager. Not only did they value his prestige as a strategist; they recognized the possible use of his name as a great star in luring players from the National League.

McAleer became very prominent and useful in later expansion of the American League, but he was discouraged in 1900. Jim was able to pick up some fair players from the wreckage of the Grand Rapids team. The best of these was Ollie Pickering, an outfielder who batted .324 for his new employers. The top-notcher among the Blues was a third baseman owned by the Chicago Cubs, Charley Buelow. The Blues stayed high in the race until Buelow was hurt in the third month of the season.

All through the summer of 1900, Ban Johnson was planning his circuit's release in 1901 from any affiliation with the National League and also expansion that would take the American League into the heart of the older loop. The Western division was all set, with Cleveland, Chicago, Detroit, and Milwaukee. Philadelphia, Boston, and Washington were established in the East. John McGraw and Wilbert Robinson were persuaded to head a team in Baltimore.

Though the Cleveland team finished a bad seventh, its debut in the American League was not without honor, excitement, and humor. There were new faces, stars recruited from the National League.

Manager McAleer built his Blues around two young in-fielders, third baseman Bill Bradley and first baseman George "Candy" LaChance, and an established outfielder, Ollie Pickering.

Bradley was one of four National Leaguers scooped up in Cleveland's first raid on the National League. He had been with Chicago, but a promise of more money induced the big but graceful infielder to switch leagues. Outfielder Jack McCarthy and pitcher Ed Scott also were lured away from the Cubs while a steady catcher, Bobby Wood, was taken from Cincinnati.

Two of the more valuable of the new Blues were bought from minor-league teams or tossed in as favors in other deals. Earl Moore, a promising pitcher, was purchased from Dayton, while a left-hander named Harry "Pete" Dowling was turned over to the Blues by Milwaukee in a friendly gesture. This pair was to figure in some historically important incidents that summer.

There was marked apathy toward the new league and new club because the Cleveland fans couldn't visualize a loosely knit circuit presenting baseball as good as they had seen in the old National League games. The *Cleveland Press*, in one pre-season story, dashed more cold water on the situation by saying, "Cleveland is a dead baseball town."

This statement was believed on Memorial Day when the Washington Senators visited League Park. The covered grand-stand was comfortably filled at one dollar a head while there were three thousand more fans in the bleachers at exactly half that price. The sky was cloudy and a few drops of rain fell.

The bleacherites made a dash for the covered stands but never made it. The holders of the reserved and higher-priced seats met the onrushing rivals with a barrage of heavy cushions. A battle royal raged for ten minutes. Finally, the players of both teams waded into the melee and put a stop to the fighting.

Such antics were duly noted in the newspaper accounts of the games, but occasionally the sports editors must have been very tired. On June 7, 1901, the Blues defeated Baltimore, 4 to 2. Pete Dowling had joined the Cleveland team a few days earlier and had been defeated in his first start. But he had won this day.

The *Cleveland Press*'s complete account of the day's baseball activities follows:

Pete Dowling: "I'm sorry I lost the first game I pitched for you, Jim."

McAleer: "I'm sorry, too, Peter. It was a pretty raw exhibition."

"I can go in today and skin 'em."

"You're on Peter."

Peter kept his word.

Later that season, Dowling was credited in the press of the day as having pitched a no-hit game against Milwaukee, but there is no recognition of the feat in standard reference books. Later Dowling pitched a one-hitter against the same team.

While Dowling didn't make the record books, Earl Moore did. He was a big handsome fellow who is honored as the inventor of the cross-fire delivery. Moore pitched nine hitless innings against the White Sox on May 9 but was drubbed in the tenth and the Blues lost, 4 to 2.

Moore had a special deal with his father, a great baseball fan who lived in Pittsburgh. Whenever Moore won a game, his father would send him a check for one hundred dollars. If he lost a tough game, his father would write him a letter of sympathy. Earl was breezing along eating up victories and checks until July 30. Then he pitched against the Athletics and Larry Lajoie.

In order, Lajoie propelled a single, double, triple, and home run, the latter with the bases filled. Earl Moore didn't hear from his father for two weeks after that.

It is doubtful if any one baseball season, including even the pair in which World's Championships were won, was as vital to the all-around welfare of the sport in Cleveland as was 1902. Regarding the American League, further expansion was in order. Johnson moved the Milwaukee franchise to St. Louis (with the help of a few more of Somers' dollars) and asked Kilfoyl and Somers to transfer McAleer to St. Louis, where his experience and personality might be used to the best advantage. As McAleer shifted to the new Browns, a grizzled diamond strategist named Bill Armour stepped up to the Cleveland club. Armour had managed the Dayton team for several years and had been credited with the development of many stars, including Elmer Flick, Wiley Piatt, Earl Moore, and Gene Wright.

Armour was a resourceful person if nothing else. After his appointment as manager of the Blues in December 1901, Armour moved to Cleveland and brought along two Dayton players, pitcher Wright and shortstop Gochnaur, both of whom he had previously sold to Brooklyn. Bill had no intention of spending an idle winter.

He, Wright, and Gochnaur went out to League Park and began to transform the grounds into a skating rink. The three threw up embankments of dirt, then turned on the water. Unfortunately, the embankments weren't strong enough. Water flowed freely and wildly over the entire neighborhood, and there was much better skating on the streets than in League Park.

Armour had the green light from Kilfoyl and Somers to grab any players available in the country. More and more National Leaguers were jumping to the new circuit. Pitcher Luther "Dummy" Taylor of the Giants, catcher Harry Bemis, infielder Frank Bonner, outfielder Jack Thoney, and outfielder Harry Bay, who had been with Detroit, were acquired.

So, too, was a pitcher who had spent the two previous seasons at Toledo. He was tall (six, three) and angular, and he threw the ball from off his right hip, hiding it from the batter until the last possible second. He looked and acted like a pitcher, and there was grace in each movement.

At twenty-two, Adrian C. "Addie" Joss became a first-string pitcher with the Clevelands. No name is more hallowed in Cleveland baseball memories than Joss's. He was, from the outset, a tremendous pitcher, a superior competitor, and a gentleman.

Armour welcomed Joss with open arms, but the astute manager knew only too well it would take half a dozen Addie Josses to make anything out of the Cleveland team. It was a jittery outfit that Armour led into New Orleans late in March. For the first time, a Cleveland team actually bedded down in a spring training camp all its own, even if the players did have to hike the three-mile stretch from hotel to practice grounds.

Gochnaur had decided to stay on at shortstop with the Clevelands instead of reporting to Brooklyn. First baseman Charley Hickman had come from Boston in a swap for Candy LaChance and the reliable and tremendous Bill Bradley was at third. But Harry Bay was the only outfielder of account, and there was a distressing shortage of pitchers, made more acute in May when Dummy Taylor and Gene Wright jumped from Cleveland to the Brooklyn Trolley Dodgers.

Not even a change in names could help the club. The players, meeting in New Orleans, decided they didn't like the name Bluebirds. This had been an informal nickname in the first place, stemming from the wearing of bright blue road uniforms not too much unlike the rococo blouses and shirts worn by the Chicago Cubs of a few years ago.

The players voted on a new name and settled upon Bronchos. That tremendous achievement recorded, they went home to Cleveland and lost 13 of their first 17 games and were deeply lonesome in the American League cellar.

Things got so tough that Armour began to pick pitchers out of the air literally. During one period in which the Bronchos were suffering more than usual, Armour was wishing he had remained in the comparatively safe precincts of Dayton. Cleveland fans were muttering into their mustachios that things never were like this in the National League days. Three of Armour's starting pitchers were crippled at the moment.

Bill happened to be a neighbor of Henry P. Edwards, the grand character of the diamond who then was baseball writer for the *Cleveland Plain Dealer*. Armour dropped in to talk to Edwards one dinner hour.

"Henry, I'm in tough shape for pitchers," he stated his case. "How about you running a story in your paper asking semipro and amateur pitchers who think they've got a chance to report to me at League Park?"

Edwards obliged in the following editions of his morning paper, and when Armour arrived at the ball yard, he was greeted by half a dozen fellows in assorted uniforms. One, a lanky blond southpaw, attracted Armour's eye immediately. His name was Otto Hess, and he had been pitching for a semi-pro team in central Ohio.

"I'm starting you against the Washington team today," Armour told the startled newcomer. When the Senators' manager, Tom Loftus, heard that a raw rookie was to pitch, he ordered his men to bunt at every opportunity. They did, fifteen times. But Hess staggered through ten innings and won, 7 to 6. He later became a twenty-game winner for the Clevelands.

If that special case is shocking to today's baseball fan, let him consider the events of the next twenty-four hours. Hess had beaten Washington, and now Philadelphia was at League Park. The mighty Athletics were to go on to win the championship, and on this particular day Rube Waddell, the inimitable, eccentric left-hander, was Connie Mack's pitching selection.

Armour paused to chat with a ticket taker, Herman Schleman, on his way into League Park. Schleman asked an obvious question, "Who'll pitch for the Bronchos today?" Armour snorted in disgust. "I don't have a single pitcher ready," he moaned.

"I know the man who can pitch for you and win," asserted Schleman. Armour perked up.

"His name is Charley Smith, and he pitches for the Cleveland Wheel Club team around town."

Armour demanded to know where he could be found.

"Inside the park in a seat," replied Schleman. "He bought his ticket and is sitting in the bleachers now."

Smith wasn't there long. In a very few minutes he had been fitted into a Cleveland uniform, had borrowed a pair of spike shoes, and was on the diamond he had admired from a distance until then.

This fairy story has the inevitable fairy-story ending. Smith zigged and zagged in his pitching, but he never collapsed fully before the hits and taunts produced by the startled Athletics. The Bronchos scored a run in the ninth inning on a single by the peerless Lajoie, to win, 5 to 4, and the young man who had come to the park as a spectator left as a hero.

CONNIE MACK'S FAVOR

CONNIE MACK was not, and is not, one to forget a friend. Thus a player who was to be acclaimed the greatest second baseman of all time served many of his banner years in the livery of Cleveland teams.

Mack had a chance to do a favor for Charley Somers, who had been a fast man with his pocketbook in the days when the tall, somber ex-catcher was trying to get a foothold in Philadelphia. This favor took the form of a gift to Somers of Napoleon Lajoie, six feet and one inch in height, 195 pounds on the scale, owner of matchless grace and smooth physical power that enabled him to field and throw with a minimum of noticeable endeavor.

Lajoie was born in Woonsocket, Rhode Island, September 5, 1875, of pure French stock. Napoleon liked the outdoors. He got a job as a hack driver in Woonsocket and played baseball in his spare hours. In 1896, when he was twenty-one, he received and accepted his first professional offer. Charley Marston, managing the Fall River, Massachusetts team of the New England League, shoved the back of an envelope in front of the young Frenchman. Lajoie signed his name and hustled off to join the Fall River team.

Lajoie led the league with a .429 average and attracted the attention of a scout for the Philadelphia Phillies. The scout took one look at the big, easy-moving second baseman and rushed him off to join the Phillies. The rookie batted a creditable .328 from August on but really got into his proper stride the next four years with averages of .363, .328, .379, and .346. He batted right-handed, and he managed to get most of his power into a swing without giving the impression of lunging at the ball or trying to "kill" it.

Mack couldn't hide his admiration of Lajoie, and when

Connie installed his American League team in Philadelphia in 1901, he talked turkey to Lajoie.

"I'll give you more than twenty-four hundred dollars a year to play with us," Connie told Napoleon, or Larry, as he was also known. "You're sure to make a lot more next year."

Lajoie listened and agreed to jump to the American League. The Phillies' star pitcher, Bill Bernhard, likewise deserted the Phillies for the Athletics. The twenty-four hundred dollars was the salary limit in the National League, and both players thought they were worth more. Lajoie led the new American League in batting in 1901 with a remarkable mark of .405.

This was too much for John I. Rogers, president of the Phillies and also a lawyer. Rogers had permitted Lajoie to play that one year with his Quaker City rivals, but now he was burning. The president went to the Pennsylvania Supreme Court and obtained an injunction to restrain Lajoie, Bernhard, and any other "jumping" players from appearing with any team other than the Phillies.

The injunction was returnable on April 21, 1902, but Mack didn't take a chance with Lajoie and Bernhard. He sent them across the Delaware River to the neighboring community of Camden, New Jersey, where they could not be served with Pennsylvania papers.

Lajoie and Bernhard were in a quandary. They refused point-blank to rejoin the Phillies, and they risked damage suits if they played with the Athletics. So they did neither for a month. Somers, meanwhile, had been seeking help for his foundering Bronchos and had stolen a fine outfielder, Elmer Flick, from the National League.

Somers approached Mack and asked for Lajoie and Bernhard. Connie considered their cases, recalled the many favors Somers had done, and said the Bronchos could have both players if satisfactory salary arrangements could be worked out.

The news that Lajoie might come to Cleveland resulted in an overnight revival of interest in baseball in the Forest City. Somers sat down with Lajoie, and a price was agreed upon. The exact salary was not announced. One report said the Frenchman was to be paid twenty-five thousand for three years, another insisted he would receive thirty thousand for four years.

The Phillies sued to prevent Lajoie, Bernhard, and Flick from playing with the Bronchos in Cleveland, but the suit was thrown out of court. The restraining order against the three appearing with any team other than the Phillies in Pennsylvania was upheld, and for the next two years the Cleveland team played in Philadelphia without those designated stars.

The Bronchos perked up considerably after Lajoie joined them in June. They were in last place when he first appeared in a Cleveland line-up on June 4, poling one of his typical clothesline doubles to help the Bronchos beat Boston. From that time on, the Clevelands improved faster and finished in fifth place, largely because Lajoie batted .369, Charley Hickman, the first baseman, .363, and Bradley .341. Bernhard became the league's leading pitcher with a record of eighteen victories against only five defeats. Joss shook off his sore arm and won sixteen while losing thirteen. Five of his triumphs were shutouts. Addie had opened the 1902 season by beating the new Browns in St. Louis, turning in a one-hit masterpiece. The lone hit was a short fly ball to the outfield that the Bronchos insisted had been caught, but the umpire ruled the ball was trapped instead.

Throughout the next winter, Lajoie's popularity with the fans showed such a tremendous increase that there were mutterings among the so-called "loyal sports" about a move Kilfoyl and Somers ought to make, *i.e.,* appointing of Larry as manager to succeed Armour. Lajoie had been the team captain from the moment of his arrival in Cleveland.

If there was any doubt of Lajoie's position in the Forest City, it was wiped out in March as the Bronchos were training in New Orleans for their second season under Armour.

The *Cleveland Press* announced a contest to select a new name for the 1903 Cleveland Americans.

"Any name you fans want to submit will be considered," cried the *Press* in a splash announcement of the contest. Some of the sports writers had proposed the name Naps in honor of Lajoie. Too, the name would fit neatly into headlines. Bronchos took up too much space.

Results of the balloting were announced with the following totals reported: Napoleons or Naps, 365 votes; Buckeyes, 281; Emperors, 276; Metropolitans, 239; Giants, 223; and Cyclops, 214. Trailing in order of votes were these rather quaint names: Terrors, Pashas, Dachshunds, Majestics, Mastodons, Midgets, Tip Tops, Crackerjacks, and Prospectors. There were at least fifty other names submitted and not all of them, according to the *Press,* could be published by a family newspaper.

Though the Naps, as they became known immediately, were to start the 1903 season with the same line-up that could do no better than fifth in the previous year, they were the national choices to win the pennant. There was a new team in New York, the Highlanders, playing in the league for the first time, and a noted baseball strategist named Clark Griffith was at the helm. This team was reinforced handsomely to compete with the entrenched Giants, and so there was much debate over the merits of the Naps and the Highlanders.

A vote of thirty-two American and National League baseball writers was taken by one of the wire services to determine the championship races in advance. Cleveland was given twelve votes to win, New York ten. But what rankled the Naps was the vote of one writer who predicted they could finish eighth.

The *Cleveland Press,* burning around the edges of its presses at the insult, struck back, "As the gentleman who voted the Naps eighth is from Brooklyn, he may be excused for not knowing anything in particular."

The brazen fellow wasn't much further off than his colleagues as it turned out. The Naps had added a pitcher, Frank Donahue, who joined Joss, Moore, and Bernhard in comprising Lajoie's "Big Four" of the mound. A rookie answering to the name of Robert "Dusty" Rhoades tagged along to learn the art of practical pitching from the aforementioned regulars. The Naps faded in midseason, and only in a tremendous stretch drive did they manage to reach third place.

Cleveland fans stuck with the club to the finish, which was a remarkable fact in view of their earlier fickleness. The Naps lost three straight in Detroit before coming home to play their inaugural at League Park. A record gathering of 19,867 overflowed the stands and bleachers. At one stage of the game, the players had to grab hands and form a ring around the outer edges of the infield to push the fans back in order that play might be resumed.

Before the Naps played the opener in Detroit, Manager Ed Barrow of the Tigers indulged in one of the maneuvers of strategy that were countenanced at the time. Barrow heard that the Naps had five pitchers who stood six feet or more.

"Get busy right now and shave all fifteen inches off our pitching mound," Barrow ordered his ground crew. "Make our mound level with the ground. That'll make those Cleveland pitchers too wild to find the plate." Obviously, something affected them as the Tigers won three in a row.

The Naps had to go to Dayton or Columbus to play their Sunday games, but no one seemed to mind very much. Baseball people were very amenable in those days, as was proved by the willingness of the Naps' management to postpone a regularly scheduled league game one day because it conflicted with a Big Six or Northern Ohio college track and field meet!

It was during several of those trips to Columbus that Somers got to know the sports editor of the capital city *Dispatch* quite well. He was E. S. Barnard, a studious, pleasant writer who had been a football and baseball coach at Otterbein College in Westerville, Ohio. Barney, as the bespectacled young man was known, started to "sell" Somers on the idea of a full-time, salaried secretary for the Naps. Until then, an office employee accompanied the team on the road during the season, or a part-time man was employed.

Somers, impressed with Barney's sincerity, hired him as regular traveling secretary and so when the Naps arrived in San Antonio, Texas, the next year to open spring training, Barney officially inaugurated a professional baseball career that grew into a permanent monument to the sport.

The Naps were red-hot choices to supplant the feared Boston Red Sox as the league's top team in 1904. Joss, Hess, Bernhard, Rhoades, Donahue, and Moore headed a magnificent pitching staff. Harry Bemis was on hand to catch these famous flingers. The effortless Lajoie was in his prime at second base. George Stovall, up from the Three Eye League, was established at first base, Bradley was an institution at third, and a towheaded rookie, Terry "Cotton" Turner, won the shortstop job. In the outfield, Bay and Flick were as good as any gardeners in the circuit.

The press of the day ignored Armour as much as possible in accounts of games and club activities. Lajoie was the fair-haired boy of players and fans, and it was around Nap that the pennant hopes of the regular fans were centered. Yet there were internal disturbances that caught up with the team in July. Until then, the Naps had battled on even terms with the Red Sox. The tension first began to show late in May. Lajoie was thrown out of a game in Chicago for flinging his well-molded wad of chewing tobacco at an umpire. In a game with the Browns, the Naps made ten errors, and a few days later they folded up before the Highlanders, 21 to 4.

In an effort to instill a winning spirit or incentive in his team, Manager Armour announced a prize for the pitcher winning a game with the Athletics on July 22.

"Whoever wins can take tomorrow off while we're playing a double-header with the A's and go out to watch Bob Fitzsimmons and Philadelphia Jack O'Brien box."

There was a rush of applicants. Bernhard won the nomination and won the game, too. But his report to teammates on the alleged fight was not one of enthusiasm.

"Those guys had it set up not to hurt each other," Bill complained. "They called it a draw, but that isn't what I'd call it."

The Naps continued to play .500 baseball until early September. The team had dropped to fifth place. Armour finally called on Somers.

"I'm resigning, Charley," he told the vice-president on September 9. "This team doesn't want to be managed. Lajoie isn't aggressive although he's a great ball player. I'm through."

Somers accepted the resignation. As team captain, Lajoie took over field direction of the team for the balance of the season and at the completion of the schedule he was given the permanent appointment as manager.

Lajoie pulled the Naps up to fourth place in the last month of play, but he never could make up the ground lost when Turner, the crack rookie shortstop, was hospitalized in midyear with typhoid fever. Bernhard won twenty-nine games, Lajoie hit .381, while Bay and Flick led the league in stolen bases. The Naps proved a better attraction on the road than at home. The team drew a total of 673,019 admissions, but only thirty-nine per cent of those were registered at League Park.

Somers took the Naps back to New Orleans for their spring training in 1905. He was interested in buying the New Orleans team, for one thing, and there was more possibility of getting some ready cash in the Crescent City if a need arose. Not that Somers was out of cash. But he had bumped into an embarrassment in San Antonio the previous spring when the Naps were about to break camp.

The training siege in Texas had been expensive. Somers had hoped to bail out the last two days, Saturday and Sunday, in exhibition games. Somers wanted to pay up to date all bills in San Antonio, but by Sunday night he still had the bills and no cash. A two-day cloudburst washed out both games. Somers didn't know where to turn for cash. His plight became known to the ballplayers.

Dusty Rhoades, the pitcher, was a handsome, strapping young fellow who dressed in the height of current fashion. He was a man-about-town in many cities, including San Antonio, so when he heard of Somers' troubles, Dusty offered help.

"How much cash can you get by with?" Dusty asked.

Somers said he needed around sixteen hundred dollars to pay bills and to buy railroad tickets to Dallas and Fort Worth for the squad that was to be split. Rhoades smiled and told Somers "not to worry."

There was a notorious gambling hall known as the Crystal Palace. Rhoades headed for the crap table. He got "on" a couple of "hot handles" and soon had piled up an eighteen-hundred-dollar profit. He took his roll and hurried back to the team hotel.

Somers took the sixteen hundred dollars and paid bills. The extra two hundred dollars was divided among the players and a crisis had been met and overcome. Present-day baseball operators might frown on Rhoades's methods but none could deny their effectiveness.

An accident to Lajoie ruined the Naps in 1905, Larry's first full year as manager. The same team that tailed off the previous year led the league on July 1, and Cleveland fans were anticipating the first clean-out championship in the city's professional baseball history. But they were destined to wait. Lajoie was spiked in a routine play at second base. He glanced at what seemed to be a minor cut and continued to play.

Dye from the stockings infected the wound, however, and blood poisoning ensued. Lajoie was out of the line-up for two months, and the Naps couldn't win without him. Elmer Flick's .306 was the top batting mark in the American League. Lajoie was off form when he returned, and there had been other injuries to Bradley, Flick, Joss, Bemis, and Bay. So once more a Cleveland championship hope was dashed. By September 5, fans had become so discouraged with the Naps' chances that the majors' smallest crowd of that year, 224 paying clients, was almost lost in League Park's seats.

Though Lajoie slumped and the Naps went down with him, the steady, dependable Bradley continued playing just about the best third base in the business. The "just about" is a doubt created by Bradley himself in the spring of 1905.

The Naps were playing in an exhibition at Atlanta en route north. A smart-aleck fan yelled at Bradley, "Who is the greatest third baseman in the country."

Without hesitating a second, Bradley replied, "Why, I supposed that everybody conceded that Jimmy Collins is."

Collins was managing the Red Sox but wasn't too busy to utter some praiseful phrases about Bradley. These were said in the fall of 1904, incidentally. The Red Sox were sitting in the lobby of the Hotel Euclid when a hanger-on asked Collins who was the best third baseman in his opinion.

"Well," Collins answered slowly and carefully, "if I could field and bat like Bradley, I should lay claim to that title myself."

Lajoie, recovered completely from his leg poisoning, regained his batting form in 1906, and it seemed, throughout the first four months of the season, that the Naps were finally going to reward their faithful flock. They were scrapping the White

Sox and Highlanders for every inch. Rhoades, Joss, and Hess were carrying the pitching burden and holding up remarkably. But they were only three, and the White Sox had six great starting pitchers, Altrock, Walsh, White, Patterson, Smith, and Owens.

Beginning on August 15, the White Sox challenged the Naps and Highlanders. A few days later, Fielder Jones's "hitless wonders" from Chicago launched their famous nineteen-game winning streak. By September 25, they were on top of the league and stayed there, ahead of the New Yorks and Clevelands.

But if the Naps blew the pennant, they won most of the individual honors. Catcher Justin "Nig" Clarke tied with George Stone of the Browns for batting honors with a mark of .358. Lajoie batted .355, outfielder Bill Congalton .320, Flick .311, and first baseman Claude Rossman .308. Rhoades won twenty-two games, Joss twenty-one, and Hess twenty. Cleveland pitchers turned in twenty-seven shutouts. Flick led the league in stolen bases and in runs scored. Even with these marks, the Naps wound up five games off the pace.

For the first time in his life, Nap Lajoie dropped below the .300 mark in batting, this in 1907. He missed by one point and his failure was typical of Cleveland's contention throughout the season. The Naps were comparatively colorless though Somers expanded the playing roster by bringing in outfielder Joe Birmingham, a freckle-faced young star fresh from the Cornell campus; Glenn Liebhardt, a home-grown pitcher off the sand lots; Frank Delahanty, one of the four famous Cleveland-born outfielding brothers; and a rookie catcher, Howard Wakefield, who became the father of the Detroit Tigers' modern outfield star, Dick Wakefield.

The Naps played winning baseball, 85 victories against 67 defeats, but still finished seven games behind the champion Tigers. Under a new president, Frank Navin, a new manager, Hughey Jennings, who replaced William Yawkey and Bill Armour respectively, the Tigers spurted to their first of three consecutive titles.

There was a growing interest in amateur baseball in Cleveland in this period and the Naps took second place in Ohio conversations for several days following a sand-lot game played on July 4, 1907. The Brooklyn Athletic Club and East End All-Stars hooked up at Brookdale Park in what was advertised as one of the leading amateur attractions of the holiday. It was all of that and more.

The teams battled through thirty innings. The game consumed five hours and fifty minutes before the Brooklyn A. C. won on two passes and a home run by their pitcher, LeRoy, who had allowed only one hit in the last eighteen innings while striking out twenty-one. Box scores of this game may be found in nearly all baseball publications of the period. For weeks after this endurance contest, the Cleveland sports writers spent more time glorifying the valiant amateurs than the slumping Naps.

THE JOY OF LAJOIE

THE 1908 AMERICAN LEAGUE pennant race, a viciously contested, sensation-packed four-team scramble, was decided either on October 5 or in early April. One guess is as good as another. For purposes of historical accuracy, the Naps were edged out of the championship by exactly four percentage points, the Tigers applying the clincher the next to last day of the regular season.

But for purposes of conjecture, an incident that occurred in Macon, Georgia, six months earlier should get equal billing with the mathematical aspects. The Naps were training in Macon. The Tigers were drilling in Augusta. Charley Somers had made his customary trip southward with the Naps and was sitting in his hotel room in Macon one evening, probably pondering the fate of a wild left-handed pitcher named John Gladstone Graney, better known as Mickey. Young Graney had joined the Naps that spring and had distinguished himself in his first pitching appearance by drilling a fast ball into Manager Lajoie's head.

The telephone rang and Somers excused himself from the conversation with some sports writers and friends from Cleveland.

"Mr. Somers, this is Hughey Jennings," Somers heard. The day's pleasantries were exchanged. Suddenly Somers' face took on a frown.

"I'd like to make a deal with the Cleveland club," the fiery Jennings said, speaking officially for the Tigers he managed. "I'll give you Ty Cobb for Elmer Flick, even up."

Somers was baffled. After all, Cobb had batted .350 for the Tigers in 1907, enough to lead the league. He was regarded as a "sure comer," though the casual observer might have doubted the wisdom of investing too much money in the stubborn

Georgian. The Augusta team had sold Cobb to Detroit for seven hundred and fifty dollars in 1905 and was glad to be rid of him.

Somers pondered Jennings' proposal. Cobb had not only batted .350, he had stolen 49 bases. Flick posted a .302 average and had stolen 41 bases.

"Tell me, Hughey," asked Somers, "Why are you so anxious to trade Cobb? Anything wrong with him physically?"

Jennings quickly assured the Naps' boss Ty was in perfect shape.

"But he can't get along with our players and we want to get him away," added Jennings. "Why, he's had two fights already this spring. We want harmony on this team, not scrapping."

Somers made his decision on the spot.

"We'll keep Flick," he told Jennings. "Maybe he isn't quite as good a batter as Cobb, but he's much nicer to have on the team."

Had Somers only guessed right on that one!

Cobb had one or two more fights with teammates, then seemed to settle down. He played fine ball, batted .324, and was easily the margin by which Detroit won the pennant. Poor Flick, on the other hand, was taken ill and was lost to the Naps for the entire 1908 season. Elmer staged a comeback the next year but never regained his presickness form.

Without Cobb, and also without Flick, the Naps struggled and scratched throughout that historic and tingling campaign. There were hundreds of thousands of shattered hopes and dreams in Cleveland in mid-October. These hopes had been built high, then torn down, rebuilt, and carried on through as hectic a last six-week period as a pennant race ever knew.

Lajoie, in spite of his marvelous fielding and tremendous batting, was not exactly a darling of the grandstand as a manager. When the Naps lost a pair of ten-inning games at the beginning of the season, the Cleveland newspapers fried Larry crisply.

"How long should a pitcher stay in a game before *everybody* knows he's no good?" asked the *Cleveland Press*. All the city's newspapers printed daily suggestions to Lajoie concerning selection of pitchers, which fielders should play, and which

Jimmy McAleer

Larry "Nap" Lajoie

Cy Young

Addie Joss

batters should bat in the more advantageous positions in the line-up.

Even so, or perhaps because of this bickering in the press, the Naps held the interest of fans from the outset. After about one quarter of the schedule had been played, the Naps were in fourth place but were only one and a half games out of first. They won a double-header from the Browns the next day and took over the league lead.

So it went, day after day. In July, the Naps went into their routine slump. By late that month they were nine games behind the first-place Tigers. Then they reversed their decline and stunned the league in August by winning fifteen games and losing only three during one stretch.

Shortly thereafter, Dusty Rhoades decided to take personal charge of the pennant race for a period. The fashion-plate right-hander was named by Lajoie to face the Red Sox in September. Rhoades had reported to the Naps' camp in New Orleans that spring with a "new pitch." He called it the Merry Widow curve. The pitch was a tantalizer, according to accounts of its use, and the Red Sox discovered to their dismay it could be epoch-making.

Dusty toyed with the Red Sox for nine innings, never allowing one to rap anything faintly resembling a safe hit. So was registered the fourth no-hit game by a Cleveland pitcher and the team's second in the American League.

Spurred by Rhoades's masterpiece, the Naps fought their way into the league lead three days later. By the last days of the month, the standings changed almost daily. The strain was terrific. The leading Tigers won three straight from Washington. Chicago blasted the Red Sox three straight. And Cleveland kept pace by hammering the A's three times!

Lajoie wasn't hitting. In fact, he was below .300 for a second year. Flick was of no use. Turner was lost for the year, and a rookie named George Perring filled in for him. Perring played better as third baseman than as a shortstop, which resulted in a shift of Bradley to short for a few games. But when the pressure was left in the last weeks, Bradley returned to third and Perring held down short.

The three leaders enjoyed a vacation on October 1. That night their standings read:

	G.	W.	L.	Pct.	G.B.
Detroit	148	87	61	.588	—
Cleveland	149	87	62	.584	½
Chicago	147	85	62	.578	1½

Each team was scheduled for five more games. The Tigers entertained the Browns in a two-game series. But the spotlight of the nation was on Cleveland. The White Sox were in League Park for two games. Little did the schedule maker dream that he was writing a clutching drama that would be unfolded in the final week of play and especially in the Cleveland-Chicago series.

ADDIE JOSS THE INCOMPARABLE

ADDIE JOSS WAS JUST twenty-eight years old, in the full physical bloom of his life. Seven years of pitching for the Naps had enabled him to "beat the rap" of having been a college man. Only a handful of players in the rough, stirring, early days of the major leagues arrived from campuses. And when they did, the shock was sometimes too much for them. Some grizzled holdovers of the late 1890's were around and they bore down heavily on the eardrums of the so-called college-boy set.

Joe Birmingham had been accorded a violent reception in 1907 when he made the leap from Cornell to Cleveland. In one of his first games, Birmingham batted against Frank "Red" Donahue, whom the Naps had traded off to the Tigers. Donahue considered himself the master of the curve, and he expected that one of his sweeping benders would baffle the eager Birmingham. But Joe slapped out a double. Donahue kicked the dirt around the mound, then walked toward the plate to yell at Joe.

"You smart college [censored]," he screamed. You'll never get another hit off me. Keep your eyes open from now on before you get hurt up there." Birmingham didn't get another hit. Donahue struck him out three times in a row.

Then there was the riotous scene enacted by Jim Delahanty, one of the famous four Cleveland-born brothers, then playing with the Washington Senators. Jim was called out at first base on a close play and proceeded to blast the umpire in loud voice and with expressions that were designed for bachelor hearers. The umpire ejected Jim from the game, and the departing player raised his voice and lowered the level of his epithets. Everyone in League Park, except a few people who may have been out of their seats temporarily, heard the verbal explosion. Strong men blanched, and the women and children in the park cringed. The next day the sports editors of the newspapers blew the tops off their typewriters demanding punishment for Delahanty.

"Baseball is a family sport now, not a game for poor sports and toughs," voiced one writer. "Come, Mr. Ban Johnson, let's have a stiff penalty imposed on this player to teach him that Cleveland is a city in which clean baseball must be played."

Whatever Delahanty said to the umpire must have been quite ripe because Johnson suspended him for ten days, ordered a fifty-dollar fine and prohibited Jim from entering League Park, as either a player or a spectator, for one year!

Joss, the college man, had soared above the criticism of jealous rivals and not a few envious teammates. And a good thing for the Naps that he had. For without Joss the Naps never would have figured in the 1908 race, one of the closest and most exciting known.

Addie won five of Cleveland's first nine games, eight of the first thirteen, and nine of the first fifteen. He won nine of the first ten games he started and had such superior control that he walked only *four* batters in his first nine appearances.

"Oh, for a Few More Like Joss," read a sports-page headline in the *Cleveland News*.

Addie faced the Senators on June 17 and retired the first two batters. The next two singled. But not another hit did he permit in the next eight innings. Against Detroit on September 1 Addie missed a no-hitter by a scant foot, a pop fly falling just beyond the infield for the Tigers' only safety.

No one but Addie Joss was in Manager Lajoie's mind when the White Sox arrived at League Park on October 2 to begin a do-or-die series for the American League championship. It was a Friday and a crowd of 10,598, excellent for a weekday turnout, was in the park, which had been enlarged earlier that year. About four thousand more seats had been constructed in a permanent grandstand and more than twenty thousand could be accommodated.

All the ball parks in the world, before and after 1908, would not have been large enough had fans known what was in store. The attraction of Joss pitching for the Naps and Ed Walsh for the White Sox, plus the tightness of the pennant race, was a good one. Joss had pitched six one-hitters. Only three days before, Walsh had pitched and won both games of a double-header with the Red Sox.

Scarcely a hint of the historical events to follow was revealed in the first two innings. Joss retired six Chicago batters in order. Walsh was even better. Big Ed's spitball was darting as it crossed the plate. Right fielder Wilbur Goode, destined to go down four times before Walsh's pitches, struck out in the first. In the second inning, Lajoie, first baseman George Stovall, and catcher Nig Clarke went down swinging.

But in the third, Walsh tried to sneak a fast ball through on Joe Birmingham. The big center fielder, a right-handed batter, lashed it to right center for a single. Joe brought to the major leagues two assets, one of the strongest throwing arms known, and a mastery of the "delayed steal." It was Birmingham, in fact, who claimed the invention of the intentional trap play that sets up a delayed steal.

On first base, Birmingham wasted no time trying to draw a throw from Walsh. He danced far off the bag. Walsh finally wheeled and fired the ball to Frank Isbell, the first baseman. But Birmingham was gone toward second. As he scanned the turf preparatory to sliding into the bag, he felt the ball hit him in the right shoulder. Isbell's peg caromed off into the outfield and Birmingham raced on to third. He stayed there as shortstop George Perring tapped to the drawn-in infield. Then Joss struck out and up stepped Goode.

Walsh fired two strikes past Goode. Ossie Shreck, the Chicago catcher, squatted to give the signal for the next pitch. Walsh nodded his head and wound up. Then he cut loose with a fireball to the outside of the plate. There had been a mix-up in the signals!

Shreck stuck out his bare right hand in an attempt to stop the ball, but it tore on through and rolled almost to the grandstand. Birmingham scored easily, and what a run that was to be! Poor Shreck, his hand ripped and bleeding, had to retire from the game. The official scoring on the play was a wild pitch for Walsh, but old-timers remember that for two decades Big Ed insisted that it was a passed ball instead.

The game wore on. Still not a hit for Chicago, still not a

Chicago runner on first base. Lajoie was magnificent. In the third and fourth innings, he retired five men in a row, four on throws and one on a pop fly. The Sox were beating Joss's fadeaway pitches into the ground, and the balls were taking some mighty queer hops through the infield. Lajoie twice raced behind the box to make great throws of slow bounders. Stovall, who had made a sensational catch of Perring's high throw in the second inning, reached in every direction to drag in the balls.

Now it was the seventh inning, and the crowd became suddenly still and silent. Even in those early days of the sport, superstition was acknowledged, and no one mentioned, other than in an aside to his neighbor, that the White Sox hadn't been able to get a runner to first.

Then, as the second batter in the seventh, Fielder Jones, Chicago's center fielder and manager, put Joss to the supreme test. Top man in the batting order because he knew how to get on base, Jones wiggled at the plate until Joss threw him three straight pitches wide of the plate. The count was three and two. A thousand fingernails hit the floor as Joss had to be careful now. He wound up and depended upon his best sidearm pitch, known to moderns as a sinker. It wasn't a good strike and there was some debate after the game that it had been a strike of any kind, but plate umpire Tommy Connolly thought it was close enough to be called. Jones, complaining, was sent to the bench.

Walsh was more erratic than his rival but more powerful, too. A total of four hits had been registered off Big Ed's pitches in the eight innings the Clevelands batted. He had struck out fifteen, a double victim having been the great Lajoie himself. The Naps couldn't capitalize upon their remaining three hits, all singles, or the one walk Walsh granted.

By the time the ninth inning was played, no one in the park was speaking above a whisper. That Joss would face three pinch hitters was certain. The first was Doc White, who grounded harmlessly to Lajoie. The second was a utility first baseman, J. Donohue. Addie whipped over three strikes, the last a "dipper" that skimmed beneath Donohue's bat.

One man to go!

No one ever will know the exact prayer that was emitted as

Addie Joss, standing in back of the pitching rubber, waited for Chicago's third pinch hitter in a row to step into the batter's box. Unlike today's ball games, which are everybody's business, due to transmission of each detail by telegraph, radio, and television, the Joss-Walsh duel was being waged for the most exclusive audience known to the sport.

Umpire Connolly turned to the grandstand.

"Anderson now batting for Walsh," he howled.

John Anderson, a big, strong, right-handed hitter, stood between Addie Joss and immortality. Men with weaker stomachs than Joss's might have been unable to locate the plate, or might have been so anxious to get the ball over they would pitch down the middle and involuntarily grant a base hit.

"A mouse working his way along the grandstand floor would have sounded like a shovel scraping over concrete," penned one press-box observer in describing the tension and the knawing quiet that prevailed.

Joss decided to pitch "in on Anderson's hands," and low. He wanted Big John to pound the ball into the dirt for a possible infield play and he figured, correctly, that Anderson couldn't get all his bat's wood on the pitch if the ball were thrown close to the body. Addie wound up and delivered his sidearm sinker. Anderson swung.

There was a shattering sound, the crack of the bat meeting the ball. Joss had got the pitch too high, too good. Anderson shot a liner down the left-field foul line into the outfield. But Anderson, like Joss, was nervous, and he swung too soon. The ball curved foul at the last split second, and ten thousand sighs from the stands sounded much like a happy whispering in a forest of plenty.

Again Joss pitched, and again Anderson swung. That time the ball struck down into the dirt and bounded toward the third baseman, big Bill Bradley. Not one chance all game had Bradley had. The White Sox, respecting Bill's strong arm and his pet pickup play on bunts and slow rollers, had not resorted to the usual strategy of bunting in the hope of getting at least one runner to first base.

Let Bill Bradley, still big and strong in his capacity as talent scout for the Cleveland Indians, tell in his own words the story of Anderson's grounder. "There have been many stories about that play," Bill says, "but there was nothing unusual about it until I threw the ball. I knew something about John Anderson. He was a powerful man who played in the outfield and at first base. Once before, when I had been playing shortstop in place of Terry Turner, who was hurt, I almost got a triple play when Anderson sent a terrific liner to me. He was a pull hitter, and so when he came up in Addie's big game, I moved over closer to the base. John hit his grounder rather sharply over the bag. I was playing deep and I took the ball in back of the cushion. I threw to Stovall, but I threw low. George made a fine pickup of the ball out of the dirt."

The arm of the colorful Francis "Silk" O'Loughlin, umpiring at first base, came up as he cried, "You're out!" Anderson, having passed the bag, turned as if to utter a protest to the arbiter. But it was too late for many reasons. Fans were pouring from the stands, eager to pat Joss on the back or touch his uniform.

Outside League Park, residents poured from their homes, begging for crumbs of information about Joss.

The perfect game!

"I never could have done it without Larry's and Stovall's fielding and without Birmingham's base running," said the modest Joss. "Walsh was marvelous with his spitter, and we needed two lucky strokes to win."

It was the sixth no-man-reach-first performance in the recorded history of professional baseball. There was to be only one other, by Charley Robertson of the White Sox in 1922. However, five of those masterpieces were put on baseball's bright canvas as purely personal efforts, without the money and the glory of teammates riding on each pitch.

Here was the strong point of Joss's perfect game. It was pitched in the heat of the end of a pennant race when the pressure on every player was at double strength. No ordinary foes were the White Sox. They, too, were pennant hungry. They, too, sought to honor Big Ed Walsh for an exhibition that would have won almost any other game ever played. Fielder Jones never let up on his enemy, Joss. He threw three pinch hitters at Addie in the ninth, men who stepped to the plate with orders to get on, never mind the method.

"Cleveland will win the pennant," claimed the *Plain Dealer* the next morning.

But the *Plain Dealer's* sports editor bragged too early. The White Sox were still in the pennant race and they fought back the next day to disappoint a huge Saturday throng of 20,729. Joss's feat and the Naps' flag possibilities had fired the minds of Clevelanders. They occupied just about every inch of space in League Park.

And they watched a game that was not as historically important as the Joss-Walsh duel but was certainly as dramatic and as tense. Lajoie called on Glenn Liebhardt to pitch for the Naps. Fielder Jones depended upon Frank Smith. After six innings, the White Sox led, 3 to 1. Then Smith got into trouble, and the Naps filled the bases.

In the bull pen Ed Walsh warmed up quickly. Ed Walsh, who had struck out fifteen Naps the day before! Ed Walsh, who had pitched and won both ends of a double-header three days before that! Ed Walsh, who was destined to win forty games that year. Now Ed Walsh came in to pitch in place of Frank Smith and standing at the plate was the mightiest batter of his time, Larry Lajoie!

Two were out; the count was two and two on Lajoie. Walsh stood calmly on the mound. Behind the plate squatted Billy Sullivan, Sr. A splint encased a broken finger on his right hand. He couldn't catch the day before, and he wouldn't have been catching now except that Ossie Shreck's hand had been split and there was no one else.

"There's a bonus of one thousand dollars in it for you if you catch this game," Fielder Jones promised Sullivan after a conference with owner Charley Comiskey.

Sullivan signaled for a fast ball. Lajoie stood behind the crude line he always drew across the batter's box. He waved his big mace. He wondered, of course, what the next pitch would be—one of those spitballs that broke every which way or a curve that might tantalize him?

Lajoie didn't think Walsh would dare throw him a fast ball. But Big Ed dared, and the great Frenchman never removed the bat from his shoulder. Lajoie took a called third strike, and the Naps had muffed their best chance. They scored a run off Walsh in the eighth but lost the game, 3 to 2.

Still, there was a chance for the pennant. The Naps moved to St. Louis, the White Sox to Detroit. Doc White beat the Tigers on Sunday, and it was up to the Naps to whip the Browns. After eight innings, the score was tied, 3-3. Joss had gone in to pitch, and it seemed his tremendous heart might pull the Naps through.

In the ninth, with two out, Joss himself was on third base. Bill Bradley was on second and Bill Hinchman at bat. Hinchman pounded a grounder over the box. Bobby Wallace, the Brown's shortstop and one of the best according to contemporaries, raced toward second, knocked the ball down, retrieved it, and threw in the general direction of first base. The ball and Hinchman arrived at approximately the same split second.

As Hinchman crossed the bag, Tom Jones, the Browns' first baseman, wheeled and threw the ball to the plate. Joss had gone in, and Bradley had dashed for home. Bradley stopped, turned, and raced back safely to third. Jones, quite obviously, thought that Hinchman was safe at first, and he hoped to cut off at least one run at the plate.

But in the confusion, Umpire Jack Egan ruled Hinchman out claiming that Wallace's throw and Jones' pickup had been in time to make the third out of the inning. Hence Joss had not officially scored from third base, the side was out, and the Naps were till tied, 3-3. They rushed Egan, but the umpire would not reverse himself. He said Hinchman could have beaten the throw but "didn't hustle." Two more innings were played without a run being scored, and Joss's fine relief stint of six and two-thirds innings in which he permitted only two hits had been wasted.

The game was ordered replayed the next day as part of a double-header. The Naps couldn't afford to lose. But they lost the first game to the Browns, 3 to 1, and formally conceded the pennant to the Tigers. The Naps were eliminated mathematically. The race was concluded October 6 with the Naps four percentage points behind the Tigers. The White Sox were third, one and a half games behind the new champions.

The night of October 5, after the split in St. Louis, Larry Lajoie permitted himself the relaxation of a good, man-sized cry. He was not the only disconsolate Nap. Addie Joss alone seemed to feel that all had not been lost. The gentlemanly pitcher remarked, "We'll win next year. We had some bad breaks this year, but watch us in 1909."

The 1908 race had been too strenuous for President Kilfoyl. Jack's health failed, and he gradually stepped out of the administration of the Cleveland team. Somers, who had been the virtual ruler for eight years, assumed the presidency and elevated Barnard to the vice-president's position. Together, Somers and Barnard planned a general expansion of the Cleveland baseball empire. Barnard had envisaged a farm system and with Somers' money was employed to build one. The Naps soon controlled franchises in Ironton, Ohio, Waterbury, Connecticut, Toledo of the American Association, Portland of the Pacific Coast League, and New Orleans of the Southern Association.

CHAPTER IX

AN INTERLUDE

EVERYONE IN BASEBALL started out to watch the Naps in 1909, but at the finish only a handful of people knew or cared what had happened to the team that "couldn't miss" winning the championship. There was one notable aspect to the Naps' failure. When they flopped, they didn't totter. They disintegrated.

The hopes of Cleveland fans, high because of the club's spectacular finish in 1908, were brightened further when Somers made a deal with the Red Sox for the return of Cy Young.

Old Tuscarawas was about to be forty-two, and there was a gathering around his waist that was not entirely wool. Cy had won twenty-one games for the Red Sox in 1908, but the dashing president of the Boston club, John I. Taylor, thought that the hero of three no-hit games was about washed up.

So he offered Young and Cy's pet catcher, Lou Criger, to the Naps for three youngsters, two pitchers named Ryan and Chech and a catcher called Spencer. None of the three was considered promising enough to include in the Naps' roster. As it happened, the three were gone from the Red Sox before the season's end, too.

But Taylor knew that Criger was a sick man—he never got to play a game for Cleveland—and that Young was aging. He didn't expect Cy to be good for nineteen triumphs, one of these a two-hit shutout of his former mates at Boston. Yet not even Young and Lajoie, who regained his batting form with a .324 mark after two years in the dumps, could save the Naps.

Joss began to fail physically, and without Addie the Naps had no peg upon which to hang their future. The Cleveland newspapers, reacting to early season reversals, shouted, "Naps? ...They ought to be known as the Napkins, the way they fold up." It may have been the day of frank journalism in baseball, but it also was the day of free-wheeling coinage of critical diamond terms. Lajoie was under fire for his handling of pitchers, and fans were saying that, as long as Cy Young could be so good at forty-two, maybe Somers ought to get rid of all his players and sign an entire new team of men forty and over.

Lajoie took it as long as he could. His tongue became sharper with each setback. Competitively, his playing remained on a high plane. He was still graceful, still sufficiently agile, and still a force with the bat. But his temper got out of hand, and many harsh words found their way through his spells of anger to land heavily on hapless athletes who might have lacked major-league graces.

"You can't win in the major leagues unless you have players who know the game," Lajoie said many times during that sorrowful summer. "We don't have time to teach and train youngsters up here. Our job is to win pennants, not run schools."

So Larry Lajoie reasoned and so, as his team lost game after game, did his patience with his players slacken. Finally, on August 17, he walked in to talk to Charley Somers.

"Maybe they'd do better with some one else running the club," the disconsolate Frenchman said. "I'd like to keep on playing for you, but I'd suggest a new manager."

Somers asked Larry to think it over. Larry did briefly. Then he told Somers he had determined to quit and that if the boss wanted to do so, a salary adjustment could be made. Lajoie was getting ten thousand dollars a year as the highest salaried player in the American League.

Five days later, Somers announced that Jim McGuire, one of Larry's coaches, would become the manager. First baseman George Stovall was named field captain. Lajoie remained what he had been for years—the game's greatest second baseman. It is interesting to point out that Lajoie finished that season as a player and spent the next five in Cleveland livery under three other managers, one of them his former player. Freed of the burden of management, Larry batted .384 in 1909. This was his highest mark as a Cleveland player.

With Lajoie no longer at the club's helm, the peppery *Cleveland Press,* having determined the Cleveland team's nicknames once before, jumped into the breach immediately, and ran a contest to select a new name. Much to the *Press's* consternation, its readers preferred the name Naps even with Larry Lajoie in the role of player. So Naps they remained.

Though they wound up a miserable sixth, the Clevelands did come up with some neat prospects, outfielder Brisco Lord and catcher Ted Easterly among them. Too, shortstop Neal Ball placed the Naps and himself permanently in baseball's record books by registering an unassisted triple play.

Young was the beneficiary of Ball's thrilling play on July 19, 1909. Cy was pitching against the Red Sox in the first game of a double-header at League Park. Two batters, Heinie Wagner and Jake Stahl, beat out infield rollers. The next was Ambrose "Ambie" McConnell, who worked his count to three and two.

Neal Ball edged over as Young delivered the next pitch. McConnell caught the ball flush with the "fat" of his bat and sent a liner screaming past Cy Young's ear. Crashing into Ball's glove went the liner. Neal took a few more strides forward, stepped onto the second-base bag, and then moved perhaps three feet down the base line toward first. Stahl, who like Wagner had started running on the pitch, walked smack into the waiting Ball.

"No one among the ten thousand persons in the park said anything for a full minute," observed one of the writers covering the game. "They were too stunned by what had happened. The Boston players didn't know right away that there had been an unassisted triple play. Then pandemonium reigned suddenly and Neal Ball was congratulated by all his teammates as he came to the bench."

By way of pouring it on the Red Sox, Ball went to the plate in the last half of that same second inning and hit an inside-the-park home run. Young was an easy 6-to-1 victor over the Red Sox as a result. The triumph was one of nineteen achieved by the forty-three-year-old Young for a sixth-place team.

McGuire's team in 1910 wasn't any better than the 1909 failures, and it was a practice in the daily press to refer to the Naps as the Molly McGuires. Young was just about through; Joss was slipping more. Somers and Barnard were thinking about rebuilding the team from the basement up. They had a great pitching prospect in Willie Mitchell, a young southpaw. Great things were predicted, too, for a rookie hurler by the name of Fred Blanding.

After two years in exile at Portland, Mickey Graney returned to the Naps as an outfielder. His wildness as a pitcher, plus his talents as a batter, runner, and thrower, had convinced the Naps he should be converted to an outfielder. Just another candidate when the team opened spring training at Alexandria, Louisiana, Graney became the lead-off man and left fielder, as a highly touted newcomer from Columbus, Art Krueger, failed to make the grade.

Also in the Alexandria camp was a bandy-legged Cleveland youngster fresh from the study halls of East High School. Roger Peckinpaugh could scoot to any given quarter of a baseball infield and come up with ground balls. Somers first heard of Peck from Principal B. U. Rannells of East High. Before many weeks of spring training had passed, baseball people throughout the country began hearing of Peck. The Naps soon learned that curves mystified the kid. After two years in the minors, Peck was still baffled by hooks, and the Naps traded him to the New York Yankees for outfielder Jack Lelivelt.

When the Naps came home to open their schedule on April 22, 1910, they gasped at the contour of their new abode. Gone were the wooden grandstand and pavilion. In their places were steel and concrete stands, fitted with individual seats. No longer would the average baseball fan sit on a crude bench. Now he was a spectator, a paying guest of the management.

The biggest and most startling feature in the new League Park was a wall in right field. It was forty feet high. It started at the juncture of the right-field pavilion and the foul line, two hundred and ninety feet out from home plate, and extended east on Lexington Avenue for more than four hundred feet. It was not a barrier of solid concrete. Only the lower twenty feet were permanent. The upper twenty feet were covered by a screen.

Alas, the new park with its green wall and bright stands was to be well nigh empty many days that summer. The Naps had a palace to play in but their tastes were definitely lower class.

The team spent the entire season in or around fifth place, a condition that sent Somers and Barnard out to the open market to do a bit of buying and swapping.

Early in September, Somers talked to Connie Mack about a young outfielder the Athletics had farmed out to New Orleans, a team in which Somers was financially interested. A New Orleans sports editor had tipped off Somers that the youngster had the makings of a big leaguer.

His name was Joe Jackson and he had been reared in North Carolina, in the deep backwoods. No readin' or writin' ever penetrated Joe Jackson, and he became known as Shoeless Joe because he slipped out of his store boots at every opportunity. But he had the greatest natural swing Somers' friend had ever seen, and Charley offered Mack one of Cleveland's own promising stars, outfielder Briscoe Lord, in exchange. Mack accepted the offer and Joe Jackson came up from New Orleans to join the Naps in mid-September of 1910. Jackson got into twenty games before the close of the season and batted .387.

Lajoie's .384 missed by one point in his personal duel with Ty Cobb, though the St. Louis Browns, who detested Cobb, tried their best to help Larry. In a final double-header in St. Louis, Lajoie was credited with eight hits in eight times at bat. Some of those were bunts to a third baseman who played far back on the grass. The intent was so apparent that President Ban Johnson of the American League investigated and fined two St. Louis players for their actions.

"If all you fellows will stick with me, we'll force the Detroit club to cancel this opening game."

George Stovall, captain and first baseman of the Naps, was speaking to his teammates on the eve of the opening of the 1911 schedule. There was a strong reason Stovall and the other Cleveland players wanted to be elsewhere than in Detroit.

Their teammate, the great and grand Addie Joss, had passed on in Toledo April 14. Only thirty-one, the lovable pitcher had succumbed to tubercular meningitis. Addie's funeral was scheduled on the opening day of the championship season. Neither the Detroit nor Cleveland managements, according to correspondents of the period, were especially anxious to call off a traditional game sure to bring a big crowd to Navin Field.

"We'll all sign a petition and give it to McGuire," Stovall suggested. They did, but they didn't wait for Manager McGuire to turn it over to Somers. The entire Naps' aggregation went to Toledo for the funeral, and the scheduled inaugural game was set back, of course.

"Cleveland Players Strike," shouted the headlines of many newspapers, including those in Detroit, when it was learned the Naps had taken the law into their own hands. But the Naps didn't care. They weren't very fond of McGuire, they thought Stovall would make an ideal leader, and they were losing faith in Somers, who was beginning to lose much of his fortune.

Not even the playing of Cleveland's first American League Sunday game could arrest a dissension in the ranks. An Ohio law permitting Sunday baseball had been legislated by State Representative Joseph Greeves. Finally, on May 14, 1911, Somers scheduled Cleveland's first game on the Sabbath and presented Representative Greeves with a solid gold lifetime pass as a part of the ceremonies. For the embattled manager, McGuire, a better part was a 16-to-3 beating the Naps gave the New Yorks. Cleveland churchmen bitterly opposed the advent of Sunday baseball, but the game's popularity was strong enough to withstand the criticism.

In late May, the Naps were almost last, nine games out of first place. McGuire had attempted to rebuild the team, but Lajoie ruptured a leg muscle, the brittle Turner was hurt again, and the manager was hard pressed to present the same line-up throughout any one series. New faces showed among the old— pitchers Vean Gregg and Bill James, catcher Steve O'Neill, shortstop Ivan Olson, and outfielder Tom Hendryx.

Bill Bradley, the peerless third baseman, had rounded out nine years with the Naps and had made a deal with the Toronto team of the International League. Later he officially ended his big-league career with the Detroit Tigers.

And Cy Young was forty-four.

The grand old man of the pitching mound had altered his style in deference to the years. No longer did he blaze his fast ball over the plate. Now he was throwing curves and "faking" an occasional spitball. No team in the American League could use Old Tuscarawas. But the Boston Braves thought he had some value, not only as a "spot" pitcher but also as a gate attraction.

Cy earned his keep in his first start. He beat Grover Cleveland Alexander and the Philadelphia Phillies, 1 to 0. Cy had won three games while losing four for the Naps that year, 1911. He posted four triumphs for the Braves and lost five games. There was some hope among the Braves he could enjoy one more year as a big-league pitcher, especially after his great start.

But Cy couldn't coax the kinks out of his forty-five-year-old arm in the spring of 1912. He quit the Braves before the start of the National League schedule and went home—home to his ample bank account, to his prosperous farm, to his Irish setters, and the neighborly folk he had known twenty-five years before. They were plain people, farm people, Cy Young people.

Debates over the name of the world's foremost baseball pitcher rage on and on but anyone placing Denton True Young at the top of the list has a pretty fair advantage. In twenty-two years, in pioneer baseball and modern baseball, in eras of skintight gloves and padded protection, the big Ohioan pitched superbly. He won 511 games, lost 315, and retired with a lifetime percentage of .609.

Cy played for Patsy Tebeau, a tough *hombre,* and for Larry Lajoie, who never tried to hide his worship of the farmer-pitcher. He ducked rocks and garbage in Baltimore in the Temple Cup Series and pitched with extreme care to the immortal Willie Keeler, who Cy insists was the most difficult man to fool he ever faced. There were fights with Muggsy McGraw and with every umpire in the old National League.

There was history and adventure in baseball for Cy Young, and there is wealth in the lore of the sport in Cleveland because of him.

At the time Young was waived out of the American League, Manager McGuire turned in his mythical badge, partly because of disgust with his team's showing, partly because the front office was making odd noises of displeasure. Somers, who had been very friendly with Connie Mack all those years, made a deal with the Philadelphia manager for Harry Davis, Connie's fading first baseman who also was a sort of assistant manager. But the deal was to be secret, Davis not being scheduled to assume management of the Naps until 1912.

"George Stovall will succeed McGuire," Somers announced to the press. The Naps themselves were delighted. They perked up. Joe Jackson batted .408. From seventh place, the Naps advanced to third. They were scrappy and ambitious. They won seven more games than they lost.

Imagine the howling at the outset of the 1912 season when Somers announced that Davis would be the new manager of the Naps! Stovall had been shipped down the river to St. Louis. Davis was an innocent victim of circumstances. He tried to rebuild the Naps. He issued an order banning handshaking and conversations with players of rival teams before and during games. The Naps, who had been happy and friendly under Stovall, rebelled. There was much grumbling and when the team slipped deep into the second division, Somers began to look around for help.

So did Manager Davis. At one stage of the race, in June, Davis talked Somers into asking waivers on two-thirds of the Cleveland team. The jitters were affecting Harry. He may have known, too, of the devotion of the Cleveland fans for Lajoie and the holdovers of the 1911 team. The day that Larry marked his tenth anniversary with the Naps, fans presented him a floral horseshoe studded with more than a thousand silver dollars.

The Naps wanted to have as much fun in 1912 as they had had the year before, and there was a hint they might in a few thrills that preceded their arrival in the North that spring. Henry Edwards told the story many times of the trip from the New Orleans training base through Memphis and Louisville to Cleveland. This trip was frequently a battle with waters of the Mississippi, Ohio, and lesser rivers that covered the countryside in typical spring floods.

The Naps' train was stopped at a small town in Kentucky to permit the players to eat breakfast since it appeared impossible to get through to Louisville. The town's lone restaurant was owned and operated by an elderly man who was clearly befuddled by the intrusion of thirty-five to forty young giants.

Lajoie took charge. "You sit down and don't worry," he told the proprietor. "We'll get our own breakfast. Just tell us where everything is."

Vean Gregg, the great southpaw pitcher, took care of the cooking of ham and eggs. Steve O'Neill made the coffee. Jack Graney and a rookie shortstop, Ray Chapman, squabbled over which should cut the bread.

At meal's end, the club secretary, Bill Blackwood, asked the total cost.

"Well, our breakfasts are twenty-five cents per person," the proprietor answered slowly. "But I suppose I ought to take somethin' off that, seein' as how you fellers did your own cookin'."

Today's major leaguer gets almost as much "meal money" for one day ($7.50) as thirty-five breakfasts cost in 1912!

In August, the Naps were mired in the second division. Somers recalled Chapman from Toledo and brought in Wheeler "Doc" Johnston, a clever first baseman. Chappie batted .321 in twenty-one games, Joe Jackson batted .395 for the season, Gregg won twenty games, and a comparative rookie from the University of Michigan, Fred Blanding, turned in eighteen triumphs.

But the Naps were sixth late that month, and Davis quit. Joe Birmingham, only twenty-eight years old at the time, took over. It was a rough decision for Somers to make. A year before he had replaced a bench manager with the popular Stovall. Somers had ignored the improvement in the team under Stovall and had brought in Davis. This time he was determined to avoid that mistake. He made up his mind to keep Birmingham indefinitely.

One man who wished Somers had not made that choice was Lajoie. The new manager and the big Frenchman, then thirty-eight years old, clashed head on many times. In June of 1913, Lajoie fell into a slump, and Birmingham benched him. Larry was furious. He cursed Birmingham on the bench and to the press.

Oddly, despite this bit of dissension and numerous other battles, the Naps kept on winning. They were in the thick of the pennant race from the first week of the 1913 season until the last. The club had good balance, sound pitching, and a crack outfield. Yet the inevitable jinx worked its inverted magic on the Cleveland team. Something was forever happening to the Naps and 1913 was no exception.

The club had second place all but clinched and had a fine chance to oust the Athletics from the league lead on the eve of the Naps' final trip throughout the East. The Naps handled the New Yorks without trouble in the first series, then boarded a train to move down to Washington to meet the pesky Senators, in third place and invariably bothersome to the Naps.

Once on the train, Vean Gregg and Cy Falkenberg, a pitcher who had shown enough promise with the Toledo team earlier in the season to be brought up to the parent Naps, got into a friendly wrestling match. They fell, locked, in the aisle of a Pullman car, and in a freak accident each man came down hard upon his pitching arm. Neither was in condition to pitch in a series as crucial as the one coming up with the Senators.

Gregg tried it in the first game and was knocked out. Fred Blanding was routed in the second game. Gregg came back in the third game only to be nosed out, 2 to 1. Bill Steen and Blanding were thrashed by the Nationals in other games, and the Naps had dropped five straight! Falkenberg, who had been sent home for an examination of his injured arm, rejoined the Naps in Philadelphia and beat Chief Bender and the A's, but the Cleveland team lost the next two games in Shibe Park and was out of the race. The Naps finally wound up third.

Everything happened to the Naps in 1914. Somers' business affairs were becoming more and more complex. His money was running out. The Federal League was threatening to come into Cleveland. To forestall such a move, Somers decided to give Cleveland daily baseball in his own park. Hence, he transferred the Toledo team in the American Association to League Park. Too, the Toledo team was not whirling its turnstiles at home, and Somers had nothing to lose by a shift.

Players were shuttled between the teams. Jimmy Sheckard managed Toledo and proved luckier than Joe Birmingham.

The Toledo club finished fifth in the American Association, while the Naps wound up eighth. No other Cleveland team finished in the cellar. Worse, the Naps established a permanent low average for Cleveland teams by winning only 51 games while losing 102 for a mark of .333. Cy Falkenberg had jumped to the Federal League, and his loss hurt the Naps plenty.

Many men who were destined to attain great prominence in baseball moved between the Naps and their Toledo farm. Sheckard's roster included Billy Southworth, Jay Kirke, Josh Billings, Sad Sam Jones, Elmer Smith, and Greasy Neale, all of whom might be playing for Toledo one day and Cleveland the next.

Disinterest in the Naps reached such proportions in 1914 and 1915 that amateur baseball in Cleveland boomed miraculously. A mob estimated at more than eighty thousand persons moved into the natural ampitheater in Brookside Park in 1914 to watch the Telling Strollers beat the Hanna Street Cleaners in a decisive city-championship game. The following year, a legendary one hundred thousand crowd filled Brookside as the Cleveland White Autos defeated the Omaha Luxus for the world amateur championship. The White Autos' star pitcher, Louie "Big Six" Crowley, was better known and more popular in the city than any pitcher the Naps or Toledo could produce.

Lee Fohl, a big ex-catcher, had joined the Naps as a coach in 1914. He was a capable baseball man and had the respect of his players, including Larry Lajoie. But Lee Fohl never was to manage Lajoie. The great slugger faded further in 1914, and at the end of that season Charley Somers released Larry to the Athletics, for whom he played two full seasons before retiring permanently with a lifetime batting average of .338. Though living within a few miles of Cleveland's major-league baseball activities for several years, the great Napoleon Lajoie made, so far as is known, only one trip to the ball park in the next three decades, this to participate in an old-timers' ceremony several years ago.

Somers fired Birmingham as manager early in the 1915 season, saying, "My reason for dismissing Birmingham is because I felt the Cleveland fans demanded a change in managers."

74

How many times that excuse was to be used in later years!

With Lajoie gone from Cleveland, there was speculation in the daily newspapers about a new nickname. The usual slang-touched and colorful names were introduced. But one was outstanding—Indians. So the Naps became the Indians and now, more than 30 years later, modern fans don't recall any other name for the home favorites.

There is a story, still heard frequently, that the Indians were named after a real Indian known as Sockalexis, a wild slugger who joined the National League Spiders in 1897. Sock was strong and fast, and there was fire in every movement. But there was fire in his throat, too, and it needed extinguishing. Between remedies for this and the discovery by enemy pitchers that left-handers who threw curves could baffle the redskin, Sock enjoyed a rapid demise as a big leaguer.

However, his presence caused many persons to refer to the Cleveland team as Indians, and this interlude in nicknames was brought to the attention of the 1915 newspaper readers when they were voting on an alias to succeed Naps.

Fohl elevated the Indians to seventh place in 1915 despite the sale of Joe Jackson to the White Sox. The colorful Jackson, owner of the smoothest swing known in baseball's big time, went to the Chicago club along with Harry "Nemo" Liebold, a stumpy outfielder. Somers was desperate for ready cash to keep the Indians rolling along and so he accepted a rumored fifteen thousand dollars, plus pitcher Ed Klepfer and outfielder Bobby Roth, for Jackson and Liebold.

Roth finished that season as the league's leading home-run hitter with a total of seven! Steve O'Neill became the Tribe's number-one catcher and such names as Bill Wambsganss, Joe Evans, Elmer Smith, Billy Southworth, Fritz Coumbe, and Guy Morton appeared in Cleveland box scores and baseball reports with greater frequency.

SOMERS AND THE BANKERS

CHARLEY SOMERS, who had been so ready with his money fifteen years earlier when the American League needed a teething ring of silver dollars, found himself up against a concrete wall, and it wasn't the one he had built in League Park.

Bankers, those men who appraise business through glasses that reflect only profit and loss, were pushing Somers every day to straighten out his various accounts and activities. Charley had made some costly investments in real estate. His coal business had slackened. The Indians had fallen upon lean seasons.

Charley Somers was 1,750,000 dollars in debt!

A Cleveland bankers' committee took over the management and direction of his various enterprises. On this committee were John Sherwin, Sr., president of the First National Bank; George A. Coulton, president of the Union National Bank; C. A. Paine, president of the National City Bank; Clifford Hubbell, president of the Central National Bank of Buffalo; and A. B. Taylor, president of the Lorain County Banking Company of Elyria, Ohio.

"Get rid of the ball club or we'll get rid of it for you," was the committee's ultimatum to Somers. "Without the ball club, you can save your coal mines. Take your choice."

Charley Somers had no choice, not when he was close to two million dollars in hock. It was up to Somers and his friend Ban Johnson, president of the American League, to dispose of the Indians. Somers asked to retain only one property, the New Orleans team. There was a personal attachment to the Pelicans, as the club was known. The bankers permitted this lone concession in a distribution of the magnate's sports properties.

Remember, this was in 1916. Charley Somers died at Put-in-Bay, Ohio, June 29, 1934 at the age of sixty-five. The gray-thatched, still handsome coal baron had recouped his fortune. He left approximately three million dollars, a notable comeback for a man who was 1,750,000 dollars in the hole. And at the time of his passing, Charley Somers, the man without whom the American League might be a mythical project even today, owned one baseball club—New Orleans.

The burden of disposing of the Cleveland Indians fell upon the American League, more directly upon Ban Johnson. The league president talked many hours with Charley Comiskey, owner of the White Sox. They proposed a dozen schemes, several based on money to be provided by Comiskey and his friends, to save the Indians for Somers. It had been Somers who financed Comiskey in Chicago fifteen years before. The Old Roman never forgot.

In Chicago at the time was a club of jolly drinkers known as the Woodland Bards. To their meetings, official and casual, went the city's leading sports. There was little poetry recited in the rooms occupied by the Bards, but there was considerable extemporaneous prose spouted.

The sad case of Charley Somers and the Indians was a favorite topic of conversation, so there were no ears flopping at special attention one evening when a group of men, including Ban Johnson, Comiskey, and a saloonkeeper named John Burns, were speaking of the Cleveland problem.

Suddenly, Johnson turned to one of the men at the table, Jim Dunn, and said, "You're going to own the Cleveland ball club."

James Christopher Dunn, born in Marshalltown, Iowa, partner in the railroad construction firm of Dunn, McCarthy and Company, gulped. "Me?"

"Yes, you," repeated Johnson. "How much money can you get together in a hurry?"

Dunn fondled his glass, eyes on the ceiling. "Well, I could lay my hands on fifteen thousand dollars right this minute, but I might be able to get more if I had some time."

Pat McCarthy, Dunn's business partner, spoke up. "I'll put in ten thousand dollars," he volunteered.

"And I can get together some money myself," put in John Burns, the bartender.

Another voice chimed in. It belonged to Tom Walsh, who had caught for the Chicago Cubs ten years earlier. Tom had forsaken a baseball career in favor of the construction business, and he had prospered. "I'll take a good block of that stock off your hands," Tom Walsh promised.

It would take about five hundred thousand dollars to swing the deal. Johnson pledged one hundred thousand dollars on behalf of the league. Comiskey agreed to another hundred-thousand-dollar loan. Jim Dunn returned to Iowa and interested several of his friends in purchasing small blocks of stock.

Jim Dunn—Sunny Jim they called him—was not a shrinking violet in any sense of the expression. He began to revel immediately in his new, though unannounced role as head of a major-league baseball team. Jim was bursting at his vocal seams to get the story to the world, but he was not an impractical man.

"Look, Ban," he said to Johnson. "I know nothing about this business of baseball. I've got to have some help."

Johnson told him to cast aside that particular worry. "I've got just the man for you, Bob McRoy. He used to be my secretary until he went to the Boston club. He'll buy five thousand dollars' worth of stock and be your general manager. He knows baseball and how to run a ball club."

Dunn, highly pleased, met the Cleveland newspapermen in a well-stocked parlor at Hotel Statler. Jim was new in dealings with writers, but he got a stand-off with them because they never had heard of Jim Dunn either. After the first announcement of the transaction had been made, the reporters clustered around Dunn and asked him his immediate plans. Would there be changes, etc.?

"Hardly any," he promised. "Lee Fohl stays as manager. I'm told he's very good and can help us build up the team. McRoy will be general manager, as you know, and I'll be president. Bill Blackwood remains the road secretary."

The reporters sensed something more to come. They asked about Somers' vice-president and general manager, the friendly and beloved E. S. Barnard.

"He goes," replied Dunn bluntly.

The Statler hasn't been rocked with such an oral explosion since. Ed Bang, the highly respected and powerful sports editor of the *Cleveland News*, got to his feet. Henry Edwards of the *Plain Dealer* went white.

Both tore into Dunn. Not only were Bang and Edwards going to the aid of a friend. They stormed at Dunn that Barney was the best versed man in the entire baseball world, that he knew baseball law, that he had built up the Cleveland farm system and was acquainted with each detail.

Actually Dunn knew very little about Barnard. All he knew was what Ban Johnson had told him, and Ban Johnson saw in the Cleveland executive a strong rival for power in the American League. Johnson was no sure bet to hang onto the league presidency. He was not popular with several owners, and it is very likely that he had heard more than once the insinuation that Barney might make a pretty good league president if a change had to be made one of these days.

So Johnson blackballed Barnard to Dunn. Still Jim was convinced by the cries of anguish sent up by the Cleveland reporters that he was speeding on slippery bricks when he arbitrarily announced he would fire Barnard. Jim backed slowly but finally agreed to let Barney stay on as an office employee. Barney never whimpered though he was not much more than a flunky for the next couple of years.

Jim Dunn was not blind mentally. Two years later he went down on bended knee to Barney. Bob McRoy was desperately ill. There was no one to run the ball club.

"I've been silly about this thing," Jim apologized. "You're the general manager around here from now on. Write your own salary on this contract and then sign it."

Barney penned a moderate figure.

"You're worth much more," Dunn objected. Barney said it was enough for him right then, and they could talk at a later date.

Jim Dunn not only had a new friend. He had a smart one.

CHAPTER XI

THE GRAY EAGLE

THE TOWN OF Hubbard, Texas, boasted of some sixteen hundred residents in 1916, but it crowed more about one native son than about all the others put together. The favorite was Tristam Speaker, born in the heart of the Cow country on April 4, 1888. Before young Tris could swing a baseball bat he could rope a calf, and before he could throw a baseball across the corral he could stay on an ornery bronc.

Tris practiced both rope tricks and baseball, but he turned to the latter as a professional outlet. Many years later Speaker was to have two illustrious pupils in rope twirling, Will Rogers and Fred Stone. But as a senior in Hubbard's all-purpose school, he was more interested in baseball, especially in pitching.

At seventeen, Tris traveled the comparatively few miles north to Fort Worth to enroll in Polytechnic College there. He stayed not quite two full years. There was less allure to Polytechnic College in 1905 and 1906 than there is today to the nationally known institute of learning into which it grew, Southern Methodist University.

Came spring in 1906 and came the call of the Texas outdoors. Young Tris yearned to feel a saddle beneath him, to pat a pinto, or maybe throw a baseball. Because he could rope, ride, shoot, play baseball, and win just about any popularity contest in his vicinity, the attractive collegian was enormously well known. After he expressed a desire to try to pitch baseball professionally, someone told him that the Cleburne team in the North Texas League was looking for pitchers.

The Cleburne team was in Waco, and Tris showed up at the ball park, asking for a tryout as either a pitcher or an outfielder. The manager of the Cleburne nine was also the first baseman, one Benny Shelton. He took on Speaker as a

80

pitcher. Many tales of Tris's life refer to a number of defeats he suffered as a pitcher. The facts are not those, he insists.

In one of his first starts as a pitcher, Tris allowed only two hits but lost the game because Shelton failed to cover first base on a grounder. Then only eighteen, Speaker popped off and bawled out the manager. Later that night, the owner of the Cleburne team returned from a search for pitchers. He heard about Speaker's fine performance in the afternoon.

"Can he really pitch?" the owner asked Shelton.

"He can pitch, all right," replied Shelton, "but he's the freshest busher I ever met in my life."

Speaker made up his mind he would try some other position on the Cleburne team after he soaked up a 22-to-4 shellacking. Shelton made the youngster stay on the mound and face one extra base hit after another. He made for the outfield, to stay there. At nineteen, he batted .314 for Houston in the Texas League. At twenty, the Boston Red Sox bought his contract from Houston for exactly four hundred dollars!

The Boston Club trained at Little Rock, Arkansas, in 1908 and trained pretty much in private, too. The natives did not demonstrate extraordinary enthusiasm over the visit of the big leaguers, and when the Red Sox were ready to leave, they found they owed a considerable sum as rental for the grounds. Would some players be acceptable as part payment, the Little Rock club was asked?

Yes, the Travelers needed talent. Tris Speaker was one of those left as collateral and proved to be worth many dollars more than the Red Sox owed. He batted .350 and by early September had been recalled to Boston.

Seven years passed....

Again it was spring in Hubbard, Texas, and again there was a tremendous urge in the heart of Tris Speaker to get outdoors and play baseball, to ride and shoot and rope. But it was a troubled urge, unlike the unfettered longing of an adolescent.

Just turned twenty-eight, Tris Speaker was a major-league holdout. He wanted more money than the Red Sox offered; he wanted much more money, and he wasted little time in declaring his case before his old friends in Hubbard.

For six years, Speaker had been Boston's star center fielder; with Duffy Lewis and Harry Hooper he formed the dream outfield. He batted .300 in the 1912 World Series in which the Red Sox beat the New York Giants. It was Speaker who had singled off the great Christy Mathewson in the tenth inning of the eighth and last game, to score the tying run and put the winning run on third base.

It was Speaker who had made one of the most renowned catches in World Series history in 1915 when the Red Sox walloped the Philadelphia Phillies. In the second game, Speaker had leaned far over the center-field bleacher barrier in the last of the ninth to grab Dode Paskert's tremendous smash for the last out. Boston won, 2 to 1, and leading the applause for Speaker was President Woodrow Wilson, the first chief executive to attend a World Series game.

In the third game, Speaker tripled to score a rally-topping run, and for the Series he batted .294. Throughout the championship season, Speaker had played sensationally. His outfielding was without an equal, and he batted .322.

Tris Speaker sat in the living room of his mother's house in Hubbard in the spring of 1916 and opened an envelope bearing the return address of the Boston club. He knew the contents, a contract. He anticipated a raise. Why not?

But the small figures in the contract, nine thousand dollars, were for same salary he had been paid in 1915.

"I'm sending this back, Mother," Tris said. "They've offered me only nine thousand dollars. I'm going to ask for fifteen thousand dollars. I think I deserve it."

Speaker sat tight in Hubbard, not too greatly concerned with his immediate future. No wolf was stalking Hubbard's main street, and besides the young star thought he was entitled to better treatment by Boston.

The Red Sox soon reported to Hot Springs, Arkansas, to begin spring training. Manager Bill Carrigan telephoned Speaker.

"Come up here and let's talk this over, Tris," advised Carrigan. As the field manager, Bill had had nothing to do with the contract negotiations. But he knew he needed Speaker to make another pennant bid.

Speaker soon met Carrigan at the mineral baths resort. Tris was adamant. He would not sign for nine thousand dollars or for ten thousand dollars. He demanded fifteen thousand dollars.

Carrigan put in a long-distance call for Joe Lannin, the president of the Red Sox, who was in Boston. Lannin had ordered the figures inserted in Speaker's contract, and Lannin had refused to budge a dollar in his battle with his star.

"We need Speaker," pleaded Carrigan. "Suppose I work out a temporary arrangement with him for the spring trip, and then you and Tris can sit down later and settle your differences."

Lannin agreed. Carrigan turned to Speaker and proposed a per-game pay plan to be in effect during the trip north and east to Boston. Speaker was willing, and he jumped into the line-up immediately. Never far away from playing condition, Speaker was further advanced than most of the Red Sox when he pulled on his uniform the first time that spring.

The Boston caravan moved toward the Atlantic seaboard. Speaker was anticipating his salary conference with Lannin. But what Speaker did not know was that the Red Sox owner had been sending up trial balloons in the form of inquiries among American League teams about their willingness to bid for Speaker.

"I'm not going to pay him any fifteen thousand dollars," Lannin said many times. "I'll trade him first."

On the mid-April Saturday preceding the opening of the championship season, the Indians and Red Sox had moved into different cities for their last exhibition appearances of the spring. The Indians stopped in Cincinnati while the Red Sox went to Brooklyn. Jim Dunn and Ban Johnson were with the Indians in Cincinnati, Joe Lannin with the Red Sox in Brooklyn.

Ed Bang, sports editor of the *News*, had preceded the Indians to Cleveland to clear the decks of his newspaper for the opening of the pennant race. That Saturday he noticed a story that came over the press-association wires. The average sports editor might have regarded as routine the news that Lannin was disgusted with Speaker's holdout campaign and wanted to trade him. Owners put out those stories frequently and just as frequently back up and sign the star after the test of publicity has been milked dry.

Bang reached for a telephone. He called Bob McRoy, the Indians' general manager, in his League Park office.

"Bob, I think we can get Tris Speaker, and I think we ought to grab him," Ed told McRoy. "I know Lannin, and I know he'll sell any player for enough money. Besides, he's mad at Speaker. I'd suggest you get hold of Jim Dunn and have him call Lannin."

By late Saturday afternoon, Dunn had been in contact with Lannin. There was the usual bickering and the promise of more telephone conversations the next day.

Little did Tris Speaker know then that his baseball life was being decided in a series of long-distance telephone calls. Tris knew that Lannin had met the Red Sox at Brooklyn, but he had had no chance to talk to the club president. He just assumed that he would accompany the Red Sox into Boston on the sleeper that night, and then he'd see Lannin the next day, Monday.

The Red Sox were tied with the Dodgers in the ninth, and the great Rube Marquard was pitching for the home team. Tris Speaker stepped to the plate. Here was a great chance to be a hero and to force Lannin to meet his terms if he could only deliver a big base hit. Speaker did more than that. He clouted a home run over the right-field wall to beat the cursing Marquard.

The first man to greet Speaker as he trotted toward the dugout runway after the game was Joe Lannin. He threw an arm around Tris's shoulder.

"That was great, Tris," he beamed. "And I'll tell you this now. Your terms are okay. We'll sign when we get to Boston tomorrow."

Tris Speaker was in an extra jovial mood as he showered and dressed. Not only had he hit a game-winning home run, he had earned his salary increase. On the eve of another title campaign, Tris felt as if every good fortune in the world was his for the asking.

After dinner that evening, Tris returned to his hotel room

Steve O'Neill

Ray Chapman

Fritz Coumbe

Tris Speaker

to pack. The Red Sox would take the midnight train to Boston. It was now 9 o'clock. The telephone rang.

"Tris," the voice said, "this is Bob McRoy, the general manager of the Cleveland ball club. I'd like to talk to you."

Puzzled, Speaker invited McRoy, whom he had known by reputation only, to come up to the room. The men chatted for a few moments, Speaker wondering what had occasioned the visit.

Finally McRoy asked, "Tris, how would you like to go to Cleveland?"

Speaker frowned and without hesitation replied sharply, "I wouldn't consider it." McRoy asked the reasons.

"I think you've got a bad ball club, for one thing. You finished seventh and eighth in two years. Cleveland isn't a good baseball town, either. Boston is great, and it looks like we might win another pennant there. I don't want to go to Cleveland and wind up in the second division."

McRoy was silent for perhaps fifteen to twenty seconds. Then he blurted, "Well, we've made the deal for you. We've bought you."

Speaker gulped. The words staggered from his mouth, "But Lannin told me only this afternoon we'd get together in Boston tomorrow."

McRoy explained patiently that Lannin and Dunn had conferred by telephone after the game and had agreed upon the terms.

"I won't go. I'll quit baseball first. Hold up the announcement of the deal," said Speaker emphatically.

"It's too late to hold up the announcement," McRoy countered. "The deal is being printed in the morning papers. They're on the streets right now in New York, just below this hotel window.

"Just think, Tris, it's the biggest deal in the history of baseball. We've paid the Boston club fifty-five thousand dollars in cash—think of that—and we're sending two players to boot."

Speaker sank back in his chair. Outside the newsboys were yelling about the most expensive transaction in the sport—fifty-five thousand dollars plus Sad Sam Jones, a pitcher, and

Freddie Thomas, a rookie infielder. The Red Sox had wanted Bill Wambsganss, a kid second baseman, but the Indians convinced Lannin that Thomas was a much better prospect, a bit of understandable chicanery that became evident when Wamby became a fine second baseman for the tribe.

Even then, all the gray in Speaker was not in his hair. Known as the Gray Eagle because of his prematurely white hair, the cagey Texan also had plenty of gray matter inside his skull. He realized that he must go to Cleveland if he wished to remain in baseball.

"All right, I'll go to Cleveland on one condition," Spoke said in resignation. "I want ten thousand dollars of the purchase price."

McRoy said he had no control over disposition of the money. The Cleveland club was to pay Boston fifty-five thousand dollars. What Joe Lannin did with the money was no concern of Jim Dunn's or his stockholders.

Speaker reached Lannin by telephone and presented his demand for the money. The Boston president objected vehemently, but when Speaker threatened to catch the next train to Hubbard, unless he got his ten thousand dollars, Lannin gave in.

It was the morning of the scheduled home opener for the Indians. Tris Speaker had agreed to terms with Cleveland and arrived in the Forest City the morning of the game. He called Jim Dunn.

"I haven't received my ten thousand dollars from Lannin, Mr. Dunn," Spoke said "And I'm not playing until I do."

A minute later he had called the transportation porter at the Hollenden Hotel and ordered a reservation to Hubbard. The demand for the ten thousand dollars was no idle gesture. Speaker meant business.

Dunn tried to reach Lannin by long distance but was not successful. He called Speaker. "Okay, I'll give you the ten thousand dollars," he promised. Spoke refused the offer and told his new boss the money must come from Lannin.

Frantic, Dunn then telephoned Ban Johnson in Chicago. Johnson reached Lannin in Boston and ordered him to mail the check to Speaker. Then Johnson called Dunn, who called Speaker.

"That's not satisfactory yet," objected the stubborn Speaker, who had made it pretty plain he didn't care for any further business dealings with Lannin. Dunn asked if he could have Johnson call Speaker direct. Spoke agreed.

And only when the President of the American League assured Tris in his own words that Lannin and no one else would be required to pay the ten-thousand-dollar bonus did Speaker agree to put on a uniform for the Cleveland Indians.

"What about a Cleveland contract?" asked Dunn. "We've agreed on salary, but we haven't signed anything."

"We're late now," Speaker yelled, "It's almost two thirty and the game starts at three. We'll worry about a contract later."

Jim Dunn wasn't Joe Lannin in Speaker's book.

There was a flow of joyful comment in Cleveland when the Speaker deal was made public. The new owner, Jim Dunn, would put the city back on the baseball map, the erstwhile critics of the Indians shouted. For the first time since Lajoie departed, the fans had a bright, broad star upon whom to hang their enthusiasm. Tris Speaker, most magnificent of all outfielders, strong batter, a scrapper in uniform, a hail-fellow in street dress, was an Indian!

Suds and conversation flowed at a terrific pace in Cleveland, but on a stone curbing at the intersection of Boylston and Massachusetts in Boston's fabulous Back Bay sector, a stocky newsboy sat, head buried in his arms. Beside him was his stack of newspapers, carelessly spread.

"Take it easy, Lefty," consoled a buddy, "the deal's been made. There's nothing you can do about it."

Lefty—Max Weisman—fought back the tears with all the strength in his nineteen-year-old body. The man he idolized more than any other, Tris Speaker, would be gone from Back Bay, from the apartment the great baseball player shared with Doc Tingley, the hockey referee.

Speaker and Lefty had met the first time when there was a large chip on Tris's shoulder. Lefty was delivering newspapers to the apartment building in which Tris lived and there was nothing except song on the mind of the youngster, who had quit school many years before to become the sole support of a large family.

But there was sleep on Speaker's mind.

"Pipe down, kid!" Speaker ordered as Lefty made his tour of the building. Lefty pulled up short and silent.

"Hello, Mr. Speaker," he grinned. "I'm sorry I was singin'. I'll be quiet after this."

It was a promise never kept 100 per cent, to Speaker or anyone else, because Lefty Weisman had to talk or sing then, even as he has to perform one of those oral functions today. Yet Speaker took a liking to the newsboy, and soon Lefty Weisman was running his errands, picking up groceries, and developing for the baseball star a worship seldom confessed in sports.

The first time that Speaker visited Boston with the Indians in the spring of 1916, Lefty Weisman was waiting at the railroad station. He "smashed the bags" of his hero. He tailed him to the hotel, to the ball park, to the restaurant.

"Lefty, I don't know what's going to happen in Cleveland as far as our ball club is concerned," Tris said, "but I do know this much. If we ever win the championship there, you'll be my guest at the World Series."

Four years later, he was.

ASSISTANT MANAGER

Lee Fohl was a big, trusting man who was understandably bewildered by all the shooting in Cleveland's baseball gallery between the close of the dull 1915 season and the opening of a 1916 campaign. Speaker, the city's top-ranking star since Lajoie, provided a major share of Fohl's befuddlement.

Not that Fohl resented Speaker or was distressed in any way by his arrival. In fact, Lee was extremely joyous, as any manager would have been who suddenly acquired a player of Speaker's rank. It was just that the Indians, who were so hopeless and bedraggled only five months before, now had new owners, new blood, new hopes.

Speaker, who had batted .322 in Boston's park with its deep right field, welcomed the sight of League Park's wall along Lexington Avenue, only 290 feet from home plate. Spoke, always a straightaway hitter, shifted to the right a mite so that he could "pull" pitches with his left-handed swing.

"It was only natural for me to try to hit that wall," Spoke has said many times since, "as it would be for any batter. You try to take advantage of the style of your home field." Speaker did. He batted a mighty .386 to win the American League individual championship. For nine years running, Ty Cobb had been the titleholder. Now Ty was good for a mere .371, and the man he disliked most cordially—mainly because Speaker was such a graceful and expert outfielder whereas Cobb was a mediocre fielder—beat him out by fifteen points!

Tris was an aggressive, commanding player with the Indians from the outset, and the team reacted to his personality most favorably. Fohl was a fine handler of new pitchers, and in the winter overhauling of the club Dunn and McRoy had come up with several promising freshmen hurlers, Jim Bagby, Stanley Coveleskie, Otis Lambeth, and Joe Boehling. The 1916

Indians were overloaded with prize catchers, too. O'Neill was the work horse, of course, but such capable receivers as Josh Billings, Hank DeBerry, Bob Coleman, and Tom Daley also were on the staff.

A medical student at Washington University in St. Louis, Joe Evans, had come along to challenge the veteran Terry Turner for the third-base assignment. The sure-fielding Wamby was at second and Chapman at short. Chick Gandil, who had come over from Washington, and a promising young Italian, Louis Guisto, divided the first basing. The outfield was set with Graney and Roth flanking Speaker. There was a big pitcher named Pete Des Jardien, who had been Walter Camp's All-American center in 1913 as a University of Chicago star.

Through April, May, and June, the Indians were on top, due chiefly to Speaker's batting and forceful field leadership. But there was an absence of balance in the line-up and two men, Fohl and Speaker, were quick to realize that the Tribe was playing over its head and would slip. It did, into sixth place with a .500 rating.

The Fohl-Speaker combination was formed almost immediately upon arrival of the Texan in Cleveland. Spoke was the natural field leader, and Fohl recognized his strength and adaptability promptly. Yet not even the players on the team knew the scope of the teamwork.

The manager and his center fielder worked out a set of signals, from bench to garden. If there was to be a change of pitchers, or batters, during a game, Fohl and Speaker exchanged signals. Tris had a voice in the selection of starting pitchers, too, though this was not generally known inside the club's family of players.

Yet there was evidence that Speaker's influence in team affairs extended beyond the limits of Fohl's office. Smokey Joe Wood, once owner of a terrifying fast ball, was acquired from the Red Sox on waivers. Wood injured his arm in the 1912 World Series and had had trouble since. But he was trying a comeback, and the Indians took him on a gamble.

And, suggested the wiser followers of the Tribe, on Speaker's say-so. There were whispers that Speaker was loading up the

Indians with his old pals on the Red Sox. Undoubtedly, Wood came to the Indians on Tris's recommendation. After trying in vain to recapture his pitching form in 1917, Wood, always a fine batter, went to the outfield, and it was there that he played a major role in Cleveland's 1920 pennant campaign.

There were great things forecast for the Indians of 1917, and the largest opening-day crowd in the city's history, twenty-one thousand, jammed League Park for the inaugural. There were many other "firsts" for the Indians.

Ross Tenney, sports editor of the *Press,* publicly expressed his astonishment because Steve O'Neill lost his temper during a game with the Browns late in April.

"Never since 1912 had we seen O'Neill let his temper get the best of him," wrote Tenney. "Steve got so mad at the decision...at the plate that he threw the ball into left field in the ninth inning and the Brownies beat our side, 6 to 5."

There was the season's first banishment of Speaker. As team captain, Tris darted in from center field to protest a decision by Umpire Tommy Connolly at second base.

"Keep goin'," Connolly yelled at the onrushing Speaker. "Don't stop until you get in the shower."

Speaker slowed his pace some, dropped his hands to his side, and kept going. But as he passed Connolly, he nudged the umpire with his shoulder. Tommy staggered a couple of feet, enough to cause him to write a report to Ban Johnson that night, and the league president plastered a three-day suspension on Spoke.

On May 19, Speaker made another dash from center field, but this time he disdained conversation or contact with an umpire. Players of both teams—the Indians and Senators—were startled to notice Speaker race at top speed to the third-base dugout, where he shouted for Frank Van Dellen, the grounds keeper.

"There's a fire in the bleachers, Frank," exclaimed Spoke. "Get the fire brigade out before those wooden seats all burn down."

Then there was one more "first" in Cleveland's American League record. On Sept. 9, the Indians were in Comiskey Park. For nearly three hours, the Tribe and White Sox had battled and wrangled. In the first of the tenth, the Indians had the bases filled. Graney was on third base, two were out.

The fast, smart outfielder took a long lead off third. Ed Danforth, pitching for the White Sox, fired the ball to Ray Schalk, his catcher, who immediately threw to Fred McMullin, the third baseman. Graney turned to slide back into the bag and in so doing upset McMullin. Schalk's throw rolled several feet from the bag.

Graney struggled to get to his feet, only to discover that McMullin had him by the belt. Graney wrenched free and raced across the plate. So did Chapman, who had been on second.

Umpire Clarence "Brick" Owens, at the plate, threw up his hands and indicated that Graney was out and that no runs had scored to break the 3-3 deadlock. Owens claimed that Graney had interfered with McMullin on the throw to third. Graney and Terry Turner charged Owens and had to be pulled off the umpire by Fohl.

The umpire on bases, Billy Evans, went to Owens' rescue. Owens "pulled his watch" and ordered the Indians to take their positions in the field. There was a long delay before he was obeyed.

In the argument, Turner had been ordered out of the game and was replaced by Ivan Howard, a utility third baseman. In the last of the tenth, pitcher Danforth was the first batter, and he struck out. Then O'Neill and Owens got into an argument. Steve got madder and madder, and finally he wound up and threw the ball far over Howard's head, into left field.

Owens promptly forfeited the game to the White Sox, charging deliberate delaying of the contest by the Indians. It was one of the few forfeitures in so-called "modern" baseball.

In spite of these flare-ups, in spite of the imminence of war, the 1917 Indians were one of the most dangerous teams in the league. They lost nine men to the service draft during the season. Yet the pitching was so good that the Redskins spent almost the entire summer in third place and finished up there, too.

From a competitive standpoint, the high light of the season was Guy Morton's bid for immortality in a game with the

Red Sox on June 1. Morton mowed down the Beantowners for seven innings without one of them hitting safely. In the eighth, the Boston pitcher stepped to the plate and rammed a single to right field. That was the only hit off the tall, drawling Morton that day, and the culprit's name was Babe Ruth. Coveleskie and Al Gould also pitched one-hitters that season. Covey won nineteen, Ed Klepfer thirteen, while the extremely cagey Jim Bagby turned in twenty-five triumphs.

From a historical standpoint, the high point of the season was the drilling instituted for big-league players. At the instigation of the two major leagues, the Army assigned drill experts to each team. With bats serving as rifles, the pantalooned athletes went through formations daily. Near the end of the season, contests were held to determine the championship drill team. The Indians were judged third best in the league, the Browns winning a five-hundred-dollar first prize while the Senators were second.

From a tragic standpoint, the 1917 routine of the Indians was interrupted by the death on July 25 of Larry, the world-famous dog owned by Jack Graney. Larry accompanied the Indians on the road and performed tricks in all ball parks. His death resulted in deep grieving by all the Redskins.

The Indians very probably would have won the pennant in 1918 except for the "work or fight" order issued by Secretary of War Newton D. Baker. There was enormous uncertainty concerning the fate of the major-league baseball season until late in July. Then Mr. Baker agreed to let the schedules run until September 1, after which date all ballplayers were to go into the armed forces or take jobs in shipyards or other essential activities.

But Labor Day fell on September 2, and double-headers were scheduled in all cities, the Indians being booked in St. Louis. Most teams expected to stretch over by one day the stipulated deadline for baseball. In the final week of August, the Indians were within four games of the Red Sox, who even then were notoriously weak on the road. The Indians were improving speedily, and there seemed little doubt that the team would have caught up with the Sox had the latter not been saved from an impending tour of the West.

As matters developed, the Indians concluded their schedule on September 1, though the others played the next day. Speaker had been tossed out of a game for arguing and had been suspended in the last week of the season, just when the Redskins thought they might make a move to overhaul the leading Red Sox. With the best batting team in the league, despite a patched line-up, the Indians lacked stability in the pitching department to pull away from the field earlier.

Mathematically out of the race, discouraged because of Speaker's absence, and thoroughly disgusted because they would not get the chance to overtake the Red Sox, the Indians disbanded after September 1. Before or during that season, the Redskins lost Wamby, Morton, Guisto, Harris, Klepfer, Lambeth, Billings, and two others in the military draft. They had been playing with makeshift line-ups.

The Browns had been advised that the Indians would not show up for their scheduled double-header in St. Louis on Labor Day. So the Browns put nine players on the field and had the pitcher toss a total of ten balls, five for each game. Then the games were claimed on forfeit. It made no difference. The Indians still finished second.

A number of incidents of interest and import were packed into the first few months of this shortened campaign. In fact, within one week in May there was enough food for conversation to feed the fans for the rest of the summer. During an Eastern trip, the Indians were in Washington on May 19 to help the Senators celebrate the lifting of the ban on Sunday baseball. The tribe did its part by losing, 1 to 0, mainly because Walter Johnson, the obvious choice to have the honor of pitching this important game, was in rare form.

The tribe moved up to Boston. Carl Mays, the Red Sox submarine hurler, was Manager Jack Barry's pitcher. There had been accusations that Mays threw certain pitches very close to batters, but some of these may have stemmed from Carl's unorthodox delivery. He was one of the last and foremost of the underhand pitchers, and batters found following his pitches quite difficult.

Speaker either didn't follow one or was completely fooled in this particular game, because Mays bounced the ball off Tris's skull. Fortunately for the Texan, the blow was glancing, but it didn't stop Speaker from getting to his feet and challenging Mays.

"I was on the same team with you long enough to know what you do," yelled Speaker. "If you throw at anyone else on this ball club, you might not even walk out of this park."

Tris wasn't the last Cleveland player Mays beaned!

Perhaps the finest game Coveleskie pitched for the Indians up to that period was fashioned in New York two days later. The stalwart Pole went nineteen innings before Cleveland edged the Yankees, 3 to 2. Five days later, Covey came back to beat the White Sox by the same score. Cleveland newspapermen quickly pointed to the "iron man" feat of Coveleskie as being greater than that of Walter Johnson a few weeks previous.

"Johnson pitched 18 innings, then had to wait 11 days before he could come back," crowed the Ohio press. "Covey pitched 19 and came back in five days. We'll take Covey for our side."

Cleveland newspapermen have been charged in recent years with overindulgence in secondhand managerial acumen, yet no modern reporter would think of charging into his team's dugout during the progress of a game to shout a suggestion to a pilot.

Henry Edwards had many favorite stories of his days as a reporter following the Indians but the one that caused him the greatest mirth in later years concerned the season's opening game in Detroit in 1918. A flu epidemic hospitalized half of Fohl's squad. Fritz Coumbe, the slender southpaw, was fit to pitch. Speaker, Roth, and O'Neill were in their positions.

Elsewhere were substitutes, rookies, and rank beginners. "But they were about all we had," Edwards' story goes. "Everyplace else were substitutes, raw rookies, or maybe a semipro or two. We were in tough shape. A bull-pen catcher, Williams, was on first. Germany Schaefer, a coach, played second. A young fellow by the name of Halt, who'd played some semipro ball around Ohio, was at short, and Getz, a utility man, at third. Graney was sick, and Jack Onslow, a minor leaguer we had picked up to try out in the spring, had to play left.

"Coumbe was going great. In the sixth or seventh inning, I forget which, the Tigers got another run because Onslow had misjudged a fly ball in left. He'd messed up one earlier. My heart was bleeding for Coumbe, and I couldn't stand it any longer. I rushed out of the press box and hurried to the Cleveland dugout. I called Fohl to one end.

" 'Get that Onslow out of there before he ruins Coumbe and loses the game,' I said excitedly. Fohl, a placid man, held up his hands, remarking that he didn't have an outfielder well and able.

" 'I saw Joe Wood playing the outfield in spring training,' I pointed out. 'Why don't you try him? He's better than Onslow.'

"Fohl nodded his head and turned to say something to Wood. But by that time Joe was running toward the outfield. He'd heard my raised voice."

Incidentally, this decision pleased Speaker no little bit. Spoke had wanted Joe to stay in the outfield, but there was the hope he might be able to regain the strength in his right arm and be a winning pitcher again. He never was.

The Indians' front office went into the postwar years with new faces in prominent pictures. Bob McRoy died, and Barnard moved up to the vice-presidency and general managership of the Tribe.

And a new traveling secretary, Walter McNichols, came over from Chicago to succeed Bill Blackburn. The McNichols brothers, Walter and Frank, had run the Chicago West Ends, an amateur baseball team, and had come to know Jim Dunn. When Dunn sought a replacement for Blackburn, he turned to his old Chicago friend, Walter, and the Indians had the same road secretary for seventeen years thereafter.

NEW MANAGER

THE YEAR 1920 STANDS OUT in Cleveland baseball history with the unconscious prominence of a foreign-made automobile parked on the main street in Eldorado. As every tot in the state of Ohio will verify at the drop of a chocolate bar, the Indians won their first American League championship in 1920 and defeated the Brooklyn Dodgers in the World Series.

Yet to those who peruse the diamond history of the period, and in the minds of the older set who remember in tremendous vividness each snap of the pitcher's wrist nearly thirty years ago, the summer of 1919 included events so portentous they dwarfed the next twelvemonth.

The war was over. Every star the Indians owned before the struggle across the Atlantic began had returned to the Cleveland fold. Some, it is true, were not in good condition. Guisto, the personable first baseman, was gassed, and finally exhausted himself in attempts to breathe the smog-laden air of the industrial metropolis. Joe Harris, also a first baseman, was cracked up in a truck accident while in service. Handsome Ed Klepfer, who had been blossoming into stardom as a pitcher, won a lieutenant's commission but lost his pitching arm, figuratively not literally.

Fohl and Speaker sat down with Jim Dunn before 1919 spring training was to start.

"Spoke and I think we can win this year if we can help ourselves a little," Fohl told the owner. "We need a third baseman and a little boost in the outfield."

Elmer Smith, who had been traded to Washington, was bought back. Joe Wood was improving. Together they could protect right field. Speaker was set in center, Graney in left. The pitching was satisfactory, the catching the best in the majors with O'Neill, Les Nunamaker, and Chet Thomas comprising the force. Dunn, Fohl and Speaker agreed on one point: the Indians could be a dangerous team throughout with a minimum of revision.

All eyes turned to Larry Gardner, Connie Mack's third baseman, who had played with Speaker at Boston a few years earlier. A good pitcher, Elmer Myers, was on the staff of the Athletics. There were some others, of lesser renown.

It was agreed to talk to Mr. Mack. In a conference made most unusual by the presence of an ordinary player-without-portfolio, Speaker, the trade was discussed. Connie finally agreed to take Bobby Roth, the Tribe's regular right fielder, in exchange for Gardner and Myers.

"I think we ought to include a third man in the deal, Mr. Mack," interposed Speaker. "It will look like a much bigger project all around, a three-for-one trade. You've got a youngster named Charley Jamieson. How about throwing him in?"

Jamieson, then twenty-six, had spent four years in the minors before Washington bought him, only to pass him along to Connie at the waiver price. Connie agreed. Speaker still claims that deal as one of his prizes of all time. Jamieson played seventeen years in the majors and finished with a lifetime batting average of .304!

The addition of Gardner, Myers, and Jamieson seemed to be just what Dr. Dunn had prescribed for his swiftly growing patient—the Cleveland Indians. The team showed improvement immediately. Until the first week in July, it seemed certain the Indians would either win the championship or surrender the diadem to the White Sox or the Yankees.

The Red Sox were beginning to make frequent use of the bat of Babe Ruth. When the giant left-hander wasn't pitching, he was playing the outfield. Between assignments, he was complaining that he didn't have enough to keep him busy. The baseball seemed more lively than ever before. At least, it could be hit longer distances. There was agitation among club owners to abolish the freak pitches that cropped up almost daily, the emery ball, the licorice ball, the spitball, etc. Ruth was hitting all these pitches out of all ball parks, and his mighty smashes were reflecting the temper of the times. The world with all its minor mechanisms, including the game of baseball, was speeding!

Babe Ruth caused many baseball managers searing headaches, but only one big-league operator lost his job because of the Babe, so far as can be determined. Whether the Bambino was the disease or the instrument, the moon-faced orphan cost Lee Fohl his job as manager of the Indians. Of equal historic importance was the home run by Ruth that brought Speaker into the managerial fold in Cleveland baseball. The two events are more closely related than twin brothers, yet each can be and should be identified separately.

Early in July, just when it seemed the Indians could move into the best position of contention in the flag race, Ray Chapman and Jack Graney were injured. A series of minor mishaps followed. Instead of setting the league pace, the Indians were barely hanging on.

Fohl was taking some unhealthy raps in Cleveland. His team was a hot contender, but the figure and personality of Speaker became so dominant in the daily play of the Indians that the general public's confidence in Lee was undermined subconsciously. There was only moderate criticism of Fohl in the daily press, but in that preradio period the word-of-mouth grapevine was probably more effectual than the opinions of the newspapers. In short, the fans "got on" Fohl.

It is doubtful if any one game ever played in the major leagues surpassed the dramatic contest unfolded in League Park on July 18, 1919. The significance of the crushing outcome and the human equations that came to the fore will be permanent signposts on Cleveland's baseball boulevards.

The Red Sox had not been able to beat the Indians in nine attempts before that fateful Friday. So confident were Fohl and Speaker of handing the sixth-place Beantowners, then managed by Ed Barrow, a tenth straight lacing that a rookie, Hy Jasper, was given the pitching assignment for the Indians. Other than serving a home-run ball to the fear-inspiring Ruth, Jasper had pitched creditably. In fact, he was holding even, 3 to 3, going into the eighth.

Then the Indians, thanks to a base-cleaning pinch triple by Joe Harris, moved out ahead and were guarding a 7-to-3 lead going into the ninth. Elmer Myers, one of the objects of Cleveland's affections in the trade with Philadelphia, had succeeded Jasper but had not succeeded in much else. The Red Sox scored one run, loaded the bases, but had two out. The next batter—

It had to be, as if in a plot, Babe Ruth!

Pitching to the Bambino in League Park with its right-field wall inviting the big guy to wheel and slash in that direction always was a job for a trained combat veteran, preferably an expert in suicides. The wall was only 290 feet away. Its height of forty feet was a restraining influence on many batters, but to Babe Ruth walls were built to hit baseballs over, not to scare him.

Three pitchers were warming up in the Cleveland bull pen in the right-field corner, in the shade of the big wall. Two were right-handers, the third Fritz Coumbe, a left-hander who threw a wide and bothersome curve.

As Ruth dawdled outside the batter's box, wiping his hands across the letters of his uniform, Fohl yelled to the umpires to stop the game. He looked to center field to pick up a secret signal flashed by Speaker. The signal was one of dozens employed by Fohl and Speaker.

A right-hander should relieve Myers, read Speaker's signal. Fohl looked to the bull pen and made a motion with his left arm. Coumbe threw one last warm-up pitch and turned to walk to the mound.

The Tribe infielders looked sharply at Speaker when they heard his voice in back of them.

"No! No!" the Gray Eagle was shouting. "No, no, not Coumbe."

But Fohl had sat down on the bench, and Coumbe was warming up by then. Speaker turned his back to the plate, and there was a slight droop to his shoulders. Bobtailed thoughts coursed through Speaker's mind. Had Fohl read the sign right? Should he run in and argue with Lee? Or had Fohl decided that a left-hander, even if he threw "slow stuff" such as Coumbe practiced, was a better bet against the left-handed Ruth than any right-hander?

The fans noticed Speaker's confusion, and there was a

murmur throughout the stands. There was a mass gasp a few seconds later when Coumbe wound up and delivered what was described by observers as a "perfect curve." The ball cut across the plate, waist high. Ruth swung with a vicious grunt, but the speed of the ball had fooled him. His bat had completed the arc before the sphere reached the plate.

Steve O'Neill, the burly catcher, called time and trotted out to the mound.

"Look, pitch this guy very low, in the dirt if you have to get down that far," he told Coumbe. "But don't give him anything up high or inside. Put him on if you have to, but keep that ball out of the pocket."

Again Coumbe wound up, and again he pitched. And again it was a beautiful slow curve. But again, alas, it was in the groove, and that time the mighty Ruth had followed the ball perfectly. Some say the ball was found later on top of a laundry building on the far side of Lexington Avenue. Some say it bounced and rolled to Euclid Avenue, a dozen blocks to the north.

Three happy Red Sox crossed the plate in front of the grinning Bambino. The greatest slugger of all time was just getting the feel of home runs then. He had almost completed the transition from pitcher to outfielder, and home runs were nails useful in barricading himself against a return to the rubber.

That particular home run was one of twenty-nine Ruth hit in 1919, but it did the damage of a thousand. The Indians, their spirits crushed, couldn't score in the last of the ninth and soon they were taking the dreary walk through the passageway to their dressing room, losers by an 8-to-7 score. The game might be retrieved, they told themselves, but the implications were eternal.

Fohl changed clothes in a hurry. The players sat in front of their lockers, heads bowed. Speaker, always one of the slowest dressers, lagged behind most of his mates. The clubhouse boy tapped him on the shoulder.

"Mr. Dunn wants to see you in the office upstairs," he told Speaker. Tris completed his toilet and climbed the one flight of iron steps to the small rooms above the ticket windows. These comprised the League Park offices, the cashier's room, the auditor's room, and Jim Dunn's private quarters, scarcely the size of a twin-bedded room in a medium-priced hotel.

Speaker looked at the men in the room as he went in. Dunn and Barnard had company. Ed Bang, Ross Tenney, and Henry Edwards, baseball writers for the Cleveland dailies, fidgeted in the silence that only reporters who are waiting for an important announcement know and appreciate.

"Lee has resigned as manager, Tris, and we want you to take over," Dunn said.

Speaker shook his head.

"I'm not sure that I'm qualified to be a manager, Jim," replied Spoke. "Besides, I prefer to play, and I'd rather play for any manager than run the club myself."

Dunn repeated the invitation, pointing out that Fohl had quit and that there had to be a new manager named immediately, whether he was Speaker or someone else.

"If Lee will ask me to succeed him, I will," Tris decided finally. "I don't want him to think that I asked for the job."

Fohl was agreeable. After all, he had quit. His confidant had been Speaker. He blamed only himself, not Speaker or anyone else, for the home run that brought on a crisis.

The announcement that Speaker would become the manager of the Indians was greeted with joy throughout Cleveland. Tris's qualities of leadership were apparent to all fans in the stands when he was the mere field captain. He was doughty and scrappy and a great ballplayer. His men knew that he knew his business. On such knowledge is the faith of baseball players built.

The Indians were in third place, one game behind New York and five and a half behind the White Sox. In the next month, Speaker led his Redskins on an even keel. They stayed in second or third place, but they could not prevent the White Sox, recognized as one of the finest teams ever assembled, from pulling away from the pack.

Speaker recognized the futility of the chase. So he looked toward 1920. A Cleveland sand lotter, George Uhle, had been taken to the spring training camp and had been carried along most of the summer so that he could pick up pitching tricks in observation of stars. Speaker tossed Uhle into a tight game with the Senators on August 14. In two innings, the husky right-hander granted only one hit and won the game, 4 to 3. Six days later, Uhle made his first start in the majors. Imperturbable, and showing a mixture of pitches that elicited favorable comment by his opponents, George turned back the Red Sox, 5 to 2, and a headline in a Cleveland newspaper shrieked, "Uhle, the Sandlotter, Arrives."

Under Speaker, the Indians won forty games and lost only twenty-one. But the Gray Eagle's batting fell off following his appointment as manager. He slumped to a final mark of .296, but his fielding and personal guidance were of such high quality that the other Redskins took up their manager's slack. For example, Graney led the league in walks with 105. On September 15, the Tribe was in second place, eight games behind the flying White Sox. After the season's last game, the Speaker men had slashed the Chicago lead to three and a half games.

The White Sox faded noticeably in the closing weeks. Those were the days immediately preceding the World Series with the Cincinnati Reds. It was in this period that gamblers "reached" the Pale Hose, and it is not unlikely that some of the players spent sleepless nights during bouts with their consciences.

Speaker, always alert to signs of ability among rival players who might help the Indians if they could be acquired, was impressed by one man more than any other in the league, that is, one man he suspected he might get.

The Yankees had a problem child, a tremendously talented right-handed pitcher by the name of Ray Caldwell, known in the trade as Slim. He had two weaknesses evident to the public and to his employers. One was whisky, the other was a complex that showed its synthetic head each spring. Slim held out invariably for a salary of nine thousand to ten thousand dollars. He seldom received more than five thousand dollars, the rest going in fines for breaking training.

Miller Huggins, the mighty mite who became manager of the Yankees in 1918, hit upon a plan of action to keep Caldwell in line. Ruth was on the same team, but the Babe hadn't yet taken to free-wheeling extracurricular activities that were, in the years to come, to drive Huggins to the brink of self-destruction.

Huggins assigned two private detectives to the trail of Caldwell. But Slim was no amateur strategist. He eluded the detectives most of the time. Eventually Huggins threw up his hands and looked around for a trade that would include the pitcher. The Red Sox, country cousins to the Yankees in baseball deals of the period, were very willing to talk about Caldwell.

They took the pitcher and three players whose names have been forgotten long since in exchange for pitchers Ernie Shore and Hubert "Dutch" Leonard and outfielder Duffy Lewis, who had been one of Speaker's pals in Boston's great outfield of half a dozen years previous.

The Red Sox, not interested in spending money to tail Caldwell and fed up in a hurry with his drinking, handed Slim his release. Earlier, Caldwell had mentioned to Speaker the possibility of going to Cleveland, but Tris told him to forget it until he was free of all other commitments. Fired by the Red Sox, Caldwell hurried to Speaker.

"I won't drink any more, Tris," promised Slim. Speaker grinned. There was a familiar sound to that lyric.

"I'm not sure I want you if you say you won't drink any more," Spoke mused. Then he shoved a contract in front of Caldwell.

"Now I want you to read this carefully, Slim. Then if you want to sign it, okay."

Caldwell's eyes traveled to the salary figures, of course, and they bulged. "This is more than I got at either New York or Boston," he exclaimed. "Give me that pen. I'll sign."

Speaker held up his hand. "I told you to read this contract very carefully. You've looked only at the money. Now read every word in it."

Slim buried his head in the printed sheet. "After each game he pitches, Ray Caldwell must get drunk. He is not to report to the clubhouse the next day. The second day he is to report to Manager Speaker and run around the ball park as many times as Manager Speaker stipulates. The third day he is to pitch batting practice, and the fourth day he is to pitch in a championship game."

Slim looked up.

"You left out one word, Tris," he said. "Where it says I've got to get drunk after every game, the word 'not' has been left out. It should read that I'm 'not to get drunk.'"

Speaker smiled. "No, it says you *are* to get drunk."

Slim shrugged his shoulders. "Okay, I'll sign," he conceded.

Caldwell won eleven games while losing only five, and had he been a revengeful sort instead of a happy-go-lucky good guy, he would have derived extreme pleasure out of beating one of the teams that let him go, the Yankees, on September 10, 1919.

Perhaps beating the Yankees is an understatement. The rubber-armed Caldwell, fast and tricky that day, threw a no-hitter at the Yankees! There is no record of Caldwell's private behavior the night of September 10.

Slim was mad at the Yankees that day. Not only had they sold him up the river to the Red Sox, they had failed earlier to get him any sizable quota of runs. In fact, during one forty-five-inning stretch by Caldwell, the Yanks had scored exactly one run. Slim had made that stand up for a 1-to-0 triumph over the Tigers.

Caldwell is the only pitcher on record who was hit by lightning that was correctly lightning and not flashes off enemy bats. Shortly after he joined the Indians, Slim was pitching in Philadelphia. It was the ninth inning, two were out, and one strike had been called on the last batter.

Then the electric storm enveloped Shibe Park. Rain and lightning arrived at the same second. A bolt came hurtling from the sky and smashed into the ground near the pitcher's mound. A direct hit would have killed any mortal. Caldwell was struck, a glancing blow fortunately. He was flattened and knocked unconscious for five minutes.

First aid was rendered, and Slim was resuscitated. Whereupon he stood up, informed Manager Speaker that he was all right, though a bit dizzy, and proceeded to throw two more strikes to the batter to end the game!

In 1920, a friend of a Cleveland banker saw Slim in a

state of distress in a speakeasy. The banker, an ardent Indian rooter who knew nothing about the private contract under which the pitcher worked and lived, thought he was doing everyone a good turn by notifying the ball club's officials.

Colonel J. J. Sullivan of the Central National Bank called Dunn and Speaker to his office and told him that his friend had seen one of Cleveland's star players drinking quite liberally in a guarded rendezvous.

Concerned, Dunn and Speaker asked the banker to identify the culprit.

"Ray Caldwell," answered Colonel Sullivan. Dunn and Speaker relaxed. They never worried about Caldwell, but some other player might have created a problem or a situation.

"Did your friend know what Caldwell was drinking?" asked Dunn, himself a firm believer in conviviality. The banker replied in the negative.

"If he knew, I'd tell some of our other pitchers to drink some of the stuff," gagged Dunn. "They're all five drinks behind Caldwell right now according to the pitching records."

Caldwell won twenty games in 1920, but in the closing months of the season, when it appeared the Indians had a chance to win their first American League pennant, Slim went on the wagon.

WORLD SERIES, 1920

THE ONLY PIECE OF Royal Doulton in Sunny Jim Dunn's collection of baseball china at the outset of the 1920 campaign was Tris Speaker. He had cost the Indians fifty-five thousand dollars and two players. The others who reported to Spoke in New Orleans for spring training were either waiver-price ballplayers or run-of-the-mine performers who had been acquired in slick deals or by cagey trading. Yet this team had finished a good second the year previous!

Three men, General Manager E. S. Barnard, Lee Fohl, and Tris Speaker, were credited with either the engagement of nearly the entire squad or the development of players after they had been obtained. Stan Coveleskie and Jim Bagby were "working agreement" ballplayers, sent to the Tribe by minor-league teams as payment of talent debts. George Uhle came off the Cleveland sand lots. Slim Caldwell was a free agent, Guy Morton a firebrand from Alabama who had been plucked from the Cotton States League.

Other than Speaker, the coterie of outfielders—Elmer Smith, Joe Wood, Charley Jamieson, Jack Graney, and Joe Evans—hadn't cost Dunn or his predecessors much more than a total of seventeen thousand five hundred dollars. Larry Gardner, the third baseman, was in the Jamieson-Myers-Roth trade. Ray Chapman had been brought up from Toledo, Wamby purchased for the staggering sum of twelve hundred and fifty dollars. The first basemen, Doc Johnston and George Burns, didn't represent a seven-thousand-dollar investment between them. Steve O'Neill's purchase price, paid to Worcester in the New England League in 1911, was so negligible no one remembered the exact figure.

Yet Speaker knew he was managing a good ball club. For one thing, his fiery personal leadership made up for some of the lack of brilliance in the play of his men. Then, taking much the same club Fohl and he had guided in 1919, Speaker began to experiment with batting-order shifts. He replaced Graney with Jamieson and used Jamey against right-handed pitchers. Against left-handers, the converted infielder, Doc Evans, got the call. He switched the right-handed Wood and the left-handed Smith in right field and the right-handed Burns and the left-handed Johnston at first.

In the first few weeks of the season, the Indians got squared away and took command of the pennant race, if leading the White Sox and Yankees by only a few games or by scant percentage points can be termed "taking command." In any terminology, the Indians were on top of the league.

From the days of spring exhibitions and continuing through the early weeks of the championship schedule there had been gossip about the White Sox's conduct in the 1919 World Series with Cincinnati. Gangland's lovely characters were talking, and many baseball men, including Speaker, who had watched the Series six months before, knew they had seen some strange happenings.

Yet the White Sox gave no intimation in the 1920 race that they were putting forth efforts shy of the best. Week after week rolled by, and either the White Sox or the Yankees were passing the Indians so closely that the league's top three places could change on the results of one day's games.

Speaker set up a big three of his pitchers, Coveleskie, Caldwell, and Bagby. Each was a work horse. Caldwell had everything in a pitcher's repertoire and was forever attempting to repay Speaker for the manager's confidence in him after he seemed on the way to the minors. Covey was the prototype of the tall, stoical Pole. He had a bright sense of humor, however, and would allow it free sway except on the days he was scheduled to pitch. Then he would be sullen and snap at questioners.

Covey operated pretty much on his own judgment. If the Indians were locked in a tight game in late innings, the spitball artist was certain to saunter toward the bull pen, much as Dizzy Dean did in a later service with the St. Louis Cardinals. Covey would warm up slowly, and if it appeared his services might be needed, he would increase his practice pace. Then he would turn to Speaker and signal with a nod that he was ready.

Bagby, six feet and slender, knew the strength and weakness of every batter in the league. Jim could exhibit marvelous control if an occasion arose. Jim usually met a crisis with a variety of offerings, carefully ordered by O'Neill, whom Speaker insists was the smartest caller of pitches he ever saw.

To lead what he considered to be a pennant procession, Speaker bounced back on his own with a brand of hitting remindful of his sensational 1916 season. The Indians picked up Speaker's spark and forged into the league lead as early as late April. The interest of fans in Cleveland was ignited by the same spark. Weekday congregations of ten thousand to twelve thousand were common in League Park's limited confines. On June 13, a crushing, pushing mob of 29,266—largest in the park's history—forced its way into the East Side plant, only to leave disappointed when the Yankees romped to a 14-to-0 triumph to cut Cleveland's lead to six percentage points!

With the exception of two days in May, when the Red Sox took over, and four days in July when the Yankees replaced them, the Indians led the league in the face of terrific competition by the White Sox and Yankees. They even survived a three-game rout by the Yankees in the Polo Grounds in July. The hot days of August arrived, but the Indians refused to crack. Speaker was batting sensationally, close to .400. Half a dozen others—Jamieson, Graney, Smith, Evans, Nunamaker, Uhle—were above .300. But the Yankees had acquired the biggest power plant in baseball, Babe Ruth, from the Red Sox.

On August 16, 1920, the Cleveland team was in first place. True, the Yankees were only a game and a half to the rear. Pressing the Yanks, from the unsafe distance of mere percentage points, were the White Sox. The Indians were making their third visit of the season to the Polo Grounds, the cavernous arena set beneath Coogan's Bluff on the fringe of New York's hauntsome Harlem.

The Indians could have used a good left-handed pitcher.

But Bagby and Coveleskie were going great. Caldwell was running a hot third to the two aces. Morton brought up a weary fourth in the big four of the mound. Yet the combination was a winning one, and whenever the Indians would drop out of first place, one of these hurlers would deliver a masterpiece, some regular would deliver a hit in the clutch, and another crucial crossroad would have been passed at top speed.

There was an ethereal fog extending over the Polo Grounds that Monday afternoon. By the fourth inning, a drizzle had set in. The sky over the huge U-shaped park, used by both New York major-league teams, was ominous. The fifth inning rolled around. The lead-off man for the Indians was Ray Chapman, the shortstop.

Chappie had joined the Cleveland family in 1912. He was now twenty-nine years old and had earned a place of rank among major-league shortstops. No magnificent "pair of hands" did Chappie own. He was not as graceful as Larry Lajoie had been, or as Lou Boudreau was to become. But he could cover a shortstop's territory beautifully. He had a fine arm, and he was aggressive. He could run the bases with skill and daring. and he was one of the best bunters in the history of the league.

At the plate, Chappie, a right-handed batter, assumed a crouch stance. He crowded the plate as a habit, and he was forever ducking in the nick of time to allow a swift pitch to sail past his head. Of all the pitchers Chappie should dare by proximity to the plate, he was destined to choose on this fateful day a man who had poured his pitches into five other batters earlier that season.

Carl Mays threw the ball with an underhand sweep. They called him the submarine twirler, and his pitches were not the easiest in the league to follow. Too, there was a suspicion that Mays did not always aim his pitches at the plate. He had hit Speaker two years before and had come dangerously close to many other batters.

It was Mays pitching to Chapman, and there was rain in the air. The baseball was damp as Mays started his right-handed warm up. Down went his body. His arm shot out from the top of the open bleachers in the deep background at the park.

"Mays tossed an inshoot that seemed to hypnotize Chapman," reported the *Cleveland Press*, "or else he miscalculated it and believed the ball would sail by. Anyhow, it struck him on the temple, fracturing his skull, and paralyzing the nerve chords, making it impossible for him to talk."

Chappie's bat had been held high and close to his head. He was a constant threat as a bunter, and the Yankee catcher that day, Herold "Muddy" Ruel, was on his toes in anticipation of an attempted bunt. Chappie took up a goodly portion of the mythical "strike zone" with his over-the-plate stance and Ruel was hard put, as was any catcher working behind the Tribe star, to follow the pitch perfectly.

Chappie turned his head a fraction as the pitch approached. There was a dull clunk, and the ball rolled out in front of the plate. Ruel ripped off his mask and in the same movement darted forward to retrieve the ball and throw to Wally Pipp, the first baseman. Ruel wasn't sure whether the sphere had hit Chapman's bat or person. But once in front of the plate, ball in hand, Ruel hesitated. He sensed something was amiss. Then he turned to see Chapman on the ground, Speaker bending over him.

Efforts at first aid failed. A doctor was summoned, and he ordered the stricken player speeded to a hospital. A delicate brain operation was performed. Chappie, unconscious from the split second of the ball's impact with his head, was dangerously close to death throughout the night.

Speaker and several others camped outside the door to Chapman's room. At five in the morning, a nurse opened the door and said solemnly, "He's gone."

No attempt was made to dam the torrent of tears. No ordinary ballplayer had been Chapman. He was a high-spirited, good-natured young man, and Tris Speaker loved him as a son. "He was the best friend I had," Speaker complimented the memory of his shortstop the next day.

It was not until then that the Indians, as a team, realized they had won the previous day's game, 4 to 3, defeating Mays. But a mere triumph or reversal was not important. The beloved Chappie was dead, and the ball game scheduled in the Polo Grounds the next day was called off.

Mays was exonerated of all blame for the accident, though in Cleveland there were murmurs that the death-dealing pitcher had best stay out of the Ohio metropolis the next time the Yankees went west. Arrangements were made to ship Chappie's body to Cleveland. Funeral services were held in St. John's Cathedral in the heart of downtown Cleveland. Nearly two thousand people crowded into the Catholic structure. More than three thousand others were turned away and waited in the streets outside.

Speaker, nervous in the heat of the pennant race, mourning his close friend and fearing a public demonstration of his grief, was so upset emotionally he did not attend the services.

The Indians went back to the East to continue their tour, but they were listless and ill at ease without Chappie. A reserve infielder, Harry Lunte, replaced Chapman. Although he was a flashy and dependable fielder, Lunte lacked the batting, bunting, and base-running skills of his late predecessor.

Five days after the Chapman tragedy, the Indians played a double-header in Boston. Speaker, himself sorrowing, could not rally his men. In eighteen innings, the heavy-hitting Redskins, who were to bat above .300 as a team for the entire season, could not score a run. Waite Hoyt and Herb Pennock painted their feathers with whitewash and so, after one month at the top of the league, the Redskins surrendered their place of honor to the White Sox.

Long before Chapman's tragic accident, Speaker had been on Dunn's coattails to get him a left-handed pitcher.

"There's that Walter Mails with Portland in the Pacific Coast League," Spoke repeated to Dunn. "I think he can help us."

Barnard thought so, too, and had been dispatched to cast a practiced eye at the pitching of the big, handsome southpaw. His report was encouraging. Though Mails had failed with Brooklyn in 1916 and 1917, he was the possessor of so much natural "stuff" that any scout was certain to be impressed. Then, too, the Indians could not be choosers at that juncture. The club needed a helpful jolt. Speaker thought the arrival of Mails might boost morale. The Tribe had fallen three and a half games behind the White Sox.

On August 21, as the Indians were being shut out twice by the Red Sox and were dumped out of first place, Dunn announced the purchase of Mails. The price was announced as thirty-five thousand dollars, but this included only ten thousand dollars in cash, the remainder being in estimated value of players to be turned over to the Portland team then and later.

While the loquacious Duster Mails was en route to the East two days later, Carl Mays returned to the pitching rubber and beat the Tigers, 10 to 0. Headlines in Cleveland newspapers blared the injustice of it all. Angry readers screamed for action by President Ban Johnson of the American League, with permanent banishment of Mays as the sentence. But the Indians were on the road at the time, and the demonstration subsided without the fuel the presence of the ball players would have provided.

Mails reported to Speaker August 25 but did not make his first start until September 1 when he faced the Senators in Washington. The Tribe was received warmly in the Capital. Clark Griffith, manager of the Senators, wanted to introduce legislation that would bar the Mays's submarine pitch and other "freak" deliveries from the big leagues. There was, to be truthful, no freakish aspect to Mays's submarine pitch other than the unorthodox delivery, and there was little ground for a formal protest.

Speaker gave Mails a big assignment as a starter. The team was only a game out of first place. Mails, high-strung, pitched with such power and abandon in the first inning that he couldn't get the ball over the plate. Speaker had to replace the rookie with Guy Morton in the second inning. Morton had one of his good days, and the Tribe went on to win, 9 to 5, and leaped into first place for the first time in twelve days as the White Sox lost. The Hose were in a bad slump, having dropped six of their last seven games.

The Indians returned to Cleveland on Labor Day, September 2. Speaker was in no mood to baby any of his pitchers, even the newcomer, Mails. The Chapman tragedy had left the manager and his players with a very limited sense of humor. There was scant bantering, and jokes were relayed only in the comparative hush of private rooms.

113

The pennant race was a serious, earnest business for the Indians. First they were confident they were as good as any team in the league, even without Chapman. Second, they wanted to win "for Chappie." And third they were, many of them, players who had barely missed the World Series' rewards of 1919.

Mails was shot right smack back into action only twenty-four hours after his league debut in Washington. This time, facing the Browns, the Duster had better luck. He won, 7 to 2, to instill a brand-new life into the Redskins. First place was secure for at least a day or two, due to a vent in the schedule. The Yankees and White Sox were deadlocked, only one game behind.

In the holiday double-header, Lunte hurt his leg. Spoke did not have a utility infielder, but Doc Evans was playing only part time in the outfield, and he had been a third baseman at the beginning. So Evans went to shortstop, and Speaker went upstairs to talk to Dunn and Barnard.

"Now what?" asked the Texan.

Dunn looked out the window. Barnard turned sharply to Speaker.

"What about that Joe Sewell we've got at New Orleans?"

Speaker permitted himself a low groan. "You saw him this spring in camp," he told Barney. "He's not ready for this league, I feel certain." Yet there was something about the picture of the stocky, round-faced Alabaman that stuck in Speaker's mind.

"What's he hitting down there?" asked Spoke. The latest records showed a .289 average. He asked Dunn and Barney if there was any chance of bringing him up.

"Let's gamble on anything now," Spoke insisted. "We've got to have some help to win this race, and anyone is better than no shortstop at all."

Sewell, who had been coached, scouted, and recommended by Xen Scott, famed University of Alabama football mentor, was an expensive purchase. New Orleans squawked about giving up Joe, even if Cleveland did have first rights to him. When the deal finally was completed, the New Orleans club had been paid six thousand dollars in cash and the Indians had agreed to give up rights of option on all New Orleans players.

The new shortstop and the New York Yankees arrived in Cleveland at approximately the same hour. There was considerably more public interest in the Yankees than in the kid infielder from the Deep South. The great Ruth was hammering home runs with terrifying frequency. His forty-seventh and forty-eighth round-trippers sailed merrily over League Park's right-field wall. Yet Coveleskie was equal to the occasion, and he beat the challengers in the opener. Caldwell was victimized in the second game, the most important feature of which was the debut of Joe Sewell as a shortstop. He replaced Evans in the fifth inning after the Indians had all but dropped out of the ball game and contributed one error in the field and no hits in two turns at the plate. After the first two games, the White Sox were exactly three percentage points behind the Tribe.

The third and decisive game of the series was played Saturday. Another crowd record went by the boards when 30,805 sandwiched their way into the park, only to leave in sadness as Ruth hit one more and the Yankees won easily.

The Athletics, then in their sixth straight year of basement occupancy, arrived in League Park on Sunday. Before the game, Speaker called Sewell aside.

"Joe, I'm starting you today, and I want you to have a good 'cut' at every pitch you think is good enough to hit. Never mind too much about grabbing everything in the field. I'll help you from the outfield as much as possible."

Sewell followed Speaker's orders to the letter. He registered a single and a triple. In the field, he handled a dozen chances. Joe was getting his first taste of big-league pitching, and he loved it. In fact, Joe ate up the American League variety from that day until the close of the 1933 season, a span of more than thirteen complete seasons in which he never played fewer than one hundred games with the exception, of course, of 1920.

Sewell had helped a lot, but the Yankees had been coming along like madmen. On the night of September 12, the Indians got up courage enough to look at the standings of the leading teams: Cleveland .619020, New York .618705!

The strain of the daily changes in the league leadership were telling not only on Speaker but on the nerves of the fans, who flocked to League Park in ever increasing numbers. On September 14, the Tribe fell one and a half games behind the Yankees. Two days later they were tied. On September 17, the Indians went ahead, a game over New York, a game and a half over Chicago. Two days later Jim Bagby posted his twenty-ninth victory of the year; the Indians had won seventeen of their last twenty-one games and were leading the White Sox by a game and a half and the Yankees by three full games.

The White Sox beat the Yankees three straight in Chicago, then moved to Cleveland on September 23. This had to be the series to decide the championship. The White Sox seemed to have recovered fully from their slump of early September. The three games to be played in League Park could be the most important of the entire season. As it turned out, they were among the more significant contests played in the history of the sport.

The Pale Hose were exactly one and one half games behind the Indians at 2:59 P.M. the afternoon of Thursday, September 23. Two hours later, after Dickie Kerr, Chicago's left-handed genius, had throttled the Indians, 10 to 3, the Sox were only half a game behind.

Duster Mails had won four in a row for his new employer. Now he was given a chance to chalk up number five, at the expense of the team many experts considered the best in the business despite all those rumors that were heard as often as a person cared to listen. Mails was in rare form that day. He granted only three hits and the Indians won, 2 to 0, to square the series. Now first place was safe from the talented Chicagoans for the time being.

In the Saturday finale at League Park, played before 30,625 excited spectators, the White Sox clawed back to win, 5 to 1, thanks to some tremendous batting by Shoeless Joe Jackson. The Cracker outfielder hit safely three times, one of his blows being a home run far over the right-field wall.

Before this series was started, before the White Sox had won two out of three from their most persistent opponents, Presi-

Stanley Coveleskie

Bill Wambsganss

Elmer Smith

Joe Sewell

dent Ban Johnson of the American League had issued a dyna-mite-laden statement from his Chicago office.

"I have evidence, and much of it is now before the Grand Jury, that certain notorious gamblers are threatening to expose the 1919 World Series as a fixed event unless the Chicago White Sox players drop out of the current race intentionally to let the Indians win. These gamblers have made heavy bets on the Cleveland team."

Did the series in League Park look as if the White Sox were deliberately throwing the games? The question, asked millions of times in that period, was adjudged asinine. The White Sox not only had won two out of three games they were alleged to have been ordered to throw, but they had been defeated the one time only because of some superlative pitching by Mails.

The White Sox went home and promptly defeated the De-troit Tigers twice. Eddie Cicotte pitched one game, Kerr the other. Chicago fans, daily reading blaring headlines that cast aspersions on their American League heroes, couldn't believe the rumors. They pointed to four victories in the team's last five starts as evidence of honesty in the current pennant race.

Cleveland was under open accusation as the "nerve center" of the multimillion-dollar racket of baseball betting. On September 25, as the White Sox were beating the Indians at League Park, President John A. Heydler of the National League was working diligently in the city's downtown area, investigating bookmakers, their betting offices, and trying to tie up the Ohio gamblers with interests in Chicago and New York. Heydler charged that a minimum of one hundred thous-and dollars per day was being bet in Cleveland baseball lot-teries alone!

The snowball was gathering crust, as it had been ever since the previous autumn. There had been only lifted eyebrows by some smart onlookers during the 1919 World Series. The next winter and through most of the 1920 baseball campaign, frank discussions of a fix had replaced idle rumors and facial gestures.

Then, on September 6, 1920, on an inside page of the *Cleve-land Press,* appeared an item dealing with telegrams that had been sent to William L. Veeck, Sr., young and new president of the Chicago Cubs. These purported to show that hundreds of thousands of dollars had been poured into Cleveland bet centers by Pittsburgh gamblers to be wagered on games in which the Cubs were involved.

A report of a fix in an August 31 game between the Cubs and Phillies resulted in action by Chief Justice Charles A. McDonald of the Chicago Criminal Court. He ordered a Grand Jury investigation of gambling on baseball games, and the first hearing was on September 22 with twelve witnesses—including baseball magnates, sports writers, and one major-league player—under the subpoena.

The player was J. C. "Rube" Benton, a pitcher for the New York Giants, who was reported to have been offered seven hundred and fifty dollars by a Cub player intentionally to lose a game. Benton later was said to have won three thousand eight hundred dollars betting on baseball games through tips provided by Hal Chase, former Giants' first baseman, who had been expelled from organized baseball a year earlier.

The snowball was now rolling faster. Testimony was being heard that placed Charles A. Comiskey, president of the White Sox, in the role of a suspicious magnate. He had employed private detectives to track down rumors of a fix in the 1919 Series. In fact, Comiskey had held up the World Series' bonus checks of eight players while his private investigation was in progress.

Baseball became a maelstrom of witnesses, testimony, rumors, bets, and threats. Ban Johnson dragged in the 1920 championship race and the report of threats against the White Sox, with the result that the investigation swept out into the front pages of every newspaper in the country. One story said Chase made forty thousand dollars betting on the Reds to beat the White Sox. Another story, believed widely, was that George M. Cohan, famous actor-producer-writer, had lost one hundred thousand dollars betting on Chicago.

Johnson and Comiskey split. Harry Grabiner, secretary of the White Sox, said, "Let's have the exposure, even if it wrecks our club, wrecks our flag chances, and even forces us to close the gates of Comiskey Park."

Early in the day on September 28, the Grand Jury heard

these witnesses: Manager Hughey Jennings of the Tigers, owner August Herrmann of the Reds, Manager John McGraw of the Giants, catcher Ray Schalk of the White Sox, National League umpire Monte McCormick, and Mrs. Claude Williams, wife of the White Sox pitcher known as "Lefty."

The last witness hadn't been out of the room long enough to regain composure before indictments were returned against eight Chicago players who appeared in the 1919 World Series. They were pitcher Eddie Cicotte, outfielder Joe Jackson, pitcher Claude Williams, third baseman George "Buck" Weaver, shortstop Charles "Swede" Risberg, outfielder Oscar "Happy" Felsch, first baseman Arnold "Chick" Gandil, and utility infielder Fred McMullin. All except Gandil were with the White Sox at the time of their indictment. He had been released after the 1919 campaign.

Abe Attell, former world featherweight boxing champion, was named chief fixer of the Series, though much of the testimony included references to the big-time gambler, Arnold Rothstein, who was murdered later. Cicotte confessed his part in the swindle and hurriedly left Chicago. Ed admitted that he "gave Cincinnati batters good balls to hit. I put them right over the plate...I deliberately threw late to second on several plays." Jackson said he had "helped throw games by muffing hard chances in the outfield or by throwing slowly to the infield." Shoeless Joe said he decided to tell his part in the fraud after receiving a threat to "bump him off" unless he confessed.

As Cicotte and Jackson, and later Felsch and Williams, admitted their duplicity, Cleveland newspapers rallied their readers to the support of the Indians. Owner Comiskey had banned immediately those players indicted. The White Sox were riddled. On the day the indictments were returned, the Indians were in first place by half a game and on that day, too, Bagby posted his thirtieth victory. Sarge Jim beat the Browns, 9 to 5, although allowing his customary complement of hits, ten.

"Our Tribe would have won the pennant even had the crummy Chicago thieves been allowed to finish the season," read one hip-hip-hooray story in a Cleveland paper. The schedule was to close on Sunday, October 3. The day before, the

Indians beat the Tigers in Detroit, 10 to 1. The Tigers got eleven hits, but they couldn't get their men across the plate. The reason was understandable. Bagby was pitching for the Indians, and the triumph was the Sarge's thirty-first of the year. No other pitcher in Cleveland history, except Cy Young, ever passed the thirty-game mark.

Ray Schalk, the honest and capable Chicago catcher, and the broken-hearted Kid Gleason, the Sox manager, led the remnants of their great teams in the last week of the campaign and split two games with the Browns. But the Indians had previously beaten the Browns four straight and had piled up a two-game lead. The final 1920 standings:

Teams	Games	Won	Lost	Pct.	Games Beh.
Cleveland	154	98	56	.638	—
Chicago	154	96	58	.623	2
New York	154	95	59	.617	3

There was no such tight race in the National League. The Brooklyn Trolley Dodgers, led by Uncle Wilbert Robinson, ran away with the senior circuit's championship. They beat the Giants by seven games and the defending champion Reds by ten and a half games.

Not even the National League was immune from the dark rumors of the season. Some of the Brooklyn players were called into the club offices following reports that gamblers were trying to get them to throw the Series to Cleveland. These were only idle rumors, however. The 1920 World Series was to be played in all honesty.

CHAPTER   XV

"THE BEST TEAM"

It was astonishing to note how quickly and effectively the
city of Cleveland chose to ignore the unsavory aspects to the
1919 and 1920 seasons in order to concentrate on the imminent
World Series. Perhaps the Ohio metropolis' interest and attitude were understandable, however, in view of the fact that
never before had Cleveland won a baseball championship all
by itself, with no qualifications.

In a fine demonstration of loyalty, Cleveland fans rallied
to their Indians and threw a civic challenge at the Trolley
Dodgers on the basis of attendances at the approaching games.
And in the steel-crested eyes of the professional odds makers,
the Indians were the favorites to win the Series because of
four factors:

1) The Dodgers had agreed to allow Joe Sewell to play.

2) The Indians finished the season with ten batters who
had averages of .300 or higher.

3) The Cleveland pitching, abetted by the seven-game winning streak achieved by Duster Mails, was considered more
than adequate for a short set-to.

4) The Indians had the strongest inspirational force in the
game at their disposal in Tris Speaker, their great player-
center fielder.

In 1920, as now, players to be eligible for the World
Series must have been listed by their teams before September
1. The Indians had not acquired Sewell until ten days after
the deadline. An appeal was made by President Dunn to the
National Baseball Commission to allow Sewell to play.

The National Commission was composed of the presidents
of the American and National Leagues, Ban Johnson and John
Heydler, and a third man who ranked as the Commission's
chairman. This had been August "Garry" Herrmann of Cin-

cinnati, but Johnson and Heydler got into such a viciously personal battle over Herrmann's qualifications that the Commission's affairs were miserably unsettled.

This Commission had been the supreme power in organized baseball. In the midst of the squabbling in 1920, Herrmann finally resigned. Johnson and Heydler could not agree upon a successor. Johnson detested the nominee of Heydler, a Chicago jurist named Kenesaw Mountain Landis. It was in this period of a chairmanless National Commission that the sport was rocked by its only major scandal.

Johnson and Heydler ducked the Sewell issue but suggested that Cleveland request permission of the Brooklyn club to use the shortstop. The Dodgers were on the spot, definitely. Death had removed Ray Chapman and had brought about this special situation. Too, there would have been long and loud wails of anguish and anger in Cleveland, and throughout the country, should the Dodgers turn down the Tribe's plea. On the heels of the Black Sox exposure, even a minor disturbance would have been magnified. Not willing to risk incurring unpleasantries, the Dodgers okayed Sewell.

The short Southerner batted .329 in twenty-two games with the Indians. Speaker had compiled the remarkable average of .388, or 92 points more than he hit in 1919! The Speaker-Jamieson-Smith outfield combination was ranked among the greatest trios of all time. Jamieson batted .319 and Smith .315.

Jim Bagby's record was 31 victories and 12 defeats. The solid man, Stan Coveleskie, won 24 games and lost 14. Caldwell conquered both the other teams and Demon Rum to win 20 games while losing 10. Mails had posted seven decisions consecutively. The first three accounted for seventy-five of Cleveland's 98 victories!

The Dodgers could not match such figures, in either batting or pitching. Yet Robinson's team had better balance. Burleigh Grimes, the great spitball artist, was the club's leading pitcher with 23 victories against only 11 losses. Then there was a tremendous drop to Leon Cadore, who won 15 while losing 14. The colorful Jake Pfeffer posted a record of 16 and 9, Rube Marquard 10 and 7, Al Mamaux 12 and 8, and Sherrod Smith 11 and 9.

Zack Wheat, the left fielder, was the team's most effective batter with .328, but only two other regulars, first baseman Ed Konetchy with .308 and center fielder Hi Myers with .304, were included in the National League's small circle of .300 batters.

Moreover, the Dodgers had no one to compare with Speaker, as a player, a competitor, or a field leader. So the professional betting odds, spoken of in hushed tones at that special time, were on the Indians to win the nine-game interleague play-off.

The Series was to have been started in Cleveland. In fact, it was to have christened the Ohio field with its new, official name—Dunn Field. When he became president of the Indians four years earlier, Jim Dunn had made two promises, one that he would bring Cleveland a pennant and second that he would rename League Park as Dunn Field when that objective had been reached.

One week before the Series, Dunn ordered erection of temporary wooden bleachers in center and right fields. A contractor himself, Sunny Jim doubted that construction could be completed in time for the scheduled opener on Tuesday, October 5. The screen comprising the top half of the 40-foot-high right-field wall had been taken down, and rows of seats had been built on the concrete base of the wall. These extended over Lexington Avenue and provided the model, innocently, for the enlargement of Detroit's Briggs Stadium many years later. Then, a city street was closed permanently to permit a double-decked grandstand in left field.

When it was apparent at the last minute that Dunn Field would not be in readiness, league and club officials authorized a transfer of the inaugural to Brooklyn. The Indians had finished their schedule in Detroit Sunday and had to be rounded up hastily and bundled onto Brooklyn-bound trains the next night.

There wasn't much doubt concerning Speaker's starting pitcher. On the train, the Gray Eagle sat down with Coveleskie. The big Pole grinned and muttered a kidding remark about all the hustle and bustle.

"You're 'going' tomorrow," Spoke said.

Covey merely looked at Speaker and grinned.

Manager Robinson pulled a minor surprise by starting Marquard, a talented if slightly Broadway-smitten southpaw, instead of Grimes. Later Robbie admitted he was trying to take fullest advantage of Ebbets Field's contours. With a left-hander pitching, the Indians' right-handed batting line-up would be used by Speaker. Left field being much deeper than right in the Brooklyn park, Robbie figured he would get a better break with Burns, Evans, and Wood in the Cleveland line-up than with Jamieson, Smith, and Johnston aiming at the right-field wall only 297 feet from home plate.

And, too, Rube Marquard was thirty-one years old and a smart workman on the hilltop. In 1912, he had won nineteen games consecutively as a pitcher for the Giants. If he needed additional incentive, it was available in the story of his early baseball life. The Rube had been born in Cleveland as Richard William LeMarquis. He pitched for Forest City amateur teams before turning to the professional field.

Signed by Indianapolis and farmed to the Canton team in the Central League, the Rube was the special pet of Henry Edwards, the Cleveland scribe who had engineered the pitcher's first professional tryout. Edwards was convinced that Marquard had the makings of a great pitcher, so convinced that he insisted upon President Charley Somers and Manager Larry Lajoie of the Naps scouting Marquard personally in 1907. Two full-time professional scouts accompanied Somers and Lajoie.

The four thumbed down Edwards' pride and joy.

"They'll steal his pants in the big leagues because of his poor movement to first," the scouts told the newspaperman. "Besides, he can't field his position. They'll bunt him crazy."

The Indians didn't bunt the Rube crazy thirteen years later, but they did beat him on a blustery, cold day. A crowd of 23,573, not capacity, went to Ebbets Field to watch the scheduled duel between Covey and Rube. There wasn't too much of a duel, but there was an interesting ball game, and the confidence of fans throughout the country was boosted several notches.

The wind whipping over and around the field led to the Tribe's first run in the second inning. Burns hit a high pop fly in back of first. Konetchy backed up but couldn't keep pace with the wind, and it blew the ball just out of the first baseman's reach. Whether Pete Kilduff, the second baseman, could have caught the ball was debated freely for some months after the game. Regardless, Burns rounded first and broke for second. Konetchy fired the ball to head off Burns, but Ivy Olson, the shortstop, forgot to cover the bag and the ball rolled into the left-field corner. Burns went all the way home with the first run of the Series.

A pass to Wood, Sewell's single, and O'Neill's double added up to one more run in that second inning, and the total was sufficient for Covey. However, Wood and O'Neill tied together ringing doubles in the fourth inning for a third run to make it that much easier for the spitball exponent. Wheat rapped Covey for a double in the seventh and completed the circuit on two outs. That minor outburst finished the Dodgers for the day. Covey allowed only five hits to win, 3 to 1.

Yet the Dodgers were not to be that agreeable in the next two games. The top pitchers of both leagues, Bagby and Grimes, went to the mound in the second clash before 24,559 fans, an increase of nearly two thousand over the Tuesday gathering. It was one of the few times that the Indians were unable to get Sarge Jim a big batch of runs. They were, as the score indicates, baffled completely by Grimes's spitters. Not until the eighth did a Cleveland runner reach third base. Then three walks, one of them intentional, filled the bags. But with two out, Doc Johnston grounded to Kilduff, and the threat had been eliminated. Bagby seemed tired after the long and grueling pennant race and was officially charged with the defeat, 3 to 0, though he was relieved by Uhle in the seventh.

The morning of the third game, Speaker and Mails taxied to Ebbets Field together. Speaker had not yet named his starting pitcher. He leaned toward Mails, but Tris always hesitated to let the Duster know in advance that he was to pitch. Mails was a terrifically nervous man who might sweat away much of his strength in useless pregame fretting.

That October 7 was a bright, sunny day, and Mails responded to the weather as the hack rolled on.

"I'd like a crack at those blankety-blanks," he assured Spoke. "My arm feels great today."

Speaker did not reply. He gazed out the window, to the pancake panorama of the Brooklyn streets, stores butting into houses and houses butting into flats. Speaker was digesting Mails's boast and it was only moderately palatable.

The manager said nothing more to Mails until half an hour before the scheduled start of the game.

"You're my pitcher today, Duster," notified Speaker. "I was glad when you told me you were in shape to work."

Speaker went about other business on the field, but shortly noticed that one of his coaches, Jack McAllister, was waving wildly from the bench to attract Spoke's attention. Tris answered the fairly obvious distress call.

"It's Mails," informed McAllister. "Says he can't pitch today, claims he's got a sore arm." And there sat Mails, holding his arm. Speaker cursed, at length and at Mails.

Slim Caldwell was sitting within earshot of the fuss. He had just finished pitching in batting practice.

"I'll start for you," he said to Spoke. Tris demurred for a moment then told Caldwell to get ready. It soon developed that Slim's heart was stronger than his arm. He walked Olson, the lead-off batter.

Before Caldwell could pitch to Jimmy Johnston, next in line, there was activity in the Cleveland bull pen. A right-hander was warming up. But so was a big left-hander, and as the southpaw pumped pitches into the catcher's glove there were shotlike sounds. Speaker looked to the bull pen. There was Mails, firing his hottest pitches, though he had not been told to warm up.

When Johnston sacrificed and Sewell fumbled Griffith's roller, Speaker looked to the bull pen again. But there were no more blasting pitches by Mails. He was sitting down, holding his left arm. Speaker swore to himself and made it audible when Wheat singled and Myers got a pop hit. Spoke stopped the game and trotted in to the mound.

He took the ball from Caldwell. "That's all for you, Slim," he said. Tris signaled to Umpire Hank O'Day that he was changing pitchers. "That —— left-hander is coming in," Spoke announced.

Mails made his way to the pitching rubber, half afraid to face the raging Speaker.

"Listen, you ——," Spoke hissed, "you haven't got any sore arm. You told me this morning you wanted to pitch. Now you pitch, and you pitch with everything you've got in you."

Mails did, but it was too late to save the third game. The next two Dodgers flied out. From then on, Duster matched the sterling pitching of Sherr Smith, who lost his shutout in the fourth when Speaker doubled and completed the circuit after Wheat allowed the ball to roll through him. O'Neill got two of the Tribe's three hits and provided the fielding gem of the game with his pickup and throw on Johnston's perfectly placed sacrifice in the first inning.

From heavy favorites to long shots in exactly two days was the legend of the Indians that night. The Dodgers were leading the Series, two games to one. Sunny Jim Dunn was side by side with his ballplayers on the special train bound for Cleveland. The owner was not averse to a toddy or two in festive mood, but this night there wasn't too much happiness among the Cleveland contingent.

Dunn was on edge, wondering not only whether his new bleachers would be completed but also whether his dream, finally made true by Speaker, would be crushed by a team of Dodgers he considered inferior.

"Damn it, Spoke, I hate to think about coming all the way back to Brooklyn," complained Dunn. "If we could have just won one of those two games—"

Speaker interrupted his boss.

"You won't have to go back, Jim," he predicted. "We're going to win four straight at home."

Dunn sat up straight in his seat.

"You think so?"

"I'm sure," promised Speaker.

Ed Bang asked Speaker why he felt that way.

"It's our home field, and our fellows are used to swinging for that right-field wall," reasoned the Texan.

How many times in later years Cleveland teams were

viciously dangerous in their home park because of that right-field wall! The 1920 Indians were at the beginning of a long procession of teams that were lopsided in their balance because of the barrier.

Selection of the Cleveland pitcher was automatic. Coveleskie had been rested three full days since his triumph in the first game at Brooklyn. One day was left open for travel. But Robinson passed over Marquard and named Leon Cadore, a right-hander.

When Joe Wood heard of Cadore's nomination, he was overjoyed, a strange mental state for a man who wouldn't get to play with a right-hander on the mound for the Dodgers.

"They're beaten already," Wood said with emphasis. "Our left-handed batters will rattle that wall."

That wasn't the exact story of the ball game, but the result was about the same. The Indians did shell Cadore and for the first time in the Series they posted double figures in the base-hit column. Cadore, who had never recovered fully from the ordeal of pitching the historic twenty-six-inning marathon 1-1 tie with the Braves during the regular season, was knocked reeling by the first batter.

Jamieson pickled Cadore's first pitch and shot a liner right back to the pitcher, who threw up his hands in self-defense and managed to hold onto the ball. Cadore walked Wamby, who moved up on Speaker's single over second. Smith sent another single over second, Wamby scoring, and when Myers juggled the ball briefly, Speaker raced for third and beat the throw with a beautiful, long slide. Smith advanced to second on the error.

The *Reach Official American League Guide* takes a poke at Manager Robinson's strategy at this point. The editor reported, "Instead of passing Gardner, always a dangerous hitter, he was allowed to hit and sent a long sacrifice fly to Myers on which Speaker scored...."

Covey was off to a flying start, and though the Tribe got him three runs later, he didn't need much help. The spitball king fashioned another five-hitter to win, 5 to 1, to square the series at two-all, and to send the 25,734 paying spectators out to begin thousands of Saturday-night celebrations. They went forth to praise, too, the shortstopping of the kid, Sewell, who tried his best to make the fans forget Chapman with three marvelously executed plays.

What happened the next day in Dunn Field was believed at first only by the 26,684 mortals inside the enclosure. As the years wore on and as there were more opportunities for comparing the Sunday game, fifth of the Series, with others played, it became more and more certain that this one contest would occupy a place of honor in any gallery of athletic performances.

Before the game, Speaker was talking to Sarge Jim.

"Everything all right?" asked the manager.

"Sho' is," replied the Georgian.

Speaker advised Bagby to use especial care in pitching to such sluggers as Griffith, Wheat, and Myers because of the temporary stands in right and center fields that diminished the playing areas.

Bagby was silent for a spell. Then he turned to Spoke.

"Ah think ah'll bust one out to those wooden seats," he drawled. "They seem just about right for me to hit."

Speaker was more concerned at the moment with Bagby's pitching than with any threats to hit home runs. Again Burleigh Grimes was the Brooklyn hurler, and again Grimes seemed to be having all his usual stuff as he warmed up. Bagby had dropped the second game to the spitball star in Brooklyn. But now Sarge Jim was home, in Dunn Field, with all those friends he could nearly reach out and touch.

Never before had a World Series been played in Cleveland. The effect was electric. Business in the city was at a standstill. Thousands milled on downtown streets, eagerly seeking the latest word on the game. It was tense enough on Saturday. Now it was Sunday—no newspapers, no radio broadcasts, no television. Only telephones and a thousand grapevines.

Bagby got by the first inning, though Olson rapped him for a hit. In fact, the Dodgers got on base in each inning except the sixth, and they rattled a total of thirteen hits off the teasers and curves served up by the Sarge. But he had nothing to worry about after the first inning.

Grimes failed to fool the alert Jamieson, leading off. The

Jersey Comet laced a line drive toward right field. Konetchy, the first baseman, got one finger of his glove on the ball, but it sailed on through and rolled into the audience on the field in front of the wall. Thus, a ground-rule double was prevented. Wamby slashed a single into left field to move Jamieson around to second. Speaker crossed up the Dodgers and bunted. Grimes tried to field the ball, slipped, and went down on his seat. In no position to throw the ball, he held it for an instant, then pegged weakly to Konetchy. Speaker reached first safely, and the bases were filled.

Smith, thin of face but wiry of muscles, stepped into the batter's box. Otto Miller, the catcher, signaled for a spitter. Smith fouled it off. He looked at one wide pitch, then at a strike down the alley. Grimes wound up for his fourth pitch to the Tribe's angular right fielder.

There was a tremendous smack as Smith's bat connected with the horsehide. From the time of impact, there was no doubt about the blow. It was a home run, a blast far over the right-field wall, over the screen, over the temporary bleachers. For the first time in the history of the World Series, a four-mast home run had been hit!

By telegraph and by telephone the news traveled. By word of mouth, the most magical of transmissions, Elmer Smith's home run became known from Dunn Field to Cleveland's outer rim within a matter of minutes. The cheer that went up from the astounded but happy crowd was heard for dozens of city blocks.

In the fourth inning, Doc Johnston rattled a single off the leg of the hapless Grimes. Miller messed up a spitball pitch and was charged with a passed ball, Doc advancing. He moved to third on Sewell's infield out, after which O'Neill was passed purposely. Bagby sauntered to the plate. This was his chance to "hit one into those seats," as he had mentioned to Speaker.

The Sarge, a strong right-handed batter, looked over the first pitch, but on Grimes's second offering he swung hard. Let the editor of the *Reach Guide* speak his piece:

"Bagby's homer . . . was merely a piece of luck, as the ball fell just inside of the temporary bleachers in right center, which seats should not have been permitted to encroach upon the playing field."

If the editor was distressed, Bagby's fans were joyously proud of the star pitcher. As Johnston and O'Neill trotted to the plate ahead of the jubilant Bagby, they turned and waited to shake his hand. As a matter of fact, the Sarge was so excited he literally tore around the bases. Johnston and O'Neill barely beat him to the pay-off station. Grimes walked off the mound at that juncture, to be succeeded by Clarence Mitchell, a cagey left-hander.

The Sarge now had a 7-to-o lead, and only baseball fans of his vintage will recall how he could fool around with a big advantage. The Dodgers had been banging Bagby for hits in each inning. They had threatened to score in the second when Konetchy tripled to left. Kilduff had followed with a low liner over Sewell's head, and Jamieson had made the catch at his shoetops, straightened up, and fired the ball to O'Neill. Konetchy never had a chance. O'Neill, ball in hand, was on his knees guarding the third-base line. Konetchy hit the dirt but only slammed into the hefty catcher and was called out by Umpire Bill Klem.

At that point Robinson had charged out of the dugout and protested that O'Neill had blocked the plate in violation of base-running rules. Klem refused to allow the complaint, and when Speaker trotted in, he paused to needle Uncle Robbie.

"You're a fine one to be squawking about a block of the plate," chided Spoke. "When you were with the Orioles, they tell me a fellow had to have a plow to knock you out of the way."

Robbie broke into a grin and returned to the bench.

There was scarcely a ripple of excitement in the crowd in the fifth when Kilduff and Miller singled in succession. Batters, two and three in a row, were forever singling off Bagby, it seemed. Mitchell, the pitcher, was to be the next batter. Robinson looked down his bench and couldn't find anyone he thought might do better than the left-handed hitting pitcher, who compiled a .234 average during the National League season.

With the count one-and-one, Mitchell swung at a "fat"

Bagby pitch. The ball started on a line toward right center field. Wamby had been playing fairly close to the bag. He made a leaping stab and pocketed the liner. In three strides he was on second base to double Kilduff, and then he saw Miller, stopped in amazement a few feet away from second base. Wamby had only to touch the startled catcher with the ball for an unassisted triple play, the first and only in World Series history!

"I intended to throw to Johnston to nail Miller after I'd stepped on second," explained Wamby after the game, "but when I saw Miller was so close, I instinctively tagged him for the third out."

All this and heaven, too, thought the city of Cleveland that day and night. Small wonder that the Indians suddenly became darlings not only of Ohio but of the baseball universe. Yet the Dodgers were not through scrapping, though the Tribe held a three-to-two lead in games.

No finer pitching duel between southpaws has been known in Series competition than that staged by Mails and Smith in the sixth game. The 27,174 fans went to Dunn Field hopeful of more home runs with the bases loaded, of more triple plays, of more thrilling base hits.

Instead, they saw Mails wrap up the Dodgers in a three-hit blanket, 1-0. The Indians picked up seven hits off Smith, but only in the sixth could they change the figures on the scoreboard. Then, with two out, Speaker poked a single into left and raced around on George Burns' double to the same field.

Now the Series was within the grasp of the Indians, and it began to appear that Speaker's prophecy of a four-game Cleveland winning streak at home would be fulfilled. Tris decided to come back with Coveleskie, no matter who Robinson selected. Not only was Speaker confident that Covey could turn the trick. He wanted the Pole to gain ranking with Faber, Coombs, Mathewson, and other immortals who pitched and won three games in a World Series.

The logical Brooklyn pitching choice would have been Marquard, but the Rube was in the doghouse. In fact, he was in three doghouses at one and the same time. A day or two before, the left-hander had stepped out in front of the Dodgers' hotel with the idea of disposing of a set of box seats. A cop watched the Rube make a deal with a fellow and promptly pinched the player for scalping.

Rube was released on his own recognition, only to be fined the grand total of one dollar and costs later. But Robbie was mad enough at him to refrain from naming him to pitch the seventh game. The Dodgers' front office decided on the spot to trade the Rube (they sent him to Cincinnati later), and the stiffest blow of all was delivered about a week after the Series by Mrs. Marquard, better known as Blossom Seeley of the vaudeville stage. She divorced him.

Thus Burleigh Grimes went back to pitch after only one day's rest, but it wouldn't have mattered who hurled. Once more, Covey was great, and once more, for the third time in the Series, he restricted the Brooklyn club to five hits. The Indians iced the game in the fourth inning on singles by Gardner and Johnston with one out. Johnston started a delayed double steal. He raced toward second, only to stop ten feet from the bag. Miller fired the ball back to Grimes, who wheeled and threw toward second base, which was unprotected. The ball rolled to the outfield, and Gardner scored. Speaker's triple in the fifth scored Jamieson with a second run, while doubles by O'Neill and Jamieson were good for a final and unnecessary tally in the seventh.

The World Series ended with Cleveland's 3-to-0 triumph as Konetchy forced Myers at second base, Wamby making the putout. In a flash, he turned to look for Speaker, but before he could get his sights on the manager, Tris was racing madly toward the infield, pursued by a large segment of the Series' biggest crowd. Wamby sighted the Gray Eagle and tossed him the baseball symbolic of the world championship.

Most of the Indians made for Speaker to congratulate him, but he sped to a box adjacent to the Cleveland dugout. He wrapped both arms around a tearfully happy old lady.

"We did it, Mother," he said in her ear above the roar of the happiest mob in Cleveland's baseball annals.

The victory, and the general conduct of the Series, was hailed as typical of what baseball fans could expect to see in the future. There was no hint of the darkness that had enveloped the 1919 classic. The 1920 Series was well attended. Each Indian got 4,204 dollars and each Dodger 2,387 dollars.

Typical of their season-long play, the Indians had six .300 batters in the Series. O'Neill and Jamieson hit .333, Speaker .320, Smith and Evans .308, and Burns .300.

Cleveland got back to normal about a week later after the triumphant Indians had been honored in a civic outdoor fete at Wade Park, on the East Side, where fifty thousand fans cheered their idols and fought for autographs.

END OF THE ROAD

ACROSS THE CHESTS of the uniforms designed for the Cleveland Indians in 1921 were the words, "World Champions." There was no doubt that the ballplayers felt worthy of the billing. Such lettering of a flannel shirt might be considered corny today, but there was no room for anything except jubilation in the minds of the Redskins after their 1920 conquests.

No winning baseball team ever had been treated more liberally by employers or admirers. The day after the World Series ended, the Indians met for a farewell in their Dunn Field dressing room. Sunny Jim Dunn and Tris Speaker were there, both beaming. Sunny Jim made a short speech.

"I hope only one thing," said Dunn, "and that is you will all be back with us next season." Dunn had nothing to worry about in the way of holdouts. Raises were granted nearly all players, and before the men left the park, they had signed 1921 pacts.

Too, Jim Dunn had given each man a bonus equal to ten days' pay. In return, the Indians presented the owner with a set of diamond-studded cuff links. Speaker was given a gold watch, engraved.

During the Series, the players had been showered with material gifts as well as with worship. Doc Johnston and Elmer Smith were given new automobiles. Smith and Bill Wamby got diamond-studded medals. Dunn and Speaker received large silver trophies. Steve O'Neill, Stanley Coveleskie, and George Burns became the owners of gold watches.

Then, to bring themselves into the spirit of giving, the Indians voluntarily reduced their own Series cuts from $4,204, as set by the National Commission, to $3,986.33. This was done so that many persons who had helped in the pennant struggle would be rewarded. Walter Mails and Joe Sewell were voted full shares. Mrs. Ray Chapman, widow of the late shortstop, already had been voted a full share. Secretary Walter McNichols, groundkeeper Frank Van Dellen, scout Jack McAllister, trainer Percy Smallwood, and Miss Edna Jameson, head of the Dunn Field ticket office, were given a thousand dollars each.

But in 1921 was to be another season and the "World Champions" on the uniforms did not scare either the Yankees or the Browns to a large degree. Also, the Indians were learning, beginning that spring, the sad lesson about the fickleness of fate. In 1920, everything went great. In 1921, everything went wrong.

Wamby, hero of the triple play, broke an arm in spring training. Harry Lunte, best available second baseman, was hurt a week later. O'Neill broke a finger and didn't return to active catching duty until July 15. No sooner had Steve regained his form than Les Nunamaker, the number-two backstop, broke a leg while sliding.

Despite these physical setbacks, the Indians kept pace with the Yankees and their mighty Babe Ruth through the first five months of the race. Bagby and Caldwell slipped considerably while Mails recorded only fourteen decisions for a .600 ball club despite all his natural ability.

Ty Cobb had "found" Mails.

After the 1920 season, Cobb and Mails played in a winter league in California. Ty began to rib the Duster about his luck in winning seven games in a row, about his great break in picking up all that World Series coin, and about the game in Brooklyn that Caldwell had to start because Mails had jitters.

"So that's why Brooklyn let you go, Mails," chided Cobb. "You can't take it. You're a busher, Mails. Out here in this winter league you're not even good enough. Wait until we get you back East next summer. Buddy, you'd better cover up your ears."

Mails couldn't take it. His "rabbit ears" were tuned in to every bench jockey in the American League. Led by Cobb, these experts in ridicule drove the Duster out of the big time.

The reliable Coveleskie, who won twenty-three; Uhle, who

was good for sixteen games; and the newly acquired Alan Sothoron, spitball star of the St. Louis Browns, who contributed thirteen victories, managed to hold the Indians' heads above water until September.

The Indians had another incentive. In the midst of the 1921 race, the infamous Chicago Black Sox were found not guilty of charges of criminal conspiracy in connection with the 1919 World Series. Failure of Chicago courts to bring Eastern gamblers to the witness stand wrecked the prosecution's case. The Cleveland players were sorely griped. They felt the Black Sox, by being banned in the last days of the 1920 schedule, had prevented the Indians from winning a forthright, clean moral victory over the field.

Into September went the Indians and Yankees, with the Browns a rather distant third. Then, on September 11, Speaker tore the ligaments in a knee. These failed to mend and the team's most forceful player and field leader was through for the year. Even so, the Indians' terrific batting kept them on the heels of the Yankees.

During spring training, the Indians had formally added a University of Alabama fullback to their squad. He was Riggs Stephenson, a square-rigged 210-pound slugger who had been recommended to the Tribe by Cleveland's perennial friend, the Alabama coach Xen Scott. Stephie, as the Southern giant soon became known, was a vicious slugger, but he had trouble throwing because of an old shoulder injury incurred in a football game.

Speaker pressed the youngster into duty at second base in the early spring after Wamby and Lunte were disabled. In fact, Spoke gambled on him in the opening game with the Browns, and the rookie contributed a mighty double to feature a sixth-inning rally that led to a 4-to-3 victory. Throughout the season, the Alabaman was the team's most dangerous substitute batter and he compiled an average of .330 in sixty-five games.

The pennant race turned past the mid-September pylon. The Indians, who had won a year earlier, made their strongest move of the season. With only ten days of the season remaining, Cleveland was mere percentage points behind the leading

Yankees. Speaker squirmed on the bench, praying daily that his knee would permit him to play. But it was no use. The Gray Eagle finally resigned himself to his role of bench manager.

The Indians trooped into the Polo Grounds for their last series of the year with the Yankees—or perhaps, with Babe Ruth. For this year was one of the Babe's most spectacular. In 1920, the Bambino had come into his own as a daily performer after the Yankees bought him from the Red Sox. He had hit fifty-four home runs and had become the symbol of the new era in baseball.

Few had thought the Babe capable of doing better in 1921. But he fooled his most fanatical boosters. He was up to fifty-six home runs already when the Indians pitched camp in the Harlem orchard on Friday, September 23. He had batted in more than a hundred and fifty runs until then. He had missed only one game all summer!

The Indians were exactly two percentage points behind the Yankees! Speaker had his ace, Coveleskie, primed. But not even the calm, capable Coveleskie could stop Ruth. The Babe rattled three doubles off the right-field wall, and each time he scored. Those three hits and three runs were enough for Waite Hoyt, but the Yankees added one for good measure to let the handsome right-hander win with more ease, 4 to 2. Speaker came back with George Uhle in the second game, and it was a perfect choice. George handcuffed the Yankees all afternoon for a 9-to-0 verdict. But on Sunday, before more than fifty thousand roaring Gothamites, the powerful home forces slaughtered the Redskins, 21 to 7!

Still, if the Indians could win the Monday game, they would be no worse off than before they went to New York. They would be finished for the year with the terrifying sluggers of Miller Huggins, and they would go back to the West still only two or three percentage points out of first place.

The Yankees were pretty much a Boston Red Sox alumni association then. Ruth, Shore, Mays, Lewis, Schang, Hoyt, Harper, McNally, and a couple of others of smaller renown, had been acquired from the money-hungry Red Sox. Huggins whipped these veterans into a winning regiment, and as is

138

frequently the case with older players, their judgment was valued highly by the mite manager.

Huggins called upon his entire pitching staff for advice before that vital fourth game. In *The Babe Ruth Story*, the Bambino relates: "Hug called a meeting of the whole staff and asked the boys to help him choose the right pitcher. He said he could start Jack Quinn, who had beaten the Indians in Cleveland earlier in the month, or come back with Hoyt, who had won the first game of the series. The staff finally voted to start Quinn, with Hoyt in the bull pen." *

Speaker came back with Coveleskie, but his choice proved no sounder than the one of Quinn by the Yankee players. Quinn didn't get by the first inning. Coveleskie did, but not before Ruth had smashed his fifty-seventh home run into the right-field seats. Covey couldn't stand the gaff, however, and was out of the game by the fifth. Uhle had come in to duel with Hoyt, who succeeded Quinn, but the Babe greeted George with his fifty-eighth round-tripper, this time with one on. It was seldom that Ruth hit home runs, or anything else, off Uhle, one of his prize jinxes.

By the ninth inning, the Yankees had fought ahead, 8 to 7, thanks chiefly to a home run by Wally Schang with one on. Darkness was lowering a veil over the field. Huggins noted the gathering shadows and put in Mays, the underhanded pitcher. Mays' pitches came out of the very earth, it seemed, and were almost impossible for batters to see. It was one of these pitches that finished the ball game. With a tying run on second, Mays scraped the top of the pitching rubber with his right knuckles as he threw to Steve O'Neill. The ball dropped into the dirt at the plate, and O'Neill swung in blindness, striking out.

In that dusky setting, the World Champions of 1920 passed out. Ruth had been too much for them. In the final game, the Babe had hit a double in addition to his two home runs. George Burns, the Tribe's stalwart first baseman, tried his best to keep up to the Bambino with three singles and a triple. Each drove in four runs, but Burns was battling the master.

* G. H. (Babe) Ruth, *The Babe Ruth Story; as told to Bob Considine* (New York: E. P. Dutton & Co., Inc., 1948)

At season's end, Ruth had 59 home runs, 170 runs batted in, and 177 runs scored.

In later years, Speaker was inclined to blame himself for the loss of the 1921 championship.

"We should have repeated, even with me out of the game in the last weeks," he insists to this day, "but I didn't handle my pitching staff the best way. I should have used Uhle more, but I was inclined to go along with the older fellows."

Perhaps the Indians would have won then, despite Ruth, had Speaker been available at the windup. As it was, the defending champions finished second, four and a half games behind the Yankees. Cleveland had to wait five years for another stretch run like that one.

In the intervening seasons, the Indians aged physically. Before the start of the 1922 season, Sunny Jim Dunn's health failed and he passed away in June at the age of fifty-seven. Four possible successors were considered, Vice-president Tom Walsh, Manager Speaker, General Manager Barnard, and secretary McNichols. Barnard was the standout for a number of reasons and succeeded the man who once was intent upon firing him. Mrs. Dunn remained the largest stockholder and, to all intents and purposes, the owner.

Throughout the 1922, 1923, 1924, and 1925 seasons, players came and went—Stuffy McInnis, Louis Guisto (still suffering from gas attacks undergone in the war), Ted Odenwald, Sherry Smith, Pat McNulty. One of the best of the period was outfielder Homer Summa, who filled the right fielder's shoes more than adequately.

Giant Garland Buckeye came along, and so did a very smart left-hander named Walter Miller. Emil Levsen, of whom more will be heard later, and Joe Shaute, a singing left-hander from Pennsylvania, Carl Yowell, Byron Speece, and Ray Benge bolstered the pitching staff. Freddy Spurgeon, a second baseman, replaced the aging Wamby, and President Barnard bought a third baseman, Rube Lutzke, from Kansas City.

The regular catcher was Luke Sewell, who like his brother Joe came to the Indians direct from the University of Alabama. A good-looking medium-sized man, Luke never played in the minors. For two years he was overshadowed by O'Neill, for two more by Glenn Myatt. Then, in 1926, Luke pushed Myatt and Martin Autry out of the way and became one of the American League's top receivers.

In 1922, just before Dunn's death, the Boston newsboy who had wept such bitter tears six years earlier when Speaker was sold to Cleveland joined his idol as trainer for the Tribe. So it was that Lefty Weisman began a lifetime in the majors, though at the beginning he did not know arnica from antipasto.

"Don't worry," Speaker said, "Doc Evans is studying medicine, and he knows what it's all about. If you get jammed up, call on Doc." Lefty did, many times, in the ensuing years in which he was establishing his private pharmacy not only of bottles but of jokes.

Those were days of trials for ballplayers. Joe Sewell, who couldn't hit left-handers with a diamond-studded bat at the outset, reported to the park each morning, gathered up the neighborhood kids who threw from the south side, and had them pitch to him by the hour while he learned to follow the curving sphere. Speaker tried to make an outfielder out of Stephenson because the muscular Southerner could hit even if he couldn't throw very well. But Stephie rebelled and finally was let go.

Lutzke had been picked up from Kansas City because Pittsburgh chose Harold "Pie" Traynor instead, and so the Indians acquired a fine fielding third baseman with marvelous "hands" but a .250 batting average. Occasionally Lutzke would take to burning inwardly because Speaker had yanked him for a pinch hitter. Once he threw his bat at the manager, who wasn't looking, and the ash stick sailed over Spoke's head.

"That'll cost you twenty-five dollars," yelled Speaker, "and if you could hit with that bat as well as you can throw it, you'd be much better."

In the clubhouse after the game, Lutzke was sounding off when Speaker came in. "If that dumb manager could figure percentages, he would know I was due for a hit," Lutzke complained. "I was up three times without any luck. So the percentage was with me."

Speaker laughed at such reasoning and rescinded the fine.

The Indians took on the appearance of pennant contenders again in 1926. Speaker, who had played in only 117 games in 1925, in which he batted a husky .389, came back strong the next summer at the age of thirty-eight. There was some snap gone from his wrist at the plate, but he was still the crouching Gray Eagle, awaiting the smash of the wood against the horsehide before dashing in or back, as instinct might dictate, to make palm-crushing catches.

The Indians—fourth in '22, third in '23, sixth in '24 and '25—were making what turned out to be a last, desperate gesture. The spark plug of the team was, strangely, someone other than Speaker. George Burns, who had been passed along to the Red Sox in 1923, was reclaimed through a trade for O'Neill and Wamby. The magnificent battery of O'Neill and Coveleskie had been broken up, Covey going to Washington in 1925 and winning twenty games. Shaute had replaced the Pole as a twenty-game winner in Cleveland. But Burns was the big noise in 1926, Burns and Uhle.

The tall, erect Burns, who batted with feet together in one of the most unorthodox poses of all good batters, punched out sixty-four two-base hits for a new major-league record. He compiled an average of .358 and was declared the American League's most valuable player.

Then there was Uhle. The balding, imperturbable man who leaped from Cleveland corner lots to the big tent won twenty-two games in 1922, twenty-six the next year, then fell away to nine and thirteen victories in 1924 and 1925. But in 1926, he bounced back, stronger, more courageous, more intelligent than ever. He posted twenty-seven triumphs while losing only eleven times, and his earned-run mark of 2.83 was his lowest of all time.

The Indians started fast, faded in May and June, but in August they were closing in on the Yankees. By mid-month, only five games separated the leading Yankees and the second-place Tribe. Now the Indians got their big chance. The Yankees moved into Dunn Field for six games, four singles and a double-header, the first game on September 15.

Speaker's batting average had shrunk to .300, but Burns was hot, and there was good pitching by Joe Shaute, Garland

Buckeye, and Dutch Levsen. The cream of the casting corps remained stalwart Uhle, who could not only thread a needle with a knee-high pitch at sixty feet, six inches, but could also "help himself" with a solid rap at the plate.

It had to be Uhle pitching against the Yankees in the opener of that six-game set, and it had to rain. After the first inning, an hour's delay was caused by a downpour. Uhle fretted and cooled off. When play was resumed, George was colder than yesterday's pot roast. He staggered for several innings and finally lost 6 to 4. The pitcher who had defeated the Yankees five times that season lost his touch sitting on the bench in Dunn Field.

A double-header was scheduled the next day. Dutch Levsen pitched against Dutch Ruether in the first game with the Cleveland right-hander winning, 2 to 1, as he gave up only two hits and personnally subdued his left-handed opponent with a ninth-inning single that scored the decisive run. In the second game, 240-pound Buckeye, who had been rescued from a bank teller's cage in Chicago, walked ten Yankees and hit another. But the Yankees could nail his right-handed shoots for only two hits and lost, 2 to 0, despite four passes to Ruth. When the Yankees filled the bases in the seventh, Buckeye calmly struck out Lou Gehrig.

Shaute won the next day's game, so when the fifth clash was played on Saturday, a capacity crowd of 26,782 spilled out of the stands and onto the outer regions of the playing area. Speaker came right back with Uhle while Huggins countered with Urban Shocker, the spitball expert. Uhle never was better against the Yankees, his favorite victims. He gave up only four hits and won, 3 to 1, to move the Tribe within two games of the leaders.

Two of the most famous titbits of repartee still on Cleveland tongues were products of that game. Though Uhle could strike out Ruth two or three times in any given nine innings— George whiffed the Bambino seventeen times in 1926—he had considerable trouble with Mark Koenig, the New York short-stop who was then serving his first full term in the league.

With two out and runners on third and second, Koenig became the batter. Uhle served two pitches to Mark, a switch hitter who was, naturally, swinging from the left side of the plate. Neither of the pitches was near the plate. Each was so patently wide that Speaker, halting the game, ran in from center field.

"What the hell are you doing?" he yelled at Uhle.

"I'd rather pitch to Ruth than this guy," George replied.

Speaker, flicking the dirt with the toe of his shoe, nodded his head.

"All right," he agreed, "but if you're going to pitch to Ruth, let's get the benefit of the psychology." With that Speaker and Uhle walked toward home plate. They met Glenn Myatt, the catcher, about six feet in front of the plate.

"What's up?" asked Myatt. And in a voice loud enough for Ruth, kneeling in the batter's circle, to hear, Speaker barked, "George says Ruth is a soft touch, but he's afraid of Koenig, so we're walking Mark."

Koenig was passed, and Uhle, pitching carefully, got the count on Ruth to three and two. Myatt gave the first signal. Uhle shook his head. Myatt gave another sign. Again Uhle wagged his displeasure. George walked in, almost to the plate, and said, "Let's hook him. He can't hit a curve around his knees."

The next pitch was just that, a curve around the knees, and the great Bambino couldn't hit it. He struck out!

A later intentional pass brought about a near fist fight between the managers. Huggins signaled to Shocker to walk Speaker so he could pitch to Burns.

"What's wrong with you, Hug, passing a lousy hitter like me to get at Burns?" Tris taunted. Huggins burned up, charged out of the dugout, and was all for punching Speaker. But plate umpire Bill Dineen, a big man who had been a famous pitcher in the days of rough and ready baseball twenty years earlier, knew how to handle the situation. He pushed Huggins to one side and ordered Speaker to keep quiet.

The Tribe had now won four straight, after blowing the opener, and was back in the race, or so it seemed. For the sixth and final game, Speaker chose Levsen a second time. A Sunday crowd of 29,726 swarmed over Dunn Field, many standing behind ropes in the outfield. Could Levsen beat the great Yankees again? The betting was that he could.

But Dutch's luck ran out on him. The good fortune that enabled him to beat the White Sox twice and to crack the record books on August 28, by pitching and winning a double-header with the Red Sox, was not in evidence. Ruth and Gehrig hit home runs, chased Levsen, and won 8 to 3 to clinch the pennant, just about.

The Indians fought back in the next two weeks but couldn't get within striking distance of the Yankees again. Uhle stood up, but Levsen didn't. The strain of pitching a double-header had been too much. Levsen himself didn't believe it for sure because he had not noticed any extraordinary fatigue in his salary whip.

In fact, after Dutch won the first game of the twin bill, he and Speaker walked to the clubhouse together.

"How's the arm?" asked Spoke. Levsen replied that it had never felt better.

"Want to try the second game?" the manager offered.

Levsen jumped at the chance and hung on to win that one, also, by the same score posted in the opener, 4 to 3.

The Iowa forester had put his name on file and his arm on the shelf.

CHAPTER XVII

DIRTY LAUNDRY

AT THE CLOSE OF THE 1926 campaign, Tris Speaker was tired. He and his valiant Redskins were figuratively out of breath after running a grueling race against the Yankees. At thirty-eight Speaker was starting to feel the strain in his legs. And, too, there was mental disappointment. Spoke thought his team should have won in 1921. Five years later he wasn't sure the Indians were better than the Yankees, but he was sure there would not be too many years remaining for him as a player.

In fact, Spoke had been making plans for the future. In Cleveland, the Gray Eagle formed a close personal friendship with a rising industrialist, Dave R. Jones, and this social contact led to a business affiliation. Jones wanted to take in Speaker as a partner in his stamping works. This was no temporary friendship based entirely on the glamour of a baseball career. Today, twenty-two years later, Dave Jones and Tris Speaker are still business partners.

As the two discussed and planned their futures, Ty Cobb resigned as manager of the Detroit Tigers. There had been rumors that Cobb and Speaker, most illustrious stars of their day and all-time greats, might be out of baseball by 1927. On November 2, Cobb quit. George Moriarty was named Detroit's manager by owner Frank Navin. There was no explanation of Cobb's departure. He not only had quit as manager; he had been released.

Detroit fans felt they were entitled to ask why the Georgia Peach had reached the end of the road in such an unceremonious fashion. There were the usual rumors—ill health, trouble with Navin, and, most prominent of all, scandal. A story that Cobb was forced out of baseball gained prominence and circulation.

A month to the day after Cobb resigned, on December 2,

Speaker stepped out as manager of the Indians. President Barnard announced the immediate appointment of Jack McAllister, one of Spoke's coaches, to the managership of the Tribe for 1927. Speaker announced that he was going into business with Jones.

He surveyed his baseball career and its financial rewards, which had been large. Spoke got fifteen thousand dollars his first year with the Indians. As a manager, from 1919 through 1926, he had been paid from twenty to thirty thousand dollars base salary, plus bonuses. Speaker had money to invest in private business, and there was every indication that, much as the football coach who resigns at the end of an undefeated season, Speaker wanted to get out of baseball and into business, so he could capitalize on his baseball fame at its peak.

But the game's scuttlebutt, or what passed for this in 1926, couldn't be stilled. The men who wrote about baseball refused to accept as raw coincidence the fact that two great stars, Cobb and Speaker, men who had brought the sport much of its fame and fortune, would step out without reason.

Speaker was sitting in the Dunn Field office of Barnard. The telephone jangled and Barney accepted a call from Chicago.

"This is Ban Johnson," the Tribe president heard. "I have information that Speaker, Cobb, Joe Wood, and Dutch Leonard bet on a ball game several years ago. I have before me information that Wood wrote a letter to Leonard and so did Cobb, each mentioning a bet on this particular game. Can you find out anything for me?"

Barney said he would investigate. He replaced the receiver and turned to Spoke. He explained Johnson's request.

Speaker looked blank. Then he shook his head.

"So that's it," he said slowly. "So that's why all this talk is going around. Well, I can tell you one thing, Barney. I don't know anything about Johnson's story, but I'm curious to know about it."

The Texan was to find out more, some of it unpleasant, some pleasant and gratifying.

Judge Kenesaw Mountain Landis had ascended to baseball's throne after the 1920 World Series. A hard-bitten jurist, the shaggy-maned native Ohioan had wooed and won the affections of club owners in a spirited battle with Ban Johnson, who was to be his pronounced enemy.

Dutch Leonard had been a pitcher with the Detroit team in 1919. He had been released later by Cobb, upon whom he heaped promises of revenge. Speaker, as manager of the Indians, refused to claim the southpaw on waivers, and Dutch fancied additional grievances.

Late in the 1926 season, Leonard sent two letters to Johnson. These had been written to Leonard by Wood and Cobb. Each referred to a bet alleged to have been placed on a Detroit-Cleveland game at the fag end of the 1919 season, seven years before. Johnson conducted his own investigation (including the aforementioned call to Barnard) before turning the missives over to Landis.

Landis called Speaker, Cobb, and Wood, the latter having become head baseball coach at Yale in the meantime, to his Chicago chambers. This was in late November of 1926. Landis sought to have Leonard, then living in California, come to Chicago also, but the ex-pitcher balked.

The judge went to California, interviewed Leonard, then returned home to face the three other players. Leonard had alleged that the bets were made on a Cleveland-Detroit game played September 25, 1919. He told Landis and Johnson that the four players "happened to get together under the stands three days before the end of the season," to talk baseball in general. Wood accused Cobb of stating that he wanted the Tigers to finish third (the Indians already had clinched second place).

The inference was that Speaker allowed the Tigers to win so they could finish third. Leonard then related to Landis, the judge said, that each of the players was to put up between one and two thousand dollars. A clubhouse attendant by the name of Fred West was to have made the bets, though he could not "get up" all the money, only a couple of hundred dollars.

The Tigers won the game in question, 9 to 5, and beat out the Yankees for third place. Leonard had gone home the night

148

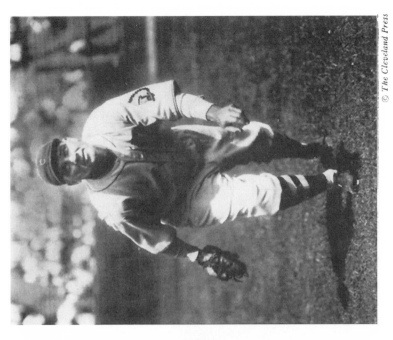

Charley Jamieson

Jack Graney

Roger Peckinpaugh

Earl Averill

Alva Bradley

before the game and did not see it. In spite of having clinched second place, Speaker played his best team with one exception. Tris had given permission to shortstop Ray Chapman to return to Cleveland and prepare for his forthcoming marriage.

Following is the letter written by Wood to Leonard. This letter and the Cobb letter were released to newspapers late in December of 1926.

Cleveland, O., Friday.

Enclosed please find certified check for sixteen hundred and thirty dollars ($1,630).

Dear Friend "Dutch":

The only bet West could get up was $600 against $420 (10 to 7). Cobb did not get up a cent. He told us that and I believe him. Could have put up some at 5 to 2 on Detroit, but did not, as that would make us put up $1000 to win $400.

We won the $420. I gave West $30, leaving $390, or $130 for each of us. Would not have cashed your check at all, but West thought he could get it up to 10–7, and I was going to put it all up at those odds. We would have won $1,750 for the $2,500 if we could have placed it.

If we ever have another chance like this we will know enough to try to get down early.

Let me hear from you, "Dutch".

With all good wishes to yourself and Mrs. Leonard, I am, always,

JOE WOOD

The Cobb letter to Leonard was less pointed. Ty mentioned that "Wood and myself are considerably disappointed in our business proposition."

The name Speaker, or any reference to him, did not appear in the Wood letter or the Cobb letter. Spoke won his main point with Judge Landis because of this.

Cobb, Speaker, and Wood were in Chicago for their private and secret hearing before Landis. They waited day after day for Leonard to put in an appearance. Landis had asked him to face the players he had accused. Speaker and Cobb were in a rage because the former pitcher would not leave California. Leonard refused to come to Chicago.

Cobb got madder and madder. He walked out of the meeting with Speaker. As they stood outside the judge's quarters, Cobb fumed, "I'm damned sick and tired of all this secrecy. I'm going to call the newspapers."

That was how the story broke officially. Once Cobb had admitted publicly there was something to the rumors, Landis stalled for a while, then released the Wood and Cobb letters on December 21.

Cobb roared, "If such a frame-up was true, why should we stop for a few minutes under the stands and arrange such an important matter?" Cobb also charged the American League, and Johnson, with having paid twenty thousand dollars for the two letters.

Speaker declared he was the goat of the entire mess. "I wanted Leonard to face me, but he has positively refused."

Baseball fans went to the support of Speaker and Cobb. Yale men rallied behind Wood, a personable fellow who had been a standout pitcher with the Red Sox and a fine outfielder-batter for the Indians.

In Cleveland, comment in the daily press became stronger and stronger. Joe Williams, crack columnist and sports editor of the *Press,* swung from all the keys on his typewriter:

Isn't it time Mrs. James C. Dunn and President E. S. Barnard quit being least actively interested and said something of the so-called Speaker scandal?

The mere fact that the majestic Landis has seen fit to force Speaker off the Cleveland club on evidence purchased by the American League from a disgruntled, revengeful man with a blackmail complex isn't sufficient in itself to stamp him as a baseball outcast. Indeed, it seems quite insufficient. Landis has been called on to open his carpet sweeper and let all the dirt fly, if he has any more to fly. The fans have that coming to them. If Landis has played all his cards, then baseball has given Speaker, and Ty Cobb, too a fiendish deal.

I have no way of knowing what happened in that scandal game of Sept. 25, 1919, which Cleveland is alleged to have thrown to Detroit, except that seven years back is a long way to go to throw mud on a man's white flannels.

Four days later, Williams added:

Ban Johnson, president of the American League, has had very little regard for Tris Speaker for seven years, and Frank Navin, owner of the Detroit Club, has wanted to get rid of Ty Cobb's $50,000 managerial contract for three years.

Landis was fond of both Speaker and Cobb personally, and his admiration for them as ball players knew no limits. This feeling may have entered into his decision, but from the evidence, and to the joy of millions, both men were cleared of all charges. On January 17 Landis issued his official decision.

"This is the Cobb-Speaker case," his verdict said. "These players have not been, nor are they now, found guilty of fixing a ball game. By no decent system of justice could such finding be made...."

Meanwhile, the American League club owners had been slapping at Ban Johnson and toasting Landis. The judge insisted that Speaker and Cobb, if they wished to continue to play, should stay in the American League. He felt if either went to the National—and each had lucrative offers—that (1) it would seem the men were no longer wanted in the American League and (2) it would be a partial triumph for Ban Johnson, the judge's sworn foe.

There was an alternative for Spoke and Ty. They could sue baseball for "defamation of character." Charles Evans Hughes, chief justice of the United States Supreme Court, was said to have proffered this advice. Or they could go back to baseball.

Speaker went to Washington and Cobb to Philadelphia. They joined forces on the Athletics in 1928, after which Spoke became manager of the Newark team in the International League. Cobb retired to an existence of luxury, thanks to investments. Wood was already established at Yale and definitely out of baseball as a player.

The Indians rocked and reeled through the 1927 season and finished sixth. Without Speaker, there was little balance on the field or on the bench. Mrs. Dunn wasn't too keen about owning a baseball club, and Barnard saw a chance to make some money for his old boss's widow if they could sell. Meanwhile, Mrs. Dunn married a man named George Pross, who owned a rather limited stable of race horses.

Cleveland was jittery about its baseball team, its operation, and its ownership. Ban Johnson was sick. There were stories that Barnard was the favorite son in the eyes of many league magnates.

An era in Ohio baseball was ending.

C H A P T E R   X V I I I

THE MILLIONAIRES

IF THE PORTERS in the private railroad car that was clicking and clacking eastbound between Cleveland and New York seemed to provide an abnormal amount of attention for their guests, it was not accidental. Not only did the gentlemen riding the plush seats own all or part of the railroad that was their carrier, they owned the rails, the ties, the car's fixtures, and probably most of the gold in the attendants' teeth.

These were millionaires, and they were on a lark in the form of a trip to watch Jack Dempsey and Jack Sharkey fight in New York in July. Some of the "boys" had got up a deal to go east for a few rounds of golf, attendance at the fight, and numerous hours of good fellowship, etc.

The group included John Sherwin, Sr., George Martin, Percy Morgan, Alva Bradley, Charles "Chuck" Bradley, A. C. Ernst, and Frank Hobson. There were some others whose identities do not fit the pattern to be cut in the following pages. Yet they had one thing in common. All were Clevelanders who had made or inherited fortunes in that city.

Sherwin the banker and Ernst the accountant king were talking about a business proposition back home.

"I hear the Cleveland baseball club can be bought," Ernst said. A sporting man, later owner of one of the country's foremost horse-racing stables, Ernst was intensely interested in baseball.

Sherwin admitted he had heard rumors through banking channels. Sherwin and Ernst "ganged up" on Alva Bradley in jest.

"Well, we have just bought the Cleveland ball club and you are to be the president," Sherwin told Alva.

Bradley laughed. "I'm certainly the man most qualified to be president," he replied, "as I know nothing whatever about baseball."

The conversation turned to other subjects, and such prosaic matters as bank balances, railroad stocks, and building rentals supplanted the sports topic. Two weeks passed, during which time Dempsey hit Sharkey on the chops as the Boston gob stood with hands down, beefing to the referee. The party long over, the millionaires returned to Cleveland's abbreviated downtown area.

Chuck Bradley said to Alva one day, "Did you do anything about buying that ball club?" Alva shook his head.

"Well, you might get busy if you want to. John Sherwin was serious about it. Why don't you look around?"

Alva called his friend, E. S. Barnard, and made a luncheon date. Yes, Barney admitted, he was authorized to sell the Indians. More important to Barney, he had been virtually promised the job of president of the American League, and he wanted to take it. But Barney felt loyalty to Mrs. Dunn and to the other stockholders.

"If I can sell the club, I'll be out of my obligations to Mrs. Dunn, and I can take the job with the American League," Barney told Bradley.

The two men returned to Bradley's office. Alva telephoned his brother Chuck to get busy on the money angle. Nearly one million dollars was required. Chuck made half a dozen telephone calls. The million dollars had been rustled quicker than a schoolboy could write the figures on a slate.

"I'm going to call Tom Walsh," Barnard told Alva. Walsh was the Tribe's vice-president and a life-long friend of Jim Dunn Though Barnard had the authority to sell the ball club, Walsh was a large shareholder and a businessman whose advice was valued highly by both Mrs. Dunn and Barney.

Alva Bradley and Tom Walsh joined several other men in a suite at the Hotel Cleveland. There was much noise, many loud voices, and other disturbing factors. Alva, a teetotaler, looked around for a refuge.

"Let's go in there," he suggested to Walsh. The two men entered a small room, closed the door. They talked for some time. The deal was set and agreed upon.

"I'll bet," cracked Bradley, "this is the first time a million

154

dollars *and* a major-league baseball team ever changed hands in a bathroom."

The completed deal was announced on November 17, 1927, though it had been quite widely exposed in the newspapers prior to that date. A couple of minor stockholders held up the transaction for several days. As was, and is, customary with deals of that magnitude, the new owners demanded the purchase of 100 per cent of the stock. One man who owned sixteen shares, C. A. Paquette, was traveling in Europe and could not be reached immediately. W. J. Garvey of Chicago owned about seventy-five shares of the stock, valued at one hundred and seventy dollars per share. Garvey demanded double the price and held up the deal while he haggled with attorneys. Garvey finally gave in, but for more money than the others were paid.

Now the final papers were in order, and a run-down of new stockholders was possible, though the press of the day did not reveal the exact holdings of each person. These were as follows: John Sherwin, Sr., 300,000 dollars; the Bradley brothers, Chuck and Alva, 175,000 dollars; Percy Morgan, head of a lithographing company, 200,000 dollars; former Secretary of War Newton D. Baker, 25,000 dollars; Joseph C. Hostetler, an attorney, 25,000 dollars; and O. P. Van Sweringen and M. J. Van Sweringen, 250,000 dollars.

The syndicate pooled exactly one million dollars. All except twenty-five thousand dollars went into the purchase of stock in line with the above figures. The million was deposited in the checking account of Alva Bradley. His personal checks were sent in payment to the former stockholders.

The stock bought by the Van Sweringen brothers, fabulous railroad and real-estate operators, was put in Alva Bradley's name. The stock acquired by the Bradley brothers was held mostly by them in person (about seventy-five thousand dollars for Chuck and fifty thousand dollars for Alva), but twenty-five thousand dollars was distributed among members of their immediate families.

Mrs. Dunn received checks for 551,000 dollars. Her former vice-president, Tom Walsh, was paid 145,010 dollars. There were a dozen checks for smaller amounts. The profit in the

Dunn operation of the Cleveland Indians was pretty close to 100 per cent!

It was only two weeks now until the winter meetings of the major leagues. The way was cleared for the election of Barnard to the American League presidency. But the new owners of the Indians had problems. They had a pretty poor ball club and 975,000 dollars in canceled checks, period.

As John Sherwin had said kiddingly on the train several months before, "Alva, you're to be the president of the Indians."

Alva became the front man for many reasons. He was a gracious, handsome individual who had maintained a lifelong interest in sports, dating from his days as a prep quarterback at Cleveland's exclusive University School. Alva and Chuck Bradley were of sturdy and wealthy lake-shipping stock. The Bradley family controlled much of the real estate in downtown Cleveland, particularly north and west of Public Square. Alva managed these properties, among other enterprises. His sharp-tongued, forthright brother was more interested in banks, stores, and railroads.

At the age of thirty-six, Alva Bradley had been the president of the Cleveland Chamber of Commerce, a post traditionally reserved for a well-to-do civic leader who could point back several branches on a family tree. Alva was suave, even-tempered, and inclined to adopt a conciliatory view of disputes. In this, the younger Bradley was the antithesis of Chuck.

Many times in the years to come, when the Indians had a running collection of the world's worst shortstops, Chuck Bradley would sit in a front-row box, watch some hapless shortstop boot one, and turn to Alva to yell, "Alva, fire that ——, fire him tonight." Only constant reminders finally convinced Chuck that shortstops did not sprout in employment agencies and that baseball players could not be discharged on the spot at an employer's whim.

Though the new owners were convinced they had an ideal president in Bradley, they all realized the need for an experienced baseball man to control the actual operation of the team. The owners were vulnerable to a baseball name. For 20 years Alva had watched an erect, broad-shouldered umpire, Billy Evans.

156

Actually Evans was much more than an umpire, because he never was content to be an ordinary umpire. Billy started out as a sports writer in Youngstown, then shifted to umpiring. But he never lost his writing touch. He wrote for or with many famous baseball personalities. He wrote under his own by-line. He became the sports editor of the Newspaper Enterprise Association, the world's foremost newspaper syndicate.

All this time he was an umpire, one of the best. He was ambitious also, so when Alva Bradley sat down with Evans and mentioned the position of vice-president and general manager of a major-league team, Billy asked only two questions: Could Bradley get him his release from the American League? How much?

On November 27, 1927, Louis Seltzer wrote in the *Press* that Evans probably had umpired his last game. The next evening Evans signed a three-year contract to operate the Indians' front office. The salary was between thirty and forty thousand dollars per year.

There was rejoicing among the stockholders. The American League foresaw happier days, too. In one of his farewell pieces for the *Plain Dealer*, Henry Edwards enthused, "Cleveland's fondest baseball hope—our Indians owned by Clevelanders, operated as a civic enterprise as well as a money-making vehicle, and eventually playing in a great new municipal stadium on the lakefront—came a step nearer realization." Henry Edwards was voicing the sentiment of the president-to-be of the American League. When Barnard moved to Chicago, he took along Henry Edwards to supervise a newly established service bureau that became the model for not only baseball but all sports within a few years.

The millionaires were making progress. They had a franchise, a president, a board of directors, and a general manager. They almost succeeded, too, in getting the American League offices moved from Chicago to Cleveland, this after Barnard succeeded Johnson as president. But there was too much tradition in the Chicago headquarters, especially because Charley Comiskey was still alive. The league officers felt Comiskey would consider any shift a personal affront.

What the Indians were most in need of was a field manager. McAllister was out. The new owners wanted their broom to sweep as clean as possible. Evans scanned the field. Names of baseball personalities popped into the sports columns daily, and each seemed to have some chance to be chosen as manager. At one point, the list included Roger Peckinpaugh, Walter Johnson, Tris Speaker, Art Fletcher, Casey Stengel, Ty Cobb, Eddie Collins, and Bucky Harris.

Peckinpaugh seemed to have the inside track from the beginning. He had gone from a Cleveland high school into the big leagues. He had started his baseball career as a Cleveland player. And now he lived in the Forest City in the off-season. His roots were as deep, if not quite as gold plated, as some of the owners of the team.

Peck won the sweepstakes, but the problem of getting his release from the White Sox remained. As a player, Roger was washed up. But Eddie Collins, then managing Chicago, had refused earlier to give the veteran shortstop his release so he could go over to the Cincinnati club and pick up a sizable piece of change by merely changing leagues. Collins wanted Peck to get a manager's job.

Once the decision had been made in favor of Peck, Evans called Harry Grabiner, the vice-president of the White Sox, and asked if he would release him. Grabiner agreed—for the waiver price or more. The Indians paid more. They paid twelve thousand five hundred dollars or five thousand dollars over the usual fee.

Once before, Peck had been a manager. As a young shortstop with the Yankees in 1914, the scooting infielder had come to the favorable notice of the team's manager, the great Frank Chance. Late in that season, Chance decided to quit. He approached Peck.

"I'm quitting," he told the startled newcomer. "I'm going to recommend you to succeed me. But don't let 'em play you for a sap. Pick up some dough for yourself. That's why I'm going to give them your name. Now, remember."

Peck did, when owner Frank Farrell of the Yankees rushed up to him in the clubhouse after a game. The club was packing for a Western trip, and there was much bustle.

"I'm going to make you manager of this team, young man," announced Farrell munificently. Peck wasn't impressed by the "rush act." He murmured thanks and in the next breath suggested a new salary arrangement. Farrell, who had expected to engineer an economical switch, pointed out the great honor being bestowed upon such a young man. But Peck stuck to his guns and got the extra pay.

There was no squabbling about salary between Peck and the millionaires. They had plenty of money, in addition to tremendous hopes. With cash handy and with the enthusiasm of a bride attacking a cookbook for the first time, Bradley, Evans, Peck, and the others took off for the December meeting of the major leagues.

Barnard was to be elected to the American League presidency, and as his assistant, the owners selected a tall, graying, soft-spoken ex-newspaperman, Will Harridge. Proper and punctilious, Harridge became the league secretary, later its acting president, and finally its president.

The first jolt any of the millionaires received came at the first league meeting Alva Bradley attended as the president of the Cleveland team. There hadn't been a league meeting for a couple of years. Landis and Johnson were feuding. Some of the club operators detested Landis; others pronounced their loyalty to the judge. Such was Bradley's introduction to his fellow magnates.

"In that first meeting, I was confused," Bradley admitted. "I asked myself what kind of a business was this I had bought into when the head of the outfit, Landis, ran the meeting but no one wanted to speak to him unless compelled to."

Alva Bradley was to find out. So was Billy Evans. And so was Roger Peckinpaugh. Until then, the Cleveland Indians had fought their battles on the diamond, with curves and fast balls and bruising, basic baseball. A pennant had been won, and several had been lost down on the dirt of the infield or on the peak of the pitching mound.

Soon, though, pennants were to be lost in the front office. Conditions unknown to any teams in the history of organized baseball appeared. The area of the Cleveland baseball operation was to change radically.

The front office, and not the perspiring athletes, came to represent the Cleveland Indians.

CHAPTER XIX

AVERILL, PORTER, FERRELL

ALVA BRADLEY said many times in the immediate years following his affiliation with the Indians, "When we bought the Cleveland ball club, we bought only a franchise and Mel Harder."
Looking five years ahead, that was exactly what the millionaires
had purchased. But Billy Evans had a different slant, that of a
practical baseball man.

Billy knew that the Indians, as he counted down the roster
before the 1928 season, were not very good in comparison with
other big-league teams. But there were a few bright spots. The
training camp was moved from Lakeland, Florida, to New
Orleans as a concession to the millionaires, a few Louisiana
bigwigs, and Huey P. Long, who had a common interest in certain railroads.

When Peck looked over his first squad, he counted fifty-two
noses that were recognizable and perhaps a dozen more that
seemed to have been left by an itinerant dust storm. Evans
had "called in" almost every player the Tribe had in the minors.
Their capabilities, on paper at least, did not send Evans or Peck
back to the Roosevelt Hotel rapping their knuckles on every
store window en route.

True, there was Harder, a right-handed pitcher of high-
school age who looked as if he might fit into a jumbo-size
straw if you could cut off his shock of hair. There was another
rookie pitcher whose talents were worn on the outside of his
right arm. His name was Wesley Ferrell, a high-strung, hot-
tempered North Carolinian who could have been easily mis-
taken for a Hollywood leading man. But, like Harder, he wasn't
quite ready for baseball's big time.

Willis Hudlin was coming into full bloom with his sidearm
sinker. A grand kid from down New Orleans way, Carl Lind,
showed exceptional promise as a second baseman, and good-

looking, grinning Johnny Hodapp from Cincinnati was playing third base and making attractive motions with a bat. Elton "Sam" Langford was hailed as the man to make Cleveland forget Tris Speaker. Eddie Morgan, a big belter, was fresh from Tulane, and Clint Brown, who side-wheeled his pitches with punishing effect, came up from New Orleans' Pelicans.

The old heads were plentiful—Joe and Luke Sewell, Myatt, Levsen, Buckeye, Jamieson, Summa, Burns, Walter Miller, Shaute, and Uhle. Lew Fonseca, a handy man in the field, could play first or second, but most of all he could mash the potato at a .300 pace in any role. The Indians opened their first season for the millionaires by beating the White Sox, 7 to 1, as Sam Langford contributed three singles. Was it possible the revival was started already?

Six weeks later, Alva Bradley was still wildly enthusiastic. The Tribe was rolling. Alva turned to Evans then and beamed, "This looks like a good team."

Evans kept his eyes on the ball game in progress.

"No, Mr. Bradley, it's a rotten team."

Evans recognized the weaknesses. He knew the need for a stable infield, for a power hitter in the outfield, and for fewer and better pitchers. In quantity, the Indians were loaded with throwers. Peck looked over twenty of them early in the year. But the tip-off on the quality was this—included in the twenty were nine whose 1928 aggregate was four victories against twenty-one defeats!

Yet the season was not a total loss. It brought to the fore a young infielder, Carl Lind, who was to become the outstanding one-year flash in the club's history. Early in the spring, Fonseca was the only second baseman on the squad. Soon there was none, because Lew and Morgan collided, and Fonseca was painfully hurt. Peck looked around for a replacement.

"I might as well try Lind," Peck told Evans in resignation. "He's the least likely looking shortstop we've got."

Lind moved across the diamond, teamed with Joe Sewell, and sparkled all summer. Carl batted just under .300 and it seemed that the Tribe's search for a second baseman, started when Wamby faded, was over at last.

Peck learned some lessons as a neophyte manager, too. One

was taught by Joe Shaute, the southpaw who had come into the league five years before. Shaute soon became one of Peck's prize packages because of his willingness to work. Whenever a pitcher found himself in a hole, Shaute would grab a glove and hurry to the bull pen to warm up. One day Evans asked Peck why he was using Shaute so much, and the manager pointed out Joe's fine spirit.

"I thought you knew about Shaute's contract," Evans said. "He's on a bonus plan and gets so much for every game he pitches in."

Shaute was called upon infrequently thereafter.

Fonseca came back late in the season to hit .327, but couldn't carry the club. Only by the grace of the Red Sox did the Indians escape the cellar.

The next winter Evans went shopping. He took one of the millionaires' spare checkbooks and headed west. San Francisco had strung together the best outfield in the minor leagues. Major-league scouts hovered over the Seals' stadium, ready to swoop down on the first unwary club official.

The outfielders were Roy Johnson, Earl Averill, and Smead Jolley. The prize was Johnson, a left-handed batter who had great speed, good power, and a strong throwing arm. Scout after scout sat far back in the stands and watched Johnson's movements. They were terrifically impressive. Evans was smitten.

But he learned, as did the others, that the Tigers had beaten everyone to Johnson. So Averill and Jolley were left. Jolley was a big man who was clumsy in the outfield. But he could drive a baseball halfway to Oakland. San Francisco scribes predicted he would break Ruth's home-run record if he got to play in those big-league parks with their handy right-field fences.

The least impressive was Averill. He was the smallest of the three, and he had a strange batting stance. He stood with feet fairly close together, crowding the plate, and he swung his bat with his body, it seemed, instead of "stepping into" the pitch with a snap and lash of the wrists.

Johnson was untouchable. Jolley didn't impress Evans. He

162

wasn't sure about Averill until he hung around the Coast for a while and talked to ballplayers out there.

"Averill's the best of the three, much the best," half a dozen stars in the Pacific Coast League informed Evans. Earl was then almost twenty-six years old and Evans wondered whether the asking price of fifty thousand dollars wasn't too high. Then Billy looked over Averill's batting mark in 1928. During the long Coast League schedule, he played in 189 games and batted .354, collecting the almost unbelievable total of 270 hits!

Evans completed the deal with San Francisco—forty thousand dollars and two players. By then it was time to report to New Orleans for the second season under the millionaires. But Averill wasn't quite ready.

"If I'm worth forty thousand dollars in cash, I'm worth some money to myself," reasoned Averill. The pride of Snohomish, Washington, said he thought five thousand dollars would be a fair share of the booty. He got it.

Evans personally conducted Averill to New Orleans. There the rookie met Bradley for the first time and flashed the president his toothy and infectious grin. Alva had been prepared to mention the hold-up for five thousand dollars. Instead, he grinned back. People were always grinning back at Averill.

"You certainly picked out a midget," Bradley commented to Evans.

"Yeah, but wait until you see him stripped down," cautioned Billy. Beneath the plain clothes that Averill affected were 165 pounds of concentrated muscle. He was as compact physically as a watch-charm football guard.

Billy wasn't finished with his shopping. He dealt out thirty thousand dollars more of the millionaires' cash to Baltimore for a combination infielder-outfielder, Richard Twilley Porter, whose batting stance reminded everyone of his middle name. Porter could hit .300 or more in any league, but he wiggled and squirmed at the plate until he gained the nickname of Twitchy Dick.

Evans was recruiting some of the power the 1928 Indians had lacked. "We'll have an interesting team," he had promised that night in Cleveland's Tavern Club when Alva Bradley first introduced him to the press. Billy was making a spectacular start in that direction.

He traded as well as bought. He sent Uhle to the Tigers for Ken Holloway and Jackie Tavener. Catcher Chick Autry went to the White Sox for outfielder Bib Falk. Unser Joe Hauser, a first baseman who could hit fifty to sixty home runs in any given minor league, came in for a trial.

Tall, blond Wesley Ferrell blazed his fast ball past American League hitters in 1929 to win twenty-one games as a freshman! Hudlin picked up seventeen triumphs, Walter Miller fourteen.

Everybody hit. Fonseca, shifted permanently to first base, batted .369, won the league championship, and was voted the circuit's most valuable player. Morgan hit .318, Porter .328, Hodapp .327, Joe Sewell .315, Jamieson .291, Falk .310, Averill .330. There was the historical opening game in 1929 when, in his first time at bat in the major leagues, Averill hit one of Earl Whitehill's pitches over Dunn Field's right-field wall.

The Tribe jumped from seventh to third. It seemed certain happier days were ahead.

Peck was to discover that base hits do not a champion make, though the easygoing manager was pretty well aware of this axiom before. The hitting improved, but there were new deficiencies. Carl Lind, after his tremendous freshman season in 1928, had contracted a bug in Cuba and failed so rapidly he never was of further use. Johnny Burnett came along to play shortstop, but he was to prove himself a much better hitter than infielder. Joe Sewell slipped and was released outright in 1930, only to catch on with the Yankees as a third baseman and turn in two seasons of steady play.

Sewell's passing seemed to be a symbol of the swift-changing pattern of the Cleveland team. After eleven years, the deep-voiced, roundish shortstop who helped win the city's only championship was tossed aside. He played in 1,103 consecutive games from September 13, 1922 to April 30, 1930. The emphasis was on raw power now. A man who couldn't hit .300, thanks in the main to the right-field wall, wasn't worth the price of half a dozen bats.

In 1930 Hodapp went up to .354, Morgan to .350, Averill to .336. Harder, with a couple of pounds of solid meat on his

164

skinny frame, came up from New Orleans to stay and won eleven games. Ferrell held out until late February in '30, then won thirteen games in a row and achieved a total of twenty-five victories. Clint Brown, who could beat the Tigers with a wink and a roundhouse, posted eleven triumphs. Hudlin added thirteen.

As became the habit of Cleveland teams, that one started 1930 at a breath-taking clip. When it lost nineteen of twenty-two in a July flop, a deluge of letters hit the editorial desks.

"Let's have a new manager," demanded the writers, one eye on the batting averages and one on Wesley Ferrell.

GIANT STADIUM

ERNEST SARGENT BARNARD couldn't keep his mind on the rummy game in the winter months of 1926–27. Consequently, Ed Bang enjoyed a moderate if temporary prosperity at the expense of the Indians' president.

Evening after evening in that period, Barney arrived at the home of the *Cleveland News* sports editor, ostensibly to play cards. But a sheaf of papers was under his arm every time, and the opening game in the two-man session seldom got beyond the first hand before Barnard had his papers spread over the table.

"Here's something else I've put in," Barney began regularly. "There'll be more seats here, and it'll be easier for people to get in and out."

The papers represented rough, home-drawn plans for a new baseball stadium in Cleveland. Dunn Field's twenty-two thousand seats were woefully inadequate. For special occasions, an additional six or seven thousand hardy souls could be wedged into the narrow arena if they cared to stand behind rope barriers in left and center fields.

Barney's dreams, penciled in almost daily, were of a stadium seating fifty to sixty thousand, something akin to the Polo Grounds, which he had also planned personally. Others in Cleveland had projected the possibility of a municipal stadium. A former mayor, Clayton Townes, had talked about one. Years earlier, Floyd Rowe of the public-school system in Cleveland had proposed a civic structure.

Barnard had powerful reasons for desiring a new home for the Tribe. The club was on the market. He was headed toward the American League presidency. If he could place the Indians in a large, new home, he could increase their sale value and also strengthen the entire league he was soon to head.

Other men had plans, some on a drawing board, some in mind, about this time. Peter P. Evans, president of the Osborn Engineering Company of Cleveland, and City Manager William R. Hopkins got together with Barnard. About that time, the Bradley interests were dickering for the purchase of the Indians. Promises were made, to and by the prospective owners of the ball club, concerning the construction and use of a stadium.

A bond issue to finance construction of the Cleveland Municipal Stadium was voted in November, 1928. The site was filled-in land on the lake front. This was to be one stadium not bounded by city streets, houses, buildings, or subject to zoning laws.

Before the bond issue was voted, the Tribe was sold. The new president, Alva Bradley, worked diligently in behalf of the issue. He formed committees and made personal appeals to voters. All this was not strictly unselfish as Bradley admitted freely.

The Bradleys and the Van Sweringens sought to move Cleveland's commercial heart to the west tip of Euclid Avenue. The "Terminal Group" had been built by the Vans. This included the famous Union Railroad Terminal, Hotel Cleveland, Midland Building, Republic Building, Higbee Building, and the city's foremost landmark, the world renowned Terminal Tower, all west or south of Public Square. Whatever business, including baseball trade in the proposed stadium, lured to "lower Euclid" would be beneficial to the buildings and stores owned or operated by the Bradleys and the Vans.

Construction was started in the late autumn of 1930. Everyone was rushing and scurrying to get the stadium ready for use late in 1931. Double speed was ordered when the Max Schmeling–W. L. Stribling world-heavyweight-championship bout was scheduled for July 3. The fight was staged there, but the stadium was not far enough along for baseball. A year was to pass.

Cleveland strutted at mere mention of the world's largest baseball plant. It cost 2,640,000 dollars. It had two decks and 78,129 permanent seats—37,896 in the main or lower deck,

29,320 upstairs, 60 in a press box, and 10,913 in uncovered bleachers in center field.

"We'll fill that place often, every Sunday," enthused the owners of the Indians.

Alas, they filled it once. Not for another sixteen years was the Stadium to be overflowing with a population the size of the city of Binghamton, New York.

As the Indians proceeded northward in the spring of 1931, the long-distance attention of their faithfuls was riveted on a home-town boy, Joe Vosmik. Broad, blond, and Bohemian, Vosmik had come off the Cleveland sand lots for two years of training in the lower minors. Now the powerful right-handed batter with the strong arm and ready smile was trimmed up for his major-league debut in the season's opener with the White Sox.

The day of the game, Peckinpaugh took the rookie to one side.

"Joe, I'm not going to let you play today," he said. Vosmik's face fell. "Nothing personal, Joe. Just this. Cleveland's your home city, and I want you to make good from the beginning here. You're bound to be nervous. We all were when we broke in. So sit this one out, and you can play tomorrow when there won't be so many people and so much strain on you. Jamieson will take over for you today."

Vosmik went to left field the next day, as Peck had promised, and the major leagues were introduced to one of the best all-around outfields in the history of any baseball team—Vosmik, Averill, and Porter. Each was a sure .300 hitter; for example, Vosmik batted .320 in his freshman year.

Peck wasn't the only manager on the field impressed by the recruit's performance in the second game. Vosmik rattled the wall that day and played spectacularly in left. After the game, Peck and Manager Donie Bush of the White Sox were walking through the common runway leading to the dressing rooms.

"Where did you find that Vosmik?" asked Bush. Peck said he had been raised right at home under the club's nose.

"Remind me to send our scouts to Cleveland after this," cracked Bush as he disappeared into the steaming clubhouse.

Wes Ferrell had beaten the White Sox, 5 to 4, in the first game and again there were murmurs on Cleveland streets that "maybe this would be the year." Evans had made another important player deal in the winter, sending Fonseca to the White Sox for Willie Kamm, a veteran third baseman who had cost the Sox a hundred thousand dollars, heavy sugar in the Terrible Twenties. Morgan took over first base and hit a terrific .361. The former Tulane star had discovered the secret of hitting in Dunn Field, or League Park, as it was being called again in the newspapers. He deliberately aimed for the right-field wall. Most of Eddie's twenty-six home runs in 1930 were over the barrier. In 1931, his home-run production fell off, but his average increased.

Seven Indians hit above .300 that year—Morgan, Bob Seeds, Vosmik, Averill, Porter, Burnett, and Falk. The great Ferrell established two batting records for pitchers, lacing out nine homers and driving in a total of thirty runs. He won twenty-two games, one of these a no-hitter. Soon after the season was opened, on April 29, Wes handcuffed the St. Louis Browns at League Park to achieve the first no-hit game by a Cleveland pitcher since Slim Caldwell's classic at the expense of the Yankees in 1919.

The Browns worked Ferrell for three passes, and two runners were safe on errors. Wes barely saved his blue-ribbon game in a late inning when a ground ball toward short almost got away from Bill Hunnefield. It was a fairly difficult chance; Hunnefield didn't get the throw to first base in time, and Ed Bang, the official scorer, ruled it an error for the shortstop.

The batter who nearly spoiled it all was, of all people, Wes's brother Rick, the Browns' catcher!

Still the Indians were disappointing in 1931. The infield was unsettled and weak. Kamm was a classy third baseman, but he had learned not to attempt circus plays. Peck tried a dozen combinations at second base, but game after game was lost there as none clicked.

Once more it was fourth place for the Tribe.

And once more, in the spring of '32, there were bright, shining hopes. Evans had swapped Hodapp and Seeds for Chalmers

"Bill" Cissell, which gave the Tribe a partial guarantee of a substantial second baseman. Harder was filling out physically and giving more promise with each pitch. Hudlin was a consistent fifteen- to seventeen-game winner. A lanky right-hander from Butler College, Oral Hildebrand, was ready for the big time, and both Evans and Peck talked faster whenever his name was mentioned. Ferrell was complaining of sore spots in his right shoulder but he had won twenty or more games for three years running. A fourth was anticipated, and Wes came through with twenty-three.

Cissell was a revelation at second base, after a series of unhappy incidents while he was with the White Sox. But not even a Cissell could save the Indians. As usual, they found their normal niche, fourth place, and were parked there forlornly on July 10, a Sunday.

Sunday baseball was still outlawed in Pennsylvania, and it was the practice of most teams scheduled there to jump back to their home lots to play the Athletics on the Sabbath. The second-place A's and the hapless Indians made the sleeper jaunt back to Cleveland and were due to catch an 8-P.M. train back to the Quaker City. They never made it.

Perhaps the daffiest game ever participated in by a Cleveland team, or any team, was unreeled that afternoon. Connie Mack left many of his stars, including Mickey Cochrane, in Philadelphia. The Indians, too, brought along a skeleton crew. Connie ordered only two pitchers to make the trip, a rookie named Harry Krausse, who lived in Columbus, and the veteran knuckle-ball exponent, Eddie Rommel, then thirty-five years old. Rommel also served as batting-practice pitcher that day.

Krausse and Clint Brown were the starting pitchers, but Krausse was no puzzle to the Indians in the first inning and left after being belted for three runs. Rommel came in, without further warm up, and pitched with his easy, tireless motion. What a break for him that he could pitch that way!

He pitched the next seventeen innings. He gave up twenty-nine of the thirty-three hits the Indians accumulated. The A's hit safely twenty-five times and Jimmy Foxx, the roundish farm boy, a slugger and first baseman, smashed three home runs into the distant bleachers in left field! Foxx also got a double and two singles for a total of sixteen bases.

But the real hitting star was the Cleveland shortstop, Johnny Burnett, a freckle-faced University of Florida product who personally engraved his name on baseball's marble columns that wild day. Johnny stepped to the plate eleven times. Only twice did he fail to hit. His seven singles and two doubles cracked all existing records for hits in one game, regardless of length.

The A's scored seven times in the seventh inning, but hardly had that score been placed on the board than the Indians bounced right back to score six times, thirteen runs in one inning. Each scored twice in the sixteenth, but the Tribe's luck ran out in the eighteenth when Foxx singled and raced home after Eric "Boob" McNair, the shortstop, hit a liner to left that took a freak hop over Vosmik's head.

It was a tough break for Ferrell, who had pitched eleven and a third innings. Brown, the starter, went six and two thirds before being relieved by Hudlin, who pitched to only two batters without retiring either. Ferrell had the game sewed up in the ninth inning when, with two out, third baseman Jimmy Dykes of the A's hit a dribbler down the first-base line. Expecting to be an easy out and thus end the game, Dykes carried his bat down the line with him. Then, as Morgan stooped to make the soft pickup, the ball trickled through his glove for an error and the game rolled on.

Three weeks to the day later, the Indians and Athletics were back in Cleveland, but not to play a farce. A milestone in Middle Western sports had been reached. The great new concrete and steel giant bearing the proper name of Cleveland Stadium was about to house its first big-league baseball game on Sunday, July 31.

There were farewells at League Park the previous afternoon. The green-walled old grounds were dripping in nostalgia. But there also was a ball game of importance. The Indians had perked up and were fighting the A's for second place. That Saturday, the Tribe lost, 7 to 2, but no result could have affected the historical event to follow. Every seat in the new stadium had been sold for weeks. Cleveland put on its celebrating clothes and rushed to the lake front.

The pregame ceremony was as impressive and probably as important as the game itself. Baseball's brass shone beneath the omnipresent sun—Judge Landis, Will Harridge, elected president of the American League after the beloved Barney Barnard passed away early in 1931, President Tom Shibe of the Philadelphia club, Ohio's Governor George White, who pitched the first ball, and the Mayor of Cleveland, Ray T. Miller, who caught it. Jack Graney, the old Naps' outfielder who became the Tribe's radio voice, introduced the stars of yesteryear, Young, Speaker, Bradley, Fohl, Flick, Elmer Smith, Wamby, Zimmer, and the peerless Napoleon Lajoie, who made one of his very infrequent public appearances.

Connie Mack took the public-address microphone and thanked Alva Bradley and Billy Evans for their roles in providing the Indians, and all baseball, with such a magnificent structure. There was naught but cheers that day, cheers sent up by a shirt-sleeved audience of 80,184, of whom 76,979 paid their way in. These included the thousands in the center-field bleachers who blocked the vision of batters so that the final score of 1 to 0, with the A's winning, was not unexpected.

Lefty Grove nosed out Mel Harder, and it is very likely, too, that Grove would have beaten the man whose turn it was to pitch, Wes Ferrell. The tall Grove brought his overhand pitches high out of the background of white shirts and restricted the Indians to four singles.

Ferrell's arm had been troublesome, and a few days before the stadium inaugural game Peck asked Wes if he would be "ready to pitch on Sunday." Ferrell shook his head.

"I'll need another day's rest, Peck," replied Wes, walking into the trap.

With that, Peck gave Harder the assignment. Later, Ferrell suddenly remembered that Sunday's game would be the biggest in the city's history; he rushed to Peck.

"I'm okay now," he told the manager. "My arm feels great."

Peck, who had favored Harder for personal reasons, refused to back down and assigned Ferrell to the game scheduled on Monday.

Harder pitched eight innings and gave up five hits, Hildebrand granting the other in the ninth. The A's pushed across a lone run in the eighth on a pass to Max Bishop, a sacrifice by Mule Haas, and Cochrane's sharp grounder that went past Harder into center for a single. Harder, whose side-wheeling pitching motion always left him off balance, couldn't get his glove on the ball as it bounded through the box.

The Indians played thirty more games in the stadium in 1932 and won nineteen. But a disastrous eastern trip ruined their flag chances, and for the third straight year Cleveland finished fourth. It was on this trip that Peck and Ferrell clashed. The manager ordered Wes to leave the mound in the first inning of a game in Boston, but Wes refused and drew an indefinite suspension. Quite obviously, Ferrell was still scorching because he had not been given seniority in the pitching order for the stadium event.

GRAVEYARD OF MANAGERS

PROFESSIONAL BASEBALL, a business, was no different than a waxworks, a foundry, a grocery store, or a hamburger stand in 1933, so far as income and profit were concerned. The Great Depression was biting its initials into the hides of the owners of the Indians, who had plenty of company throughout the country in their miseries.

General Manager Evans was instructed to keep costs of operation down. Gone were the days in which Evans could pay forty thousand dollars for one ballplayer and thirty thousand dollars for another. Gone were the homeless dollars that the millionaires kept in their wallets for tips. Ferrell's salary was cut six thousand dollars. One of the few raises was given to Cissell for his fine play in 1932. The Indians were assigned 77 games in the Stadium. Alva Bradley, seeking to tighten up all along the line, banned radio broadcasting of the Cleveland games for the 1933 season.

"It hurts attendance," reasoned Bradley.

Yet Peck was optimistic, more so than he had been at any stage of his career as the Tribe manager. Perhaps Peck saw the handwriting on the wall. Perhaps he thought he had better lift the Indians out of fourth place or look for other employment. Whatever the cause for Peck's outlook, it was widely quoted and accepted.

"I thought sure we would win then," Peck insists to this day. "But we had Averill and Vosmik hurt at the beginning. Ferrell's arm went bad after those four great years. We never got away good and never had a chance."

The biggest single factor in the collapse of a good team was the stadium's terrifying expanse. True, it was only 320 feet down the foul lines to the curving stands. But the curve continued, and only a Herculean slugger had a chance to hit a home run into the seats if the ball was not right on the line. Marvin Owen, Detroit's third baseman, had hit the first home run there, a curving liner into the right-field seats. And Owens was a right-handed batter! Cleveland's first home run was credited to Burnett, who got the ball barely into the seats. And one of the first homers in left was hit by Rabbit Warstler, a small infielder who gained his alias in the field and not at the plate.

Ruth, Greenberg, Gehrig, Simmons, Dickey, Foxx, and other long-distance batters swore in full voice whenever one of their power drives to left center or right center would be pulled down 400 to 430 feet from the plate. Batting averages of the Indians dropped from 50 to 100 points! Porter went down to .267, Vosmik to .263, Averill to .301, the first time he'd ever been that close to the rim of the so-called charmed circle. The champion Cleveland batter was a little freshman catcher, Frankie Pytlak, who lined out enough hits to compile a .309 mark.

There was the same old infield trouble, and it was felt the team had been weakened by the trading of Luke Sewell to the Washington club for Roy Spencer. However, a new pitcher from Toledo, Monte Pearson, looked like the answer to a manager's prayer.

A beer may have made Milwaukee famous but a question made Cleveland just as famous.

"What's wrong with the Indians?"

Millions asked and were told in the papers daily. Bradley was blamed. Evans was blamed. Peck was blamed. The millionaires took some raps. The fans didn't care much who was to blame. All they wanted was the answer to their question, "What's wrong with the Indians?" When they began to ask so often that Bradley heard voices in his sleep, he took a train to the East and joined the Indians in New York.

As it so happened, the team had lost seven of eight starts on that particular seaboard tour and had tumbled from first to fifth. Bradley had a long talk with Peck. When the correspondents traveling with the Tribe asked Bradley what had transpired in the conference, he answered, "I told Roger that the team would have to start winning or we would be compelled to make a change."

And with that, the president paid a visit to the club dressing room and gave a pep talk to the Indians, who were sadly in need of a hypo of some sort, oral or physical.

About two weeks later, on June 9, Bradley called in reporters.

"We have decided to make a change in managers," he said. "There is no man for whom I have a higher personal regard than I have for Peckinpaugh. But this team lacks pep. It plays loosely. And as I have said before, 'We only hire the manager, the public fires him.' "

He paused.

"The new manager, gentlemen, is Walter Johnson."

You could have blown over the reporters with a soft note. The Big Train was one of the greatest, if not *the* greatest of pitchers, a grand baseball figure, beloved idol of every Washington oldster.

"Billy Evans went over to Johnson's farm and made the deal with him. He's here now and will take charge immediately."

The more calloused of the scribes weren't impressed by Johnson's arrival. They knew he had been a failure as a manager in the majors and the minors. At the insistence of sentimental fans, owner Clark Griffith of the Washington team tried him as a manager the year before but found him wanting. Earlier Johnson managed Newark in the International League. Late in 1932 he retired to his Maryland farm. It was there that Evans found him.

Evans knew of Johnson's failures, knew the man as a ballplayer and as a manager. The general manager did not—and he said so frankly—want Johnson as a manager. He signed him under protest and made it plain to newspaper friends that he did not wish to be held responsible for any actions by Walter.

The Indians played neither better nor worse for Johnson. Their batting was far below that of previous seasons and they cursed the Stadium and its big playing area for their slump to seventh place in team batting. In the final standings of 1933, the Tribe wound up fourth for the fourth straight year, but not without the customary dosage of excitement.

Johnson revealed almost immediately that he would reserve little patience for ailing players. It was his boast that "I've never had a sore arm." Like many immortals in sports, Johnson couldn't understand why everyone couldn't perform as he had. Two months after he took charge of the Tribe, he clashed with Hildebrand.

A trigger-tempered Hoosier, Hildebrand blew up—orally—after walking three batters in a row in the seventh inning of a game at St. Louis on August 1. Johnson walked to the mound and told Hildy to leave. The pitcher slammed the resin bag to the ground and demanded he be left in. Johnson told him not to take a shower but to take the first train to Cleveland.

Hildy talked to Evans, then said, "I don't believe any pitcher can work for Johnson and be satisfied." However, Hildy telephoned Johnson, apologized for his conduct in St. Louis, and was restored to good graces.

Late in the campaign, Ferrell asked for a trial as an outfielder, and Johnson permitted it. Evans was scorching.

"How can we expect to make any kind of a deal for Ferrell if we admit to the world his pitching arm is shot?" he asked. A deal for Wes was made the next year. He and Porter went to the Red Sox for pitcher Bob Weiland and Bob Seeds, the latter back for a second whirl in the outfield.

Evans was having other troubles. Not only were the Indians losing; the turnstiles were also slowing down. Bradley called in the general manager. "I want the exact figures after every ball game so we know just were we stand," was Bradley's order.

On the last day of the season, according to Bradley, the ball club faced 70,000 dollars in unpaid bills. The Sherwin and Bradley families raised 150,000 dollars, largely in the form of their own personal checks. There were some other switches in stock about that time.

The Van Sweringen empire crashed. The 250,000 dollars in ball-club stock owned by the brothers was offered to Bradley at half price. Most of the stock—95,000 dollars worth—was bought and retired by other officers and shareholders in the

Tribe. Three sales of 10,000 dollars each were made to E. G. Crawford, president of the Cleveland Electric Illuminating Company; I. F. Freiberger, chairman of the board of the Cleveland Trust Company, and W. G. "Bill" Bernet of the family of brothers that took over operation of many of the Van Sweringens' railroad interests.

Two other widely known businessmen bought into the team, George A. Martin, president of the Sherwin-Williams Paint Company, and George E. Tomlinson, multimillionaire lake-shipping leader. Each obtained 50,000 dollars in stock from Percy Morgan, one of the original purchasers.

The axe was out for Evans after the 1933 season. The outspoken, capable general manager had worked under a pair of three-year contracts. It was time for a new contract.

"We're retrenching," Bradley told Billy, "so we'll have to ask you to take a pay cut."

It was too much of a cut to suit Evans—from 30,000 dollars to 12,500 dollars—and he quit. However, he reconsidered when the club directors met his offer of 12,500 dollars' base salary and a 5,000-dollar bonus should the team make a profit of 100,000 dollars or more in 1934. Both the club and Evans attained their goals, at least at the box office, as the games were moved back to League Park.

The Indians improved in the league, moving up to third place in 1934 but only after a summer of conflict within the ranks. Johnson and the reporters assigned to the Indians quit speaking except upon occasion. Walter was charged with poor handling of pitchers. The team played .500 baseball, but the fiery *Cleveland Press* was not contented. It yelled in eight columns:

"The Indians, Without Leadership, Have Flopped; What Are the Owners Going to do About It?"

Johnson had another run-in with Hildebrand. Also he was blamed for getting rid of Ferrell, who went to Boston and won fourteen games while losing only five. The next year Ferrell won twenty games using slow pitches mainly, and Johnson took another public thrashing.

During the minor leagues' meeting after the 1934 season,

the Indians signed Steve O'Neill as a coach. Johnson wasn't keen about the move. Not that he had anything personal against Steve. But Johnson was inclined to guard his job jealously, and he knew that he was none too secure with the fans. Further, he knew that Bradley had changed managers to put him in, and there was no assurance the great ex-pitcher himself wouldn't be removed bodily to make way for a successor.

There were no outward signs of rebellion or friction as the Indians reported to their New Orleans camp in 1935. Instead, there was a feeling Evans had provided Johnson with a pretty good ball club, and if anything should happen to the Tigers or Yankees, the Redskins might sneak through on the rail. The pitching was greatly improved as Monte Pearson blossomed into a sturdy, steady workman. Monte had missed a no-hit game in the ninth inning in 1933, his first year with the Tribe, when Ossie Bluege of the Senators led off with a sharp single past Kamm at third. The Indians were ahead, 7 to 0, at the time.

One of the younger players who had caught Johnson's eye early in '34 was a soft-spoken, laughing third baseman from Eldorado, Arkansas, by the name of Odell Hale. He had been dubbed "Bad News" Hale in the minors because of his propensity for breaking up ball games in late innings with power drives. A compact 170 pounds, Hale could send a baseball as far, yard for pound, as anyone in the game.

The Indians might not have picked up Hale except for a Louisiana downpour. C. C. "Cy" Slapnicka, famous Cleveland scout, was sent to look over two players with the Alexandria, Louisiana, team in the Cotton States League in 1929. The Indians had their choice or, if it came to a pinch, could get both men for a total of five thousand dollars.

The day Slapnicka arrived in Alexandria, rain was pelting the streets, but he wasn't sure whether the scheduled game would be played, so he hurried to the ball park. He found the place deserted except for one man and two small boys. The man was sitting astride the second-base cushion, a barrel stave in each hand, and pretending to row through choppy waters, made that way by the splashing of the youngsters.

Slapnicka said to himself, "What kind of monkey business goes on here?" Later he discovered the identity of the comedian. He was Lon Warneke, a pitcher, and he was one of the two players Slapnicka was to scout. Slapnicka, disgusted, took the next train out of town. He never saw either Warneke or the other player, Hale.

Sometime that fall, the Chicago Cubs grabbed Warneke. The Indians were still interested in Hale, so Slapnicka made a second trip to the South. He watched the young third baseman in six games, then recommended that the Tribe buy a third baseman on another team in the same league!

At the December baseball meetings, Hale's name came up again. The club that owned him owed the Indians fifteen hundred dollars.

"Will you take Hale and cancel the debt?" asked the anxious minor-league executive. Billy Evans agreed, not too hastily, but it proved to be one of the best buys of his lifetime in baseball.

The giant first baseman, Hal Trosky, had found himself once the Tribe returned to League Park, and he was on his way to becoming one of the finest sluggers in Cleveland history. Bill Knickerbocker was settling down at short, and a bandy-legged second baseman, Roy Hughes, was around to give Hale a tussle for the starting job.

Despite the improvements, despite Harder, Lloyd Brown, Clint Brown, Lefty Lee, Pearson, Hildebrand, Hudlin, Galehouse, Pytlak, Averill, Vosmik, and a likable new outfielder, Bruce Campbell, the Indians faltered early in 1935. Pitchers did not hesitate to fasten the blame on Johnson. Rumblings of trouble grew louder.

Then on May 23, all hell broke loose. Johnson revealed in Philadelphia that he had discovered an "anti-Johnson" bloc among the Indians. He ordered Kamm to go to Cleveland and handed an unconditional release to the veteran catcher, Glenn Myatt.

"Those men are influencing the young players on the team," Walter charged. "Why, not more than five players know who's

Wes Ferrell

Hal Trosky

Oscar Vitt

Bob Feller

the manager of this club. For the good of the team, I'm dismissing Kamm and Myatt."

Cleveland fans, never too friendly toward Johnson, exploded on every street corner. Petitions demanding the manager's removal were circulated and signed quickly. There were cries of "He's jealous of Kamm," and "Kamm actually runs the team, Johnson doesn't."

Kamm took his case direct to Judge Landis.

"I'm interested in clearing my name," the veteran told the judge. "I realize that my baseball future is up to the Cleveland club. But a lot of people might think I've built up a bad reputation because of the way all this happened."

Landis, in an unofficial directive, did clear the names of Kamm and Myatt but emphasized that he had no control over Johnson's decision. Almost immediately, Kamm was appointed a scout for the Indians, while Myatt caught on with the New York Giants. He turned down other offers from the White Sox and A's.

But the pot was boiling, and the overflow was catching up with Johnson. On June 6, a large advertisement appeared in Cleveland newspapers. It was headed: "Some Inside Stuff Direct From the Camp of the Indians."

The ad said, in part, "We, the members of the Cleveland Baseball Club, want the fans to know that we are not a team split wide open by dissension, arrayed against our manager..." For twelve inches of type the message carried on. Johnson was not extolled, but neither was he crucified.

The signatures of twenty-one players appeared in facsimile at the bottom of the ad. These were Hildebrand, Trosky, Pearson, Harder, Hudlin, Hughes, Lee, Clint Brown, Ab Wright, Ralph Winegarner, Bill Brenzel, Bosey Berger, Hale, Knickerbocker, Milt Galatzer, Walter Stewart, Pytlak, Vosmik, Averill, Lloyd Brown, and Bruce Campbell.

On June 8, two days after the advertisement appeared, the Indians returned to League Park to meet the Browns. The management was not napping. When the crowd of four thousand showed up to applaud and boo Johnson and his underlings, they found extra policemen inside and outside the park. Soft drinks were served in paper containers. Each scoreboard contained an inserted sheet, a reprint of a Detroit newspaper column that asked, "Is Johnson Being Persecuted?"

The fans did not absolve the Indians completely. Cries of "we love our teacher—signed, Averill" went up because the star outfielder had granted an interview in which he said he, Vosmik, and the others were "100 per cent behind Johnson."

Those same fans and hundreds of thousands of others stayed away from the ball park. Johnson was slipping in public favor. Bradley and Evans fretted. Their problem hit rock bottom on July 28, a Sunday, when only five thousand showed up to watch the Detroit Tigers, leading the league. The next day Bradley called Johnson to his office.

"We've decided to make a change," he told Walter. "I'm sorry, but something must be done. The fans are mad at you, and so we're going to put Steve O'Neill in charge and see if he can pull us up a little."

Johnson smiled before framing his reply.

"I'm sorry, Mr. Bradley, I failed you," he said. "Of course, whatever change you make is your decision, and I'll go along with it. However, I have a request to make."

Bradley leaned forward.

"We're going on a short Western trip," continued Johnson, "and we'll probably lose a lot of games. It wouldn't be fair to O'Neill to have him start in on a losing streak. I'll take the club west, and you can announce my resignation the minute we get back, regardless of the success or failure of the trip."

The President forced a smile over a rather large lump in his throat.

On August 5, 1935, Stephen Francis O'Neill, the pride of Minooka, Pennsylvania, became the thirteenth manager of the Cleveland American League team. The paunchy, rough-hewn Irishman who served as the Indians' prize catcher from 1915 through 1923, with a few extra years thrown in, coached at Toronto and managed Toledo before joining up with his old employers.

The man puzzled by the appointment of O'Neill was, curiously, Alva Bradley. When he advised Steve of his promotion, Bradley added, "I really can't understand why anyone would want to manage a ball club. It's such a thankless, nerve-racking job, and every fan is your boss."

Steve laughed at the bewilderment of his employer. But underneath, Steve was thinking already of the game on the morrow, his first appearance as a manager in the big leagues. The Indians had lost to the Tigers, 5 to 0, in Detroit that afternoon. Lefty Lee, the giant southpaw, was the only starting pitcher O'Neill, as director of the bull pen, had saved for the next day, but Johnson had insisted upon using Lee in a "lost" game.

The Browns were Steve's first opponents. He had one pitcher ready to go, but he wasn't a regular starter. Still, Ralph Winegarner, a reformed third baseman, could throw hard and often, and he got O'Neill's nod. Further, Ralph beat the Browns, 4 to 2, and an unidentified fan was so elated at the turn of managers and events he presented Winegarner with a new radio.

Under O'Neill the Indians spurted and finished a good third. Harder, who had won twenty games in 1934, increased his output to twenty-two with the finest year in his long and productive career as a pitcher for his only sponsor, Cleveland. Hudlin won fifteen but Pearson skidded to eight victories.

Three days before O'Neill's appointment, while the Tribe was playing in Detroit and composing love advertisements to the fans back home, a game was called off because of rain. A day off meant only one thing to the Indians of that time, a poker game. The grapevine was pressed into use, and within a matter of minutes, a game was scheduled for the room of the *Cleveland Press* correspondent, who happens to be the writer of this history.

Vosmik, Averill, Lloyd Brown, Pytlak, Hale, Trosky, and the loyal trainer, Lefty Weisman, were enrolled speedily. As the clan was gathering, Campbell sauntered in the room, sat down at the newly arrived round table, then stood up with a look of distress on his face. In the tenth inning of a game the day before, Bruce had gone back to the hotel, ill.

"Call me in a little bit after the game gets going," he requested. "I don't feel good, got a headache. I'm gonna lie down for a while." He didn't come back and the promised call was forgotten.

The next morning the club was amazed to discover that Campbell was in a critical condition at a hospital, victim of cerebral spinal fever, a form of spinal meningitis. The doctors said he had no more than a fifty-fifty chance to recover.

All baseball rooted for Bruce Campbell, one of the nicest guys in the trade, and in a surprising fight against permanent retirement, Bruce beat his case and was ready for more baseball the next year. However, he collapsed again in May 1936 in Boston. Doctors tested all members of the Indians and the correspondents, but only Campbell was afflicted. Again, Bruce won his battle and a month later was honored on Bruce Campbell Day at League Park. Against the Yankees, Bruce came back to bang out three singles in as many trips to the plate!

He'd won that particular fight 100 per cent.

The troubles with Johnson, the players, and the fans had affected the club's drawing power at home in 1935, and a rather short profit of seventy thousand dollars was announced. The directors asked Billy Evans to take another drastic cut in pay. Billy refused and again turned in a resignation. This one was accepted, and late in November, the office of general manager of the Indians was formally abolished.

In its place was established the office of assistant to the president and into the new job was fitted snugly, as befitted the immediate future operation of the team, the peerless ivory hunter Cy Slapnicka. The bald, Iowa-bred Slapnicka was a minor-league pitcher in his youth. Once, E. S. Barnard drafted Slap from the Rockford, Illinois, club in the Wisconsin-Illinois League. He got only as far as Toledo, and though he pitched against the Indians, he never formally joined the club. That was in 1910. In 1923, Barnard signed Slap as a full-time scout.

CHAPTER XXII

SPITFIRE ALLEN

WHEN O'NEILL had managed the Toronto team in 1931, he was entrusted with the job of schooling a fiery, square-shouldered right-hander who had the temper of seventeen wildcats and about the same vocal powers. He was Johnny Allen, who looked as tough as he talked. Toronto sent Johnny along to the New York Yankees, for whom he won fifty games while losing only nineteen in a four-year stretch. But because of his outbursts, Allen never found exceptional favor with the Yanks' manager, Joe McCarthy.

Steve wanted Allen for the Indians, and he prevailed upon Slapnicka to trade Pearson and a strong, Cleveland-born right-hander, Steve Sundra, for the spitfire Allen.

One month after the 1936 season was started, O'Neill wondered whether he had given his boss some bad information. Allen's temper was much more prominent than his pitching average, and it seemed that in the years he was with the Yankees, rival teams had discovered his weakness.

Knowing his patience was limited, other clubs spread the word that Allen "couldn't take it." Week after week, every enemy outfit operated on Allen's disposition, and most of them left their scalpels inside the wounds. Within earshot of the victim, managers, coaches, and players said to umpires, "How do you let Allen get away with throwin' spitters?" Or, "Why don't you bums look at the ball after Allen gets through with it? You'll see somethin'."

Whenever he pitched, batter after batter stopped the game and insisted that the umpire examine the ball. The championship season was only three weeks away when Allen blew his top the first time. The Indians were in Detroit. Del Baker, the Tiger's third-base coach, was talking to Allen continuously, shouting pricking cracks about spitballs, "cheaters," etc.

185

The Tigers knocked Allen out of the box. When O'Neill told him to leave, Johnny went straight for Baker instead.

"You smart heel," he screamed. "All you can do is stand around and make noise. I ought to belt you on your mouth." The ever alert umpires prevented bloodshed, if any.

The heckling continued whenever Allen took the mound, and finally on May 12 Slapnicka composed a letter to Will Harridge demanding a league curb on Allen's detractors. Slapnicka charged other teams with "poor sportsmanship" and argued that the umpires were "interfering with the pitcher's attempts to complete games."

Harridge absolved Allen of any trickery with the baseball in a communiqué made public the next day, but the news that the Indians had "cried" was all over the league, and Allen took a double ribbing. The unpleasantries so upset him that by June 4 he had won only four games while losing five and had pitched only one complete game.

That night Allen decided to relax and one Boston hotel hasn't been the same since. Reports of what followed were varied. It was generally agreed that Allen, irked by the size of the stools in the Brunswick Hotel bar, upended most of them. Then he got into an argument with (a) a hotel porter or (b) a room-service waiter. Allen snatched a fire extinguisher off the wall and either doused the porter or slugged the waiter with it, or both. A hotel maintenance man, perched on a stepladder while changing a light bulb, was grounded when Allen jerked the support out from under him. Next he attempted to remove the plaster from a nearby wall by smashing it with his new-found weapon, the stepladder.

Lefty Lee, the pitcher's roommate, eventually got him into bed, but not before O'Neill had heard of the rumpus. The next morning Allen was handed a fifty-dollar bill for damages to the hotel and a two-hundred-and-fifty-dollar fine by Steve.

It was probably the cheapest three hundred dollars Allen ever spent. He straightened up, once he had blown off all that steam, and won sixteen games while losing only five from then on to finish the year with a creditable mark of twenty triumphs and ten losses. Allen's spurt earned him a sizable increase in salary.

Then came another Boston incident, but of a less hilarious nature. By mid-June, Allen had won four games and was unbeaten. In Boston he was stricken with appendicitis and underwent an emergency operation. In two weeks he was back pitching. He won eleven games in a row for a total of fifteen and he was only four shy of Rube Marquard's all-time big league record of nineteen straight, and one shy of the American League sixteen-game mark owned by Walter Johnson, Lefty Grove, Joe Wood, and Schoolboy Rowe.

The Indians were finishing the season at Detroit. The last game was scheduled on October 3 and the Tribe pitching honor went, quite naturally, to Allen. Manager Mickey Cochrane of the Tigers sent Jake Wade, a left-hander serving his first year in the majors, against Allen. Wade, a fellow North Carolinian, had won exactly three games in all 1936 and he had an earned-run average at the moment of pretty close to six runs per game!

Johnny got a bad break in the first inning. Pete Fox was credited with a double on a hump-backed liner. Hank Greenberg then slashed a grounder right to Bad News Hale at third. The ball sizzled through Hale, and Greenberg was credited with a single, Fox scoring. Thereafter Allen pitched eight runless innings.

But Wade was even better. Jake permitted the Indians only one hit, a single by Trosky in the seventh. Allen, though restricting the Tigers to six blows, was defeated, 1 to 0, and with the loss went his chance to tie the league record.

Allen was irate in the clubhouse after the game. He accused Hale of sloppy fielding, insisting that Greenberg's grounder should have been an out instead of a base hit. Words flew fast, and only the intervention of O'Neill stopped a fist fight on the spot. Returning to Cleveland on the train that night, Allen continued his abuse of Hale.

The newest uprising was in the dining car, and just when blows seemed inevitable, O'Neill got between Allen and Hale.

"You've popped off enough, now shut up," Steve told Allen.

"I ought to kill him," the pitcher yelled. "Any bush-league third baseman would have made that play."

Again O'Neill ordered Allen to pipe down.

"Listen, John," Steve eventually offered, "If you'll only shut up and forget it, I'll buy your gasoline for the trip back to St. Petersburg. That's about twenty-five bucks. Good enough?"

Allen agreed, and the trip was continued without incident.

One twenty-game season, followed by a near record performance of fifteen victories and one defeat, caused Allen to hold out in the spring of 1938. He signed eventually in late February for thirty-eight thousand dollars, spread over two seasons. Then, at the season's outset, he was heaved out of a game by Umpire Bill McGowan and fined twenty-five dollars.

On June 7, 1938, the Indians were in Boston; Allen was again the pitcher and McGowan again the plate umpire. Allen in Boston—something was sure to happen. It did. John squawked to McGowan about the arbiter's decisions on several pitches in the first inning. McGowan, the league's number-one umpire, whose judgment is seldom questioned and properly so, held his tongue until the second inning.

Then McGowan stopped play, walked to the mound, and told Allen he would have to cut off a part of his sweat-shirt sleeve that dangled whenever he delivered the ball, thereby distracting the attention of the batter. Allen argued and refused to change the shirt.

He walked into the Cleveland dugout and sat down. Manager Oscar Vitt, O'Neill's successor, and Captain Lyn Lary pleaded with Allen to have Lefty Weisman, the trainer, slice off the offending sleeve, but John was adamant. Vitt gave up.

"Okay, that'll cost you two hundred and fifty dollars," he yelled at Allen. "No pitcher of mine can walk off the rubber without me telling him to."

"You and McGowan can both go to blazes," snapped Allen.

The shirt incident became a *cause célèbre*. President Bradley flew to New York a few days later to investigate the Allen uprising. After hearing all the evidence, Bradley turned an odd trick.

He bought the shirt for two hundred and fifty dollars, the amount Vitt had fined Allen, and returned to Cleveland with the soiled undergarment. Whereupon it was mounted in a glass showcase in the men's furnishings department of the Higbee

Company, a large department store. Bradley claimed the Higbee Company, and not the ball club, had paid the two hundred and fifty dollars for the shirt. However, it was more than coincidental that Chuck Bradley, Alva's brother, was the president of the Higbee Company at the time.

But the shirt was not yet at the end of its tail. By this time, the national baseball public knew the story of the frayed sleeve. So the shirt was placed in the Hall of Fame at Cooperstown, New York, and it is there today as a symbol of one of the game's daffiest episodes.

BOB FELLER IN PERSON

THE INDIANS engaged in more "new deals" in the space of eight or nine years than the ordinary baseball club would encounter in a lifetime. However, no one in full possession of the facts would label the Indians as an ordinary team, and the operation of their front office was fantastic and astounding. Interest of home fans was divided between executive and competitive Redskins. Many times the antics of the front office far overshadowed home runs and low-hit pitching.

Bradley never despaired of his team's chances, at least in the early part of each year. A supreme optimist, the smiling, gentlemanly president greeted each new baseball season with high hope for success. Only in August would he relax and concede. By then, an Eastern trip had taken all the poison from the Tribe's arrows, and there probably had been the customary tumble from first place to fourth or fifth.

So no one was terrifically surprised in the early spring of 1936 when the directors of the Indians tossed a luncheon, quite a private one, in the celebrated suite of the Van Sweringens in the Terminal Tower. Slapnicka, the new assistant to President Bradley, was there. So was O'Neill, starting his first full season as manager. Everything was very informal, even Alva's optimism. He did want one man to talk, however.

"Slap," he addressed Billy Evans' successor, "tell them about that young pitcher you signed."

Slapnicka cleared his throat.

"Gentlemen, I've found the greatest young pitcher I ever saw," he began. "I suppose this sounds like the same old stuff to you, but I want you to believe me. This boy that I found out in Iowa will be the greatest pitcher the world has ever known."

The directors were silent. True, they had heard promises

before, in business and in baseball. But Slapnicka was religiously sincere. And there was a note of finality in his voice. Slap was no ordinary scout. The directors knew of his skill in flushing baseball hopefuls from under haystacks and model T autos.

Slapnicka enlarged upon his opening statements.

"I found this boy, name of Bob Feller, in a small town not far from Des Moines—Van Meter, they call it. I know that country out there pretty well. My home section, you see. Well, my friends told me about this boy, so I went to see him pitch. I only saw him pitch once before I signed him. Went back to the Feller farm that same night and the boy's father and I made a deal. Got along fine, too."

The scout and Bill Feller always got along. They were plain men of the Iowa soil. Big men, bluff men, suave men had talked to Bill Feller about his son, Bob. Bill Feller didn't like those types. He was of Slapnicka's mold. The farm had never left either of them.

Bob Feller was sixteen when Slapnicka signed him, and Bill Feller, to a contract for Bob to pitch for the Fargo-Moorehead team in the Northern League in 1936. Fargo-Moorehead was, of course, a Cleveland property. Baseball prohibited the signing of a sand lotter by a major-league club direct. Only minor-league teams could sign amateur players, other than collegians.

"Bob's finishing out this school term," Slapnicka continued his narration to the directors. "We'll send him to Fargo-Moorehead in June. But I repeat to you, gentlemen, he will be the star of them all. Do you know that he averaged 19 strikeouts a game last summer?"

Slapnicka's ravings about his new pitching star were soon forgotten in the early rush of the 1936 Indians. O'Neill had been optimistic and not without due cause, it appeared early in the season. Trosky was away to a flying start toward his finest season in the big league, one in which he batted .343, hit 42 home runs for an all-time Cleveland record and led the league in runs batted in with 162. Averill outhit Trosky with a .378 mark, but he trailed in home runs with 28 and in runs batted in with 126.

A stumpy, drawling Texan, Roy Weatherly, came up from New Orleans and in his first year hammered American League pitching for a .335 average. Handsome Billy Sullivan, a catcher whose dad caught for the immortal Chicago White Stockings, was obtained from Cincinnati on waivers and hit a sensational .351.

But the shadow of June passed across the Wigwam, bearing its dreary message. The Indians lost nine out of twelve on an Eastern trip and O'Neill threatened a shake-up. Allen hadn't begun to click, Harder was going through a .500 season, Hildebrand was under that mark, while Hudlin failed almost 100 per cent, skidding from fifteen victories to one.

It was a question of whether Slapnicka was more concerned about the Indians or about his seventeen-year-old pitching wonder, Bob Feller. Instead of having Feller report to Fargo-Moorehead when school let out in June, Slapnicka ordered the youth to Cleveland. There were reports Feller had a sore arm, and they may have been accurate reports. Suffice it to say that Slapnicka was a man who trusted few others. His native suspicion boiled when he thought about sending his prize discovery to a Class D minor league and entrusting his development to a comparatively strange manager.

In his autobiography *Strikeout Story,* Feller describes his first days after arrival at League Park.

"The Indians were on the road at the time and the problem of what to do with my time remained. There have been stories that Slapnicka put me to work sacking peanuts in the concession department, but these are untrue. I worked out every day and played catch with Bruce Campbell...Campbell had been left behind when the team hit the road." *

The operators of one of Cleveland's outstanding amateur baseball teams, Max Rosenblum and I. S. Rose, had been after Slapnicka to allow Feller to pitch for their team, the Rosenblums. Slap consented and Bob beat a semipro team from nearby Akron. The next day, Slapnicka complimented the Iowa youngster and advised him of a bigger and better assignment.

* R. W. A. Feller, *Strikeout Story* (New York: A. S. Barnes & Co., Inc., 1947)

"You're going to pitch against the St. Louis Cardinals," he told the startled schoolboy.

The Cardinals were booked for an exhibition with the Tribe at League Park on July 6, one of the open dates occasioned by the all-star game. One of the conditions of the game was the promise by the Cardinals to use their highly publicized stars—Manager Frankie Frisch, Leo Durocher, Joe Medwick, Terry Moore, Pepper Martin, Dizzy and Paul Dean, Ripper Collins, and Wild Bill Hallahan.

George Uhle, who was brought back to the Tribe's fold as a coach and part-time pitcher by O'Neill, hurled the first three innings. Feller drew the middle three innings and also drew his manager, Steve O'Neill, as his catcher. Steve went two innings with Bob, then retired in favor of Joe Becker.

"That kid's too tough for me to catch any more," observed Steve as he rubbed his bruised left hand. "He throws that thing so fast it looks like a pea, a damned small pea."

The Cardinals thought so, too. They had never seen anythink like Feller; for that matter neither had the Indians or the nine thousand spectators. He wound up as if he were following the contour of a large pretzel. Then he kicked his left leg high in the air, up in front of his face. Then he threw— fast balls. No curves, just blazers. Eight Cardinals went down swinging, or ducking, in those historic three innings!

After the game, the inimitable Dizzy Dean was responsible for a saying that has been repeated thousands of times. A photographer asked Dean to pose with the mere boy who had thrown a baseball so fast.

"Why ask me?" he shot back at the surprised lens man. "Ask that kid if *he'll* pose with *me!*"

After one more sand-lot game, in which he struck out fifteen, Feller packed his bag to join the Indians for a trip east. The youngster may have been a good-luck charm, for the Indians won ten and lost only two games. In one of those setbacks, in Washington, Feller had made his first appearance in a championship game, going in after the Tribe was far behind.

By late August, O'Neill had dropped his last hope for a whirlwind finish. The Yankees were a dozen games in front of the pack. The Browns came to League Park on Sunday,

August 23. Slapnicka and O'Neill decided that the St. Louis team, mired in seventh place, might serve as Feller's first big-league victims. They did.

Bob struck out fifteen Browns while pitching to a rookie catcher, Charley "Greek" George. The national baseball front had heard thunder and lightning about him. Any pitcher, star, or raw recruit, capable of striking out fifteen batters in a major-league game was worthy of more than a paragraph on the sports pages. Bob Feller cracked the headlines in every newspaper in the country for the first time!

Three weeks later, the schoolboy started to become a legend. He faced the Philadelphia Athletics at League Park and struck out seventeen batters to tie Dizzy Dean's major-league record. He might have broken the mark with better control. Bob walked nine, hit one, inserted one wild pitch, and fumbled at the rubber as the A's stole nine bases on him. Again Bob's catcher was the rookie, George, and again Bob was thankful to him. For it was George, sensing his pitcher's growing fatigue in late innings, who walked out to the mound and gave him fatherly advice, though a bare four years separated them in age.

In the last month of the 1936 season, Bob won two more games, but the best the Tribe could do was finish fifth. Harder's arm started to give him the miseries, and Pytlak was sorely missed. For the fourth straight season, Pytlak was lost to the team for one reason or another, mainly broken fingers and stomach ailments.

He went down and out early in August after one of Monte Pearson's fast balls literally jumped into his jaw during a game in the Stadium. The crowd of 65,342, many of whom still believed the Indians had a chance to win the pennant, was spread throughout the bleachers in center, too, and their white shirts comprised a screen out of which pitches sailed plateward. There had been considerable agitation to rope off the middle section of the bleachers so that the batters would be in less danger at the plate, but nothing had been accomplished.

Then the massive audience was sickened and stunned as Pearson's pitch zoomed out of the white shirts in the fourth inning. Pytlak turned his head a trifle. He had missed the previous pitch by inches. But this one caught him on the left side of the face. Blood spurted from his mouth as he staggered. Bill Dickey, the Yankee catcher, and Joe Vosmik, who had been in the batter's circle, grabbed the little catcher. He was rushed to the hospital, where x-rays showed a triple fracture. Naturally, he was through for the season and his .321 batting average was sorely missed.

Any troubles O'Neill had about that time were minor compared to the woes piling up on Slapnicka. The daily press in Cleveland was "on" the front-office chief continually. As Alva Bradley said, "There's one thing about Slapnicka—he knows how to make money." That he did, but he pinched a few pennies in the process, and his critics seized every rumor or circumstance and were not averse to enlarging them.

Both O'Neill and Slapnicka were protecting Feller, but in vastly different ways. Steve was aware of the pressure being applied to his young pitching star, so he had him move from a nearby East Side hotel to an outlying golf club. Later Steve got Weatherly to room with Bob, and the two, in company with a man named Hub Stone, kept far removed from the temptations of a big city.

Slapnicka was less open in his maneuvers in behalf of Feller. In order to make Bob eligible to pitch for Cleveland, Slapnicka put through a series of dummy transfers of his contract. Fargo-Moorehead assigned Feller to New Orleans. The latter team, in turn, switched his contract to Cleveland. Thus, Feller got to the big leagues without the formality of ever wearing the uniform of the Fargo-Moorehead or New Orleans teams, though he had been listed in the office of Judge Landis as being the property of each at some time or another.

It was a plain "cover up" deal of the type frowned on by Landis. For three months the baseball commissioner had been examining the evidence in the Feller case. It was brought to his attention first within a matter of hours after Bob pitched against the Cardinals in the Cleveland exhibition.

Owner Lee Keyser of the Des Moines team in the Western League filed the original protest with Landis' office. Keyser said he had attempted to sign Feller in the summer of 1935 but that Slapnicka had beaten him to the punch and had violated the Major-Minor League Agreement and Rules by signing a sand lotter to a major-league contract.

Landis called Bill Feller to his office. He called Alva Bradley and Cy Slapnicka. He called Lee Keyser and Sec Taylor, sports editor of the *Des Moines Register-Tribune,* to whom Bill Feller had told a story different than the one Landis heard.

Finally, late in the 1936 season, Landis beckoned Bob Feller to his Chicago chambers. The seventeen-year-old farm boy, now 180 pounds and spreading, and his father faced the judge together. Exactly what Landis said to father and son never has been published in full. But later statements by Landis tended to show he was dubious about some of the testimony.

Yet there was one outburst by the trembling Iowa boy that probably had more effect than any other on Landis. When the judge pointed out that he might take him away from the Indians, Bob blurted, "I don't want to play anyplace else. I want to play for Cleveland."

Landis bore down on Slapnicka extra hard. He made no bones about stating that he believed the Cleveland executive was to blame for the entire mess. He drove home the point that Feller had been "covered up," that the procedure in such cases was to declare the player a free agent, and that there was invariably some form of punishment for the culprit.

No case of a baseball player commanded more national attention than the possible freeing of Feller from Cleveland shackles. Estimates as to the amount such wealthy teams as the Yankees, Red Sox, and Tigers would pay to the youngster, or his dad, for signing went as high as a quarter of a million dollars.

It was the picture of these baseball wolves waiting outside his door that had a heavy affect on the Commissioner's decision. Too, Landis was extremely fond of Alva Bradley, whom the judge had guided through early days as a club executive.

Landis didn't believe much of the testimony given by the case's principals. He said so, quite frankly. On pure evidence, his decision could go only one way, *i.e.* a severance of Feller from the Tribe.

He argued with himself for many hours. His problem had become rather a basic one. He could turn Feller loose and make him immensely wealthy immediately, or he could restrict him to the Indians and bawl the devil out of Slapnicka and the others.

On December 10, 1936, Judge Landis made the most important player decision in two decades. In several hundreds of well-couched words, he said, Bob Feller remains the property of the Cleveland club.

The Des Moines club was awarded seven thousand five hundred dollars, small balm for the loss of the greatest pitcher of the times.

Six months later, Landis wasn't so easy with Slapnicka. The Indians had "covered up" a twenty-one-year-old Massillon, Ohio, outfielder, Tommy Henrich. Henrich had a great year at New Orleans in 1936, batting .346, but his reward was a promotion only to Milwaukee instead of to the Indians. Billy Evans, general manager of the Tribe three years before, had signed Henrich originally.

Tommy complained to Judge Landis in the spring of 1937, asserting that he felt he was ready for a major-league trial but had been denied one because the Cleveland team had brought up Roy Weatherly instead. Landis freed Henrich and thus enabled him to obtain a bonus of twenty-five thousand dollars for signing with the Yankees.

During the Henrich investigation, the Indians' front office charged that Evans had "blown the whistle" by secretly advising Henrich of his rights and Bradley threatened to institute a civil suit against his former general manager for "breach of ethics."

The club that Bill Evans had assembled several years earlier was dismantled before the beginning of the 1937 season. Vosmik, Hildebrand, and Knickerbocker went to the Browns for Lyn Lary, Moose Solters, and Ivy Paul Andrews. Lefty Lee went to the White Sox for Earl Whitehill. Pitchers came and went. Vosmik's legs were bothering him, and Joe had fallen off the pedestal he occupied in 1935 when his .348 average was one point shy of the league's best.

And Bob Feller had a sore arm. After his sensational debut only nine months earlier, the eighteen-year-old fireballer came up with a lame limb early in the season. And to make O'Neill's grief complete, Weatherly fell apart at the plate. Pitchers learned that he was a sucker for slow balls. By the time hot weather was in vogue, Weatherly was back in New Orleans, a victim of push pitches and a .201 batting average as a result thereof.

During one spell, the Indians lost eleven of thirteen games in the East, and rumors spread that O'Neill was washed up in Cleveland. Two names, Bill Terry and Tony Lazzeri, were mentioned in discussions of a successor. Terry was reputed to be considering an offer of forty thousand dollars annually to serve the Tribe as a combination general manager and field boss. Lazzeri, nearing the close of a career with the Yankees, had staunch backing as a playing manager, according to gossip in the big leagues.

Midway of the 1937 season, the Indians surrendered first place to the Yankees. Bradley, prodded by Slapnicka, called O'Neill on the carpet.

"Don't worry," O'Neill soothed the boss. "We're a better team than we've shown so far. Feller's had a sore arm, Allen had an operation, and Hughes has been out. We'll get going."

Feller staged a remarkable comeback on August 25 when he struck out sixteen Boston Red Sox at League Park. For a fellow with a sore arm, Bob seemed to be doing pretty well. But at season's end, the final figures revealed there had been something wrong with his whip. He'd won only nine games while losing seven.

O'Neill rallied his forces for a great climax to a poor season. Steve won forty of his last sixty games.

"See," he pointed out to newspapermen, "we'd have figured in this pennant race if we'd had that kind of a streak earlier in the season."

But there had been criticism of Steve's handling of players. Some said he was too easy. When the Tribe was in an especially downcast state during the season, Ed McAuley, baseball writer for the *Cleveland News*, addressed an open letter to O'Neill.

"Get Mad, Steve," admonished the headline. But Steve needed more than a change in dispositions. He needed some pitchers and he needed confidence by the front office. Bradley was open to conviction. Slapnicka wasn't. Slap wasn't an O'Neill man.

The team wound up in fourth place, nineteen games behind the winning Yankees. Bradley's directors didn't think the Indians should have been that far behind. Neither did Slapnicka. So Bradley went shopping for a new manager. He found one within two weeks after the 1937 race had ended.

THE 1940 REVOLUTION

PERHAPS A HUNDRED MEN sat around a perfectly square festive board in the Hotel Cleveland one evening in the autumn of 1937. The owners and directors of the Indians were there. So were some business friends, some newspapermen, some gentlemen of the cloth, Slapnicka, and Frank Kohlbecker, the club's efficient traveling secretary.

Alva Bradley was the toastmaster.

"I have every reason to believe we will have a fighting, peppy ball club in 1938," he pronounced. "Our team should reflect the personality, the desire to win, the animation of our new manager, Oscar Vitt."

In October of that year, Oscar Vitt had been named manager of the Indians. A small, graying man with an aquiline nose and a set of teeth that were seldom hidden, Vitt got to his feet.

He was cocky, to be sure. He was fiery and jumpy.

"I don't know much about this team," he conceded, "but I can tell you one thing. We'll have the damnedest fighting team you ever had here. There'll be no loafing. Ol' Os will see to that."

That was Vitt's pet name for himself, "Ol' Os." He had been a banjo-hitting third baseman with the Detroit Tigers in Ty Cobb's heyday. Ol' Os talked a terrific base bit, and when he was spouting about his career with the Tigers, he would purposely overemphasize his batting.

"Ol' Os could hit that ball," he said, making with the motion of putting both hands on an imaginary bat he held perpendicular in front of his face.

People like Vitt at first meeting, and so it was small wonder Bradley and Slapnicka had been smitten. Too, he had achieved a miracle record with the Newark Bears of the International League in 1937. That club, pipe line to the Yankees, had won the pennant by twenty-five and a half games. Vitt's roster included Joe Gordon, Charley Keller, Buddy Rosar, Babe Dahlgren, Atley Donald, Bob Seeds, Jim Gleason, Marius Russo, and others who took the ferryboat to Yankee Stadium and often came back to Newark.

George Weiss, astute head of the Yankees' farm system, recommended Vitt highly. So did Joe McCarthy. Vitt, it seemed, was the answer to Cleveland's jackpot question of any baseball year: "What's wrong with the Indians?"

Whatever it was, Vitt would fix it. He tried hard in 1938. Slapnicka obtained Rollie Hemsley from the Browns in a swap for Billy Sullivan, Roy Hughes, and a minor-league pitcher. Weatherly came back for another trial.

From Milwaukee, the Indians acquired three highly touted players, third baseman Ken Keltner, outfielder John Geoffrey Heath, and second baseman Oscar Grimes. Two of them, Heath and Grimes, cost only the usual farm-system fees. But Keltner was a twenty-five-thousand-dollar (plus two players) package.

Vitt met a measure of trouble in his first year. Solters, who had hit .323 the year before, fell off to .201. Averill traveled a breath-taking pace for half the season, batting close to .400, but he slumped to a final mark of .299, a drop of 99 points from his '37 average.

However, Keltner and Heath got away beautifully. Heath hit 21 home runs, drove in 112 runs, and compiled a .343 average. Keltner batted only .276, but he poled 26 home runs, many of them tremendous drives into the distant left-field bleachers in League Park. Trosky chipped in with .334, 19 home runs and 110 runs batted across. Feller won 17 games, while some promising new pitchers, Al Milnar, Johnny Humphries, and Denny Galehouse, brightened Vitt's days.

The Tribe stayed high in the 1938 race until July, then ran second until late in September, when it dropped to third. There was a new battery, Feller and Hemsley, but all was not peaceful in that department. Allen refused to pitch to anyone except Pytlak. Hemsley had been in a couple of jams because of drinking, and around the first of June he broke a finger, leaving Pytlak to do most of the catching, including Feller's games.

There were rumblings among the Indians, complaints about the way Vitt made public the troubles the players thought should be settled in the clubhouse. But Vitt liked to air his team's problems to reporters, and he was not bashful about taking a good, verbal rap at his men in print.

Somehow, Vitt's personality was beginning to inversely infect the squad. There were blowups between players and umpires. Vitt changed his line-up at the slightest provocation. But nothing helped. September was over, and second place had been muffed, the Red Sox moving up to finish behind the Yankees.

Only a farewell series with the Tigers remained, but the set of three games took on a light of importance because Hank Greenberg, the slugging Detroit first baseman, was chasing Babe Ruth's home-run record. Tall, handsome Hank had fifty-eight homers. He needed two to tie Ruth's record set in 1926. He needed three, one in each game, to surpass that mark.

Hank had everything going against him. One of the games was scheduled in League Park, with its left-field foul line 375 feet away from the right-handed-batting Greenberg. Hank starved against Denny Galehouse in the first game played there. Denny beat the Tigers, 5 to 0. That meant Greenberg had to hit his home runs in the Stadium in a Sunday double-header, and no park in all baseball haunted a slugger's dreams as did the lake-front arena with its acres of outfield space, or so it seemed to the batters.

Feller was chosen by Vitt to pitch the first game and aside from a normal desire to win another game, his eighteenth of the year, Bob had no special interest in the proceedings, least of all in Greenberg's home-run campaign. All Feller wanted to do was prevent home runs by any enemy batter, Greenberg or the rawest rookie up from Galveston.

The Detroit pitcher was Harry Eisenstat, a stocky left-hander with a tantalizing curve ball. Harry's forte was control. And he had enough in his heart to make up for the lack of a fast ball. Not many pitchers would have envied Eisenstat's position, facing the fireball rookie, Feller. Yet Harry was to gain a permanent place in baseball lore because of that day's events.

By the middle of the afternoon, a new strike-out record had been written for the record books. The Iowa farm boy, who wouldn't be twenty for a month yet, struck out eighteen batters to set a new all-time, all-major-league mark! Laabs whiffed five times and Eisenstat three. Every Detroit batter excepting Birdie Tebbetts and Roy Cullenbine was a victim.

No game like that one ever was pitched before, or since. Whatever glory there was in the final score went to Eisenstat, who was the winner, 4 to 1. And there were no home runs by Greenberg.

The man most dissatisfied with the Indians' showing in 1938 was Slapnicka. He was developing an intense hatred of Vitt. Much of this stemmed from Vitt's unwillingness to co-operate with box-office schemes devised by Slapnicka.

"You run the front office, and I'll run the ball club," Vitt told Slapnicka so reporters could hear. If his opinions of players could be public, so could be his thoughts on front-office personnel. Slapnicka burned. Yet Slap paid attention to his job, which was to build up the Indians. With Averill slipping and involved in an argument with Bradley over a bonus clause, outfield help was needed. Slap got Ben Chapman from the Red Sox for Denny Galehouse. Two new pitchers, Johnny Broaca and Joe Dobson, looked promising. Skeeter Webb added strength to the infield.

Then it looked as if Feller was ready to become of age as a big-league performer. He won twenty-four games while losing only nine and pitched more innings in 1939 than anyone in the league. Only a bunt single by Billy Sullivan of the Browns ruined Feller's best bid for a no-hitter that year. Slapnicka acquired Eisenstat in a swap for Averill. Luke Sewell and Oscar "Ski" Melillo joined Vitt's coaching staff. Altogether, the outlook was good.

But when the same old hot-weather slump set in, the fans began to carp at Bradley, Slapnicka, and Vitt. They were mad at Bradley and Slapnicka for trading Averill, one of the most popular players to put on a uniform in any big-league city. Vitt was under fire by press and public for his constant juggling of line-ups. Players were complaining to friends, and friends were relaying the beefs to the reporters, who printed them.

The Tribe's 1939 season was saved by two events, the first-night game in the Stadium and a late-season desperation maneuver designed to affect the box office. The new lights on top of the Stadium's horseshoe-shaped rim were ready on June 27. Feller and Bobo Newsom were the pitchers. The Indians won from the Tigers, 5 to 0, but that was a minor aspect of the nocturnal inaugural. Feller missed another no-hitter on a single by Averill, the Tribe discard.

To get the full story of the box-office maneuver mentioned in the above paragraph, it is necessary to go back to the time of the team's spring training in New Orleans. The New Orleans Club, managed by Roger Peckinpaugh, had a working agreement with the Tribe, and the teams trained together. To prove further that Cleveland baseball lures curious bedfellows, Steve O'Neill showed up there and spent some time working out before he was due to take over the management of the Buffalo Bisons of the International League. Two former Tribe managers, Peck and O'Neill, were now in perfect working accord with their old bosses.

Peck had first crack at Cleveland's surplus material. There were more second-base combinations than oyster shells in Heinemann Park. At least two of the duos were to be farmed out. One was composed of shortstop Frank Scalzi and second baseman Jim Shilling, the other of shortstop Lou Boudreau and second baseman Ray Mack.

"I'd like to have Scalzi and Shilling," O'Neill told Slapnicka. Steve's preference was understandable. He wanted to make a good showing at Buffalo, and Scalzi and Shilling looked to be a better bet because of their experience than the raw collegians, Boudreau and Mack, each with only part of a year of minor-league play under his belt.

But Peck also wanted Scalzi and Shilling. Because Peck was working indirectly for Cleveland, he got his wish. O'Neill had to take Boudreau and Mack.

Buffalo's first league game was with Toronto. Neither Boudreau nor Mack was outstanding. In fact, each was jittery. After the game, Steve called the youngsters to his room.

"I don't want you kids to worry about what happened to-day," he counseled. "You're my second-base combination, not only for tomorrow, but for the rest of the season. And you'll get to the majors. I'm sure of it."

In mid-July, Slapnicka telephoned O'Neill and told him he intended to transfer Boudreau and Mack to the Indians. O'Neill had to agree to the move. That was one of the conditions by which he was given the pair. He called Lou and Ray together before a game in Jersey City.

"Two weeks from today you two go up to Cleveland," he informed them. The day they were to leave Steve, the Bisons were in Syracuse. Under ordinary conditions, a young player getting a chance to go to the big time is overjoyed, nervous, or both. Boudreau and Mack were neither.

"We don't want to go, Steve," they argued. "We would rather stick out the season with you."

Needless to say, Steve wasn't happy either. Buffalo was only a game and a half out of first place. Without Boudreau and Mack, the Bisons were sure to slip. They did, and Buffalo fans howled. Slapnicka assigned Webb to Buffalo, but Skeeter claimed Slapnicka had given him a bum deal and threatened to quit baseball.

On August 7, Boudreau and Mack and Two-Ton Tony Galento were the special attractions under the Stadium arcs as the Indians met the Browns. Slapnicka had contracted for a personal appearance by Galento, a boxer of sorts, though the reason has escaped all known memories. The second-base combination put on a much better show.

From the moment he trotted out to shortstop for infield practice, Boudreau had the crowd in the palm of a right hand that was to become world famous. He had the movements of the natural athlete. He was graceful and commanding. Mack, much bigger but equally fast if not as flashy, worked beautifully with his partner.

The kids were terrific, and the Cleveland sports writers, who had gone to the park armed with hot adjectives to shove down Slapnicka's throat for hippodroming the grand, national sport, wound up instead writing glowing accounts of the rookies. Boudreau played in fifty-three games and batted only .258.

Mack, in thirty-six games, hit a paltry .152. No one cared much what they hit. Their arrival gave the entire team a lift.

But there was trouble brewing. Cleveland correspondents with the team wrote of impending disaster. Vitt battled with some of his men, threatened to get rid of the malcontents. Yet in their last trip through the East, the Tribe won nine of eleven games.

Third place was accepted without much argument mostly because it looked like a sure pennant in 1940, regardless of any fights between Vitt and players or Vitt and newspapermen.

The Indians' opener in 1940 was in Chicago. Each of the writers traveling with the ball club received a telephone summons by Rollie Hemsley. "Meet me on the hotel mezzanine," he asked. Everyone did.

"It's been just a year now since the most wonderful thing in the world happened to me," he began, "so I feel safe in telling you boys about it. You know I didn't have a drink all last season. Well, Alcoholics Anonymous did that for me. I'd like to give credit to this great organization and you'll do me a favor by writing a story about A. A."

The whisky blush was gone from Rollie's face. His eyes were clear, his speech rational. How different from the Hemsley the boys knew a couple of years earlier, or the talented backstop who drank himself off the Pirates, Cubs, Reds, and Browns.

Just after Rollie joined the Indians in the Spring of '38, he bashed a bureau drawer over the head of a photographer in New Orleans. Later in the year he got in a fight in St. Louis, then one in Cleveland. He wound up invariably with black eyes and hangovers.

No wilder night in a Pullman could be imagined than the one celebrated by Rollicking Rollie as the Indians and New York Giants were nearing the end of their spring exhibition series in 1939. Rollie picked up a full head of steam before boarding the teams' special train in Richmond, Virginia. He bumped into the large and playful Jim Dawson, esteemed and personable *New York Times* correspondent, who traveled with some strange contents in his suitcases. At the moment, Dawson's prize possession was a trumpet.

Hemsley and Dawson conducted a two-man parade the length of the train. The hour was one of sleep, it said on the training bulletins. The late Lewis Mumaw, traveling secretary of the Indians in 1939, stuck his head out of an upper berth and complained about the noise.

"Oh, you've got a beef," said Hemsley. "We'll fix that."

Whereupon Rollicking Rollie yanked back the curtain and proceeded to toss lighted matches on the bunk. Later he returned with cupfuls of water and threw those inside the berth.

"We'll have to put out the fire," he yelled at Mumaw, who by that time was demanding help.

At the termination of that spring tour, Hemsley was met by Slapnicka and two strangers, nameless men who represented Alcoholics Anonymous. They took Hemsley to Akron and started him through their mental mill.

Results were 100 per cent.

The Indians were national favorites to win their first pennant since 1920 as the '40 campaign got under way. At the insistence of O'Neill, the Tribe had bought a chunky left-handed pitcher, Al Smith, from Buffalo, though Slapnicka stubbornly held off until the last minute. Smith won sixteen games against two losses at Buffalo. Boudreau was a sure bet at short, with Mack or Grimes at second. Keltner already was an established star at third, and the veteran Trosky held forth at first. The others, Hemsley, Pytlak, Heath, Chapman, Weatherly, Beau Bell (acquired for Bruce Champbell), Allen, Broaca, Dobson, Eisenstat, Feller, Harder, Humphries, Milnar, and Zuber, gave the Tribe its greatest strength in fifteen years.

Then the amazing Feller started off with a no-hit game! Bob beat the elements and the White Sox to record the first hitless opening game in history. With the temperatures in the thirties and with Hemsley behind the plate, Feller mowed down the White Sox batter after batter. Heath's single and Hemsley's triple provided the only run of the game, but it took a miracle play by Mack to preserve the classic for Bob.

With two out in the ninth, Luke Appling, the finest exponent of intentional fouling of pitches the game ever knew, fouled off ten before he drew a pass. Taft "Taffy" Wright, burly outfielder and left-handed batter, hit a wicked grounder between first and second. Mack sped to his left, scooped up the ball in his gloved hand, and flipped it to Trosky to complete a truly remarkable play. No one was more glad to see that performance than Feller.

Yet there were less glorious days ahead. Vitt was despised by most of the Redskins. His tongue continued to wag in criticism of his players. Oscar Grimes was struck in the face by a line drive during batting practice, and the bone structure of his left cheek was shattered.

Even so, the Tribe was within a game or two of first place right along. But nothing could break the tension each player could feel in the dugout. Players spoke to Vitt only when it was necessary. There were small gatherings in hotel rooms at night. The storm was gathering, slowly but surely.

There was nearly an eruption in Yankee Stadium early in June. Big Al Milnar pitched a fine 3-to-0 shutout of the Yanks, but Feller and Smith lost one-run decisions. The team's spirit was lower than ever as the move was made up the coast to Boston.

In the opening game in Fenway Park, Feller was the starting pitcher, and he took a number of bumps. The Red Sox were teeing off on Bob when Vitt is said to have cracked, "There's my star out there, the great Feller. How can I win a pennant with him?"

Word spread among the players quickly that Vitt had hit the jackpot in his criticisms of his own players. So that night, half a dozen of the older men decided to swing into action.

Frank Gibbons, king-size baseball writer for the *Cleveland Press*, was standing outside the Hotel Kenmore when Trosky approached.

"How about a walk, Frank, I want to talk to you."

The pair sauntered down Commonwealth Avenue to a pub, and over a beer Trosky asked sharply, "What do you think of Vitt?"

Gibbons ducked neatly and said he had formed some opinions. "Why?" he countered.

"We think he's impossible," Trosky declared. "We're thinking of going to Alva Bradley and asking him to fire Vitt."

Gibbons counseled patience. As a newspaperman, he envisioned a tremendous story. But as an individual, he foresaw the penalty to the players if their request ever got to the public.

"Why not wait a few days and then see what happens?" Gibbons advised. Trosky agreed. But the next afternoon the Red Sox swamped the Tribe again, and when the team boarded the train for Cleveland, there was no holding the athletes. They were determined to get Vitt.

It was decided, during a meeting on the train, to pay a formal call on Bradley the next day. Some of the Indians were not included in the organization plans. Boudreau and Mack were dismissed because of their youth, Bell because he had just joined the team. One or two of the others, notably Roy Weatherly, backed away from participation.

Harder, who had engaged in an argument with Vitt in the last game in Boston because Mel resented a slur on his endeavor, was to be spokesman. He called Bradley early the following morning, June 13.

"May I come in to see you?" asked Harder. Bradley, whose door was always open to his players and employees, told him to come in.

Within an hour, a dozen players made their appearance at the President's door. Harder was in the lead.

"Well, come in. What's this all about?" Bradley asked. He thought Harder was coming alone, perhaps on personal business. Mel stated the player's case.

"We think we've got a good chance to win this pennant, Mr. Bradley," he began. "But we'll never win it with Vitt as manager. If we can get rid of him, we can win. We all feel sure of that."

The veteran pitcher detailed the general complaints: that Vitt sneered at his players on the field, that he was double-dealing with them, praising or carping first one then another according to his immediate whim, that he held them up to ridicule before the press, that he held grudges and undermined their confidence.

At that point the telephone rang.

"Mr. Bradley, this is Hal Trosky. I just want to tell you

that I'm 100 per cent in favor of the story you're now hearing. Those are my sentiments without qualification."

The blond first baseman, ringleader in the revolution, was at the airport about to board a plane for his home in Iowa. When he arrived in Cleveland that morning, he was notified of his mother's death. So the others—Hale, Feller, Grimes, Heath, Milnar, and Hemsley among them—carried on.

Bradley looked out the window after hearing their story.

"How many people other than your group know this story?" he asked. Harder said some of the newspapermen were aware of trouble, though not in full possession of the details.

"If this story ever gets out, you'll be ridiculed the rest of your life," Bradley warned. Then he dismissed the players, advising them to play their best, and promising they would hear from him later.

As the last broad back disappeared, Bradley turned to his secretary, Catherine Kelly, and said, "Miss Kelly, those boys don't know what they're starting. They're in for a lot of grief."

An hour later, just before noon, Bradley's telephone jangled again. The caller was Gordon Cobbledick, baseball writer for the *Cleveland Plain Dealer*. Almost word for word, he repeated the complaints the players had put before Bradley.

"Is that what they said?" asked Cobbledick. Bradley had to admit the accuracy. Someone—the best guess always was Hemsley—tipped off the morning-paper scribe, and he sat down to write the story.

The man who was not tipped off was Gibbons. He had arranged with Trosky for a telephone call immediately after the meeting, verifying the visit to Bradley, so that Gibbons could break the story in that afternoon's editions of the *Press*. But Trosky, in his haste to fly to Iowa, did not reach Gibbons, and the reporter didn't know until too late that the group had met with Bradley.

Paris fell to the Germans that June 13, but you never would have suspected it from the front page of the next morning's *Plain Dealer*. So wary of a leak to a wire service or a radio station was the *Plain Dealer* that the story of the rebellion was held out of every edition until the final.

Then it got the full treatment, eight-column headlines and foot after foot of type.

There never had been a story like it. The tag "Cry Babies" was attached to the Indians immediately. Their load was not lightened on June 16 when they signed a "truce" on Cleveland Baseball Club stationery in the clubhouse. The statement read: "We the undersigned publicly desire to withdraw all statements referring to the resignation of Oscar Vitt. We feel this action is for the betterment of the Cleveland Baseball Club."

They may have signed that paper, but they didn't believe it. Bradley told them in a clubhouse meeting it would be a good idea. The strained feeling between Vitt and his players remained, though it was a different type now. Vitt became silent and spoke to his men only when conversation was necessary.

Ten days later, the Tribe was back in first place, had won twelve of the last fifteen games, and was two and a half games ahead of the Tigers. By August 22, the Indians took what most teams would consider a safe lead. They were five and a half games ahead of the Tigers, eight ahead of Boston, and nine in front of the Yankees.

Shortly before this period, Vitt had asked Slapnicka to get an outfielder from the Louisville club. Slapnicka, who was generally suspected of encouraging, if not actually instigating, the revolution, couldn't or didn't acquire the player, and Vitt just about gave up.

The torrid race turned into September. The Indians were in Detroit after losing four straight. A meeting was held in Allen's room. The leaders, Allen and Hemsley, decided that the team wasn't using the hit-and-run play enough. Reporters heard the next day that a second set of signals, unknown to Vitt, had been agreed upon by the insurrectionists.

In the next two weeks, the Indians tottered and finally surrendered the lead to Detroit on September 12. The Yankees came to the stadium that day, and the particular "hate" of Cleveland fans was coaching at third base as usual. That was Art Fletcher, who had been subjected to a barrage of fruit and vegetables. There had been trouble between the Yanks and Indians earlier in the year, mostly because of a squabble featuring Milnar and Earl Combs, the New York first-base coach.

Milnar challenged Combs to a fight after he suspected Earl was signaling to the batter on each pitch.

The Indians arrived in Detroit for the last time the night of September 19. No group was ever received with a more diversified bombardment. Five thousand fans were at the station. When the Indians walked up the ramp and through the station foyer, they were hit with tomatoes, eggs, lemons, and other edibles. Shouts of "Cry Babies" came from everywhere. The next afternoon, bottles bearing nipples were dangled from the upper deck in Briggs Stadium in front of the Cleveland dugout.

The bitter rivals were in an exact deadlock, but not for long. Mel Harder, who had held the Tigers for seven and a third innings, was yanked by Vitt, who called in Feller. Harder seemed to be in command of the situation, but with Greenberg coming up and two on, Vitt decided that Feller might be a better bet. Feller was tired out from earlier pitching and had told Vitt so. Big Hank singled and later scored the tying run. It was the hit that broke the Tribe's back. The Tigers went on to win, 6 to 5, and Vitt took a bad roasting in the Cleveland papers.

Exactly one week later, the Tigers went to Cleveland for a do-or-die series as far as Cleveland was concerned. The Tigers had everything in their favor. They were two full games ahead. That meant the Indians had to sweep the three games. All were scheduled in the Stadium. Feller was a sure bet to start the opener.

So the night before, Manager Del Baker of the Bengals called a meeting of his older players.

"This is your dough as well as mine," he said. "What should we do about the Feller game, pitch one of our regulars, or hold them back in case we lose?"

Most of the Tigers went along with Baker on his choice of Floyd Giebell, a right-hander with limited big-league experience. Only Greenberg held out for someone else. He wanted Hal Newhouser or Freddy Hutchinson.

It was Ladies Day and 45,533 persons were in the stands. Thousands of the women were armed with fruit, vegetables, and other throwable objects. They held their fire until the last half of the first inning. Then, as Greenberg circled under a fly

Dale Mitchell © The Cleveland Indians

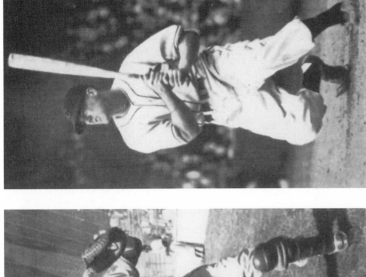

Jim Hegan © The Cleveland Indians

Ken Keltner © The Cleveland Press

Bill Veeck

hit by Weatherly, the dames pitched. Somehow, in the shower, Greenberg held onto the ball, but left field resembled a vegetable patch. Umpire Bill Summers grabbed the public address microphone near the Cleveland dugout and pleaded for order. So did Vitt.

The game was resumed, but there was an interruption and a dangerous accident in left field. Sitting in the Tigers' bull pen were catcher Birdie Tebbetts, pitcher Schoolboy Rowe, and a couple of others. Sitting in an upstairs box directly over the bull pen was an ice peddler. He had gone to the park equipped with a basket of bottles and fruit. He calmly dropped his bomb of groceries over the side, and the blow conked out Tebbetts. Birdie recovered, and as cops were leading the culprit out of the park, Tebbetts took a swing at his tormentor.

Rudy York also took a swing. He picked on one of Feller's pitches and hit a high fly ball to left field. But this one was right down the 320-foot line, and it fell into the seats for a home run, a freak round-tripper in the toughest park in the game in which to hit for the circuit! Charley Gehringer was on base, but the one run would have been enough.

Giebell, the rookie, beat Feller, 2 to 0, and the maddest pennant race in Cleveland's history was ended.

CHAPTER XXV

THE BOY MANAGER

FIFTEEN MINUTES AFTER the last out of the last game in 1940, Oscar Vitt walked around in the Stadium's clubhouse. He shook hands with player after player, even with Hal Trosky and Rollie Hemsley and Mel Harder and Bob Feller, the men he knew had hated him. Then he went outside and climbed into an automobile. With his wife, always a strong force in his battles, beside him, he drove away.

Not many principals in Cleveland baseball missed him. One who did was Ed McAuley of the *News*. When the Indians lined up against Vitt, so did the writers on the *Plain Dealer* and the *Press*. McAuley strung along with Vitt, not necessarily because he favored Vitt but because he believed that some time he might get Vitt's own story of the rebellion. Other reporters heard McAuley had been given such a promise.

In fact, Ed was all set to hear from Vitt's lips the curse of his aching heart. But Ol' Os had other commitments in California. McAuley never got his story or even a telephone call from Vitt.

Everyone knew that the little man was finished in Cleveland. Speculation over his successor was limited because (1) the city's loyal baseball followers were still crushed under the 1940 calamity, (2) there was increasing talk of war because of registrations for the military draft, and (3) Luke Sewell seemed to be a natural choice.

On November 12, Bradley invited the baseball writers and radio newsmen to luncheon at Kornman's Restaurant, a downtown sports headquarters and, incidentally, located in a Bradley-owned building.

It was, as Frank Gibbons put it humorously in the *Press* that day, "so quiet you could hear a herring drop." And it was about that quiet a few minutes later when Bradley said, "Roger Peckinpaugh is our new manager." Inasmuch as Peck had been sitting at the table for an hour, his appointment was not exactly a roaring surprise.

Bradley said privately that Sewell had been passed over because of a fear of public criticism. Luke had been the favorite of the players in 1940. He was their choice to replace Vitt at the time of the call on Bradley. Sewell stayed on as a coach under Peckinpaugh but was to go to St. Louis as manager of the Browns later in the season.

Peck, fired by Bradley eight years earlier, got to work with Slapnicka to strengthen the team that finished only one game out of first place the previous autumn. They traded Dobson, Pytlak, and Hale to the Red Sox for pitcher Jim Bagby, catcher Gene Desautels, and outfielder Gerald "Gee" Walker. A number of promising rookies were in the camp at Fort Myers, Florida, the next spring. Among them were catcher Jim Hegan, infielder Bob Lemon, pitcher Joe Krakauskas, pitcher Mike Naymick, outfielder Clarence "Soup" Campbell, shortstop Jack Conway, and pitcher Pete Center.

"We should win this race," Peck told the reporters off the record. "We've got the best team in the league."

A note of warning was sounded by Connie Mack in Cleveland early in the 1941 season. The late Rt. Rev. Msgr. Joseph F. Smith, pastor of St. John's Cathedral, was holding his fourteenth annual dinner in honor of the venerable manager of the Athletics. Invitations to the Monsignor's dinners were eagerly sought. Mack always made a spirited talk during which he referred to Boudreau (pronounced Bud-row) as "Bore-due." Bradley was eulogized by the cleric, who in turn confessed that he was probably the best grandstand manager in the entire diocese.

"This will be a seven-team race," Mack declared. "We're out of it, but every other team has a chance."

The Indians were in the race until June. Then Trosky's migraine headaches drove him to distraction. Loss of the big slugger was felt keenly. Heath staged a remarkable and commendable comeback, turning in a .340 average after a .219 season under Vitt in '40. Big Milnar, who plugged his way to eighteen victories in the rebellion year, fell down to twelve.

Harder was slipping. Feller's twenty-five victories were admirable but couldn't support an entire team.

The Yankees, driving hard under the impetus of Joe Di Maggio's great batting streak, pushed the Indians out of first place and were never headed thereafter. Di Maggio started his streak on May 15. In each of the next fifty-six games, the famed Yankee Clipper hit safely. The old record tumbled many games earlier. As Di Maggio went, so went the Yankees. They were unstoppable.

On July 16, the period's best road attraction in baseball, Di Maggio, came to Cleveland. He had hit in his fifty-fifth game in Chicago the day before, getting a single on an infield scratch. But in number fifty-six, Joltin' Joe belted Milnar for two hits and Krakauskas for one. That made fifty-six games, and the figures for those are astounding. The average was .408, computed on fifteen home runs, four triples, sixteen doubles, and fifty-six singles!

The largest turnout in the history of night baseball, 67,468, was banked around the stadium in the evening heat of July 17. Al Smith, left-hander who specialized in a screwball pitch—one that broke in on right-handed batters—faced Di Maggio in the first inning. Joe sent a screaming grounder over the third-base bag.

Ken Keltner backhanded the ball with his glove hand, straightened up, and whipped the ball to first. In a later inning, Di Maggio again pulled the ball down the third-base line. And again Keltner made the play "after the ball was past him," as observers said later, to throw out the sweating Californian. In the ninth, Di Maggio made his final bid. Bagby had replaced Smith. Joe sent a terrific smash to shortstop. The ball was hit so hard that Boudreau barely got his glove on the ball, but scooped it up and started a double play.

Maddest man in the ball park was Lefty Gomez, the Yankees' colorful left-hander.

"I'm gonna find that cabbie who brought me down to the park," he yelled. "That dirty heel said Di Mag would be stopped tonight."

Two and one half months later, the Indians, pennant favorites in the spring, finished in a tie for fourth place, having lost four more games than they won.

Within a few weeks after the end of the season, Slapnicka resigned as assistant to President Bradley. He had spent six grueling years in office. He had shaken off one heart attack. The years with Vitt had been hectic. Slapnicka, a superior judge of baseball flesh, never mastered the art of public relations.

Peck stepped up to Slap's job, and for the sixteenth time in the club's history, a new manager had to be appointed.

No narration of the Bradley-Evans-Slapnicka-Peckinpaugh regime in Cleveland baseball would be complete without reference to the eccentrics who zoomed, floated, or slid in and out of the Indians' family over a fifteen-year period.

Reporters still say that only Buck Newsom and Boots Poffenberger, among the game's quaint participants, missed Cleveland. The Indians had most of the others.

Before he joined Alcoholics Anonymous, Hemsley was probably the prize exhibit. Yet his catching buddy, Pytlak, was one to pack up and go home to Buffalo at the slightest whim, leaving behind a salary of perhaps nine thousand dollars per year in order to sit in his parlor and blow or strum the many musical instruments he cherished.

Weatherly, the drawling Texan, was the top umpire baiter of his day. His remarks to the gentlemen in blue cost him many dollars and frequent banishments. During one game in Cleveland, when Little Stormy was being kicked out of a game by Umpire Brick Owens, Roy's father, up from Pineland, Texas, charged onto the field and challenged the arbiter.

There was the inimitable Heath, who remains the enigma of all baseball players. He should have been one of the greatest players in history. But there were no valves on his temper. He grinned in the manner of a schoolboy or he snarled with the viciousness of a tiger. Once Heath and Broaca staged a fake fight on the bench. They were close friends, so everyone was surprised when Heath swung on the Yale product in the limited confines of a dugout. Heath later admitted he had hoped to catch Vitt with the wild swing.

A glance over the list tells its own story: Ferrell, the hot-headed genius who had a mad desire to win in everything, Allen the trigger-tempered, Broadway Lyn Lary, Scrappy Roy Hughes, Harley Boss, Moose Solters, whose interpretation of a football game O'Neill interrupted one night in Washington, Playboy Eddie Morgan, Cissell, Sarge Connolly, Bob Holland, Hildebrand, rebellious Ben Chapman, Pinky Shoffner, Dancing Boze Berger, Nate Andrews, Jimmy Zinn, Young Jim Bagby, trainer Weisman, Chubby Dean, Joe Heving, Oris Hockett, Good-time Roy Cullenbine, Fabian Gaffke, and unpredictable Pat Seerey.

Through the portals of Cleveland baseball passed most of the screwballs in the game, and many stayed for dinner.

Other than the night watchman, two cats, and an occasional stray executive who might want to type a personal letter in privacy, the dingy offices of the Indians in League Park hadn't had an after-dark visitor in years. So considerable surprise was expressed by newsmen when Alva Bradley summoned them to a night press conference in the ancient offices on November 25, 1941.

The reporters didn't know who might emerge from the cob-webs and closets, but they knew they were about to meet or see or hear about another new manager. The day had long passed when Cleveland reporters got excited about new managers. There were too many.

The scribes were in an outer room. A door was opened and out stepped Bradley, wearing his best smile.

"Gentlemen, meet the new manager," he said proudly.

Behind him was Louis Boudreau, Jr., twenty-four years old. Managing a major-league baseball team had been considered a job for a mature man. There were some exceptions, Bucky Harris and Joe Cronin, but Boudreau was beating their course record by several years.

On second thought, the Cleveland reporters weren't as surprised as they could have been. They saw Boudreau play through two full seasons in the big time. They saw him developing into not only a master shortstop, but a dangerous batsman and a sterling competitor. From the first minute he wore a

Cleveland uniform, in August of 1939, Lou Boudreau was the key man in the field. He was a magnet drawing to him all the responsibilities and requests for judgment usually reserved for gray managers sitting in the shade of the dugout.

Newspaper comment throughout the nation was bitter or facetious, in spite of the general acceptance of the appointment in Cleveland. The only complaints heard there were in the form of fears that the worries of managing might hamper Lou's shortstopping.

But across Lake Erie, a Detroit newspaper wept openly on its editorial page: "Being made manager of that outfit after two years in the majors and having to face the irascible Cleveland public and a press box full of second guessers is enough to warrant calling out the Society for the Prevention of Cruelty to Children."

Boudreau wasn't worried half as much as the commentators. In the first place, he asked for the job! The idea was put in his head a full year earlier by this historian. "If Clark Griffith owned the Indians, he would put Boudreau in charge of the team even if he were only 23 years old," it was written. Griffith, Washington president, was the man who appointed the first two so-called boy managers, Harris and Cronin.

Bradley read some immediate criticism of himself in the light that he was trying to save one salary by combining the jobs of shortstop and manager. Actually Bradley was strongly opposed to the appointment of Boudreau because of his youth.

Boudreau's name was proposed officially the first time by George A. Martin, a club director. Bradley and Martin, golf cronies, discussed their team's managerial candidates from tee to green day after day.

"Boudreau is the greatest shortstop in the world, George," argued Bradley. "I'm not going to ruin his career by burdening him with the problems of managing."

Martin snorted. "He's practically been the manager right along," he pointed out. "Besides, he was the captain or leader of every team he ever played on. That boy's a natural."

Bradley won out. He didn't consider Boudreau old enough for the responsibilities. Alva turned to Branch Rickey for advice, and the famous double-talking executive recommended elderly, smooth Burt Shotton, then at his winter home in Florida.

Bradley called Peck. "You might start down to Florida and have a talk with Burt Shotton," he suggested. Peck was barely outside the city limits when Bradley received a long-distance call from Boudreau.

"I'd like to come to Cleveland and talk to you about the manager's job," Lou said. "I think I can handle it." Bradley told him to come ahead.

Meanwhile, Bradley called a meeting of club directors. He put all his cards on the table.

"Boudreau wants this job, but I don't think he's old enough," said Alva. "However, I'm open to suggestions."

The directors, few of whom knew anything about baseball, favored the young star they had watched from their box seats. He was a captivating player, handsome and alert.

"All right, I'll go along with you on Boudreau if we can protect him with older coaches," Bradley agreed. A telegram reached Peck as his train was nearing Florida. "Hold off on Shotton," the message ordered.

Bradley sat down with Boudreau.

"Lou, we're going to try you in this job, but I'm going to insist upon the best possible protection. I'm going to name your coaches, because I want older men with you."

For twenty-five thousand dollars a year, Lou was more than willing to accept the advice of oldsters. Peck got a second order, to sign Shotton as a coach. Del Baker, former manager of the Tigers, was added.

The Boy Manager was off in a cloud of baseball brains!

The leading citizen of Harvey, Illinois, was born in that industrial community, thirty miles south of Chicago's loop, on July 17, 1917. His father was French, his mother German. Lou, the boy, never was to learn to speak French despite the Parisian aspect to his name. He was too busy outdoors, for one thing.

As a grammar-school fledgling, Lou was a catcher.

"Lou, if you like baseball so much and if you ever expect to

Lou Boudreau fires to first for a double play.

Bob Lemon

get any place, get out from behind that plate. Try the infield. You'll get your fingers broken catching."

So the Boudreaus, father and son, retired to the corner lot for practice. The father had been a semipro third baseman, and he wanted young Lou to be a third baseman. About that time, another father was playing catch with his boy out in Iowa, people by the name of Feller.

Soon young Lou broke away from the tutoring of his father, who could spare only limited time away from his machines in one of Harvey's large plants. Perhaps this is one of the factors in the early development of leadership in Boudreau. At the age of thirteen, he coached the grammar-school basketball team. He also coached and managed an amateur basketball team in the town.

A favorite debate in Harvey was whether Lou Boudreau was a better basketball or baseball player. He gained much more notice on the hardwood because school baseball, in Harvey as in many cities, is a secondary sport. But Harvey was immensely proud of its basketball team and of its star, Lou.

Harvey won one state championship and was runner-up twice in the three years young Boudreau played. Lou did better than his team. He made the all-state honorary five three years in a row! No wonder the University of Illinois wanted him. And Lou, of course, wanted to go to the state university. Most kids do.

But there were problems. The Boudreau family was poor. Lou was torn between seeking a college education and seeking a job in professional baseball. He decided to try the latter first and worked out with the Chicago White Sox. No one looked closely at the Harvey flash. His feelings were a little hurt for he was a big man in Harvey. Lou walked out of Comiskey Park and never went back until he wore the uniform of the Cleveland Indians.

There was only one place he could go now, to the university. Friends helped him get a small scholarship. Still, no kid could play basketball and live on a pittance. A scout for the Indians had been watching Lou. The scout wanted to make sure Cleveland would have first call on the young infielder's services after college.

An agreement was reached whereby Lou's mother was to be paid one hundred dollars per month by the Indians. In exchange, the youngster would join the Tribe upon graduation. The plan worked for a couple of years. It wasn't new or novel then or now. Boudreau played so spectacularly as a sophomore on the varsity basketball team that he gained national attention. And as if to emphasize his qualities of leadership, his teammates elected him their captain for the following year when Lou would be a mere junior!

Somebody talked and Major John L. Griffith, commissioner of athletics for the Western Conference, heard of the hundred-dollars payments to Mrs. Boudreau. It seemed Lou's college career was at an end, though he could have repudiated his agreement with the Indians, remained in school, and been made eligible for sports the following year.

Lou stayed at the university through his junior year, then reported to the Indians, who assigned him to the Cedar Rapids team in the Three-Eye League. He hit a moderately impressive .290 as a third baseman and reported back to the Tribe. That was in 1938 and if there was one thing the Indians did not need, it was another third baseman. Ken Keltner, in his first year, was a national sensation.

From that time on, Lou Boudreau was a shortstop.

Two weeks after he became manager of the Indians, the United States almost lost Pearl Harbor and Lou Boudreau lost half his baseball team. For on December 9, 1941, two days after Pearl Harbor, Bob Feller enlisted in the Navy. Hal Trosky retired to his farm.

Wartime baseball and all its bloodless horror became a reality.

BASEBALL, WAR BRAND

BEFORE BOUDREAU COULD sketch a plan for his first big-league product, players began dropping off the roster in bunches at the command or suggestion of their draft boards. Of those who remained, most had recurrent miseries in their legs or arms or hearts.

The Boy Manager himself was an immediate 4-F because of one arthritic ankle and another that was just plain weak. Countless poundings on basketball floors had taken their toll and had led to a new descriptive phrase for Boudreau. He became known as the only great athlete who ever walked on the outside of his ankles.

Lou became known, also, as a major-league manager who had lots to learn, especially in the matters of handling press relations and his own men. At the outset of spring training in 1942, Lou called a meeting of the reporters assigned to regular travel with the Tribe. It was, in fact, his first press conference.

"I'd like to suggest that in the future you gentlemen show me your stories before they go in the papers," he requested. "In that way, nothing will appear that will be detrimental to the ball club."

Gordon Cobbledick of the *Plain Dealer* choked on a piece of herring.

"Look, Lou," Cobby admonished. "You run the ball club, we'll write the stories. And while we're on the subject, we all wish you would quit referring to us as 'your newspapermen.' We work for our papers, not the Cleveland Indians."

In the next six weeks, Boudreau was too busy with his whistle, charts, and other accessories in physical training to fret much about press relations. Chances are he never thought of them. Now the conditioning period was ended and the ball club was starting north. There was a spirit of apprehension among all. The war was getting a good start, and baseball's future was as uncertain as the next day's railroad schedules.

Boudreau and his ever present coaches, Baker, Shotton, and Susce, were at one end of a dining car. Players occupied nearly all the other seats. Some of them stole glances at the slim, dark Boudreau, no more than a baseball adolescent in full command of thirty players, twenty-five of whom were his senior. This was no college basketball team whose members might be awaiting eagerly each order of the leader. This was a big-league ball club, tough and old. Snide remarks, directed at "the kid," were common.

It was in this setting that Boudreau was compelled to make his first decision in team deportment. Jeff Heath, laughing and muscular, pelted Jim Bagby, the irascible Georgian, on the back of the head with hard rolls. Whenever Bagby turned in an attempt to catch his tormentor, Heath feigned innocence. Eventually, of course, Bagby caught Heath in the act. Jim picked up a glass of water and doused Heath with the contents. Jeff doubled his fists and a few pugnacious advances were made.

Boudreau who had been observing the fracas in silence, barked, "All right, that's enough. Now sit down, both of you, before I have to pass out some fines."

With that, Boudreau turned to Frank Gibbons and sighed, "I suppose this will be in the papers." Gibbons shook his head.

"Not unless you fine them," he corrected. "You see, Lou, reporters don't print everything they see or hear when they're living, eating, and sleeping with ball players. Only if you fine someone does it become news."

Boudreau's first entry in the American League derby was a pretty good aggregation "on paper." There was balance in the pitching staff, with Bagby, Harder, Eisenstat, Smith, Kennedy, Milnar, and others of comparable reputation on deck. The veteran DeSautels was a first-rate catcher while three quarters of a prewar infield—Boudreau, Keltner, and Mack—could be called upon.

But Trosky's retirement cost the Tribe its big punch. Feller's enlistment eliminated the key winner. By midseason, the Indians had been outclassed by the Yankees. Cleveland was resigned to another fourth-place team, but the appetite of the city's fans certainly was not impaired by the Indians' failures.

The year's largest crowd, 62,094, was in the Municipal Stadium the night of July 7 to watch a special exhibition game between the American League All-Stars and the Great Lakes varsity, managed by Mickey Cochrane and starring Feller. The turnout was especially sweet to the Cleveland sports writers, who had taken over promotion of the game. The scribes imported a full-scale war show and, with the help of Alva Bradley, almost doubled the size of the crowd that had watched the American League all-star team beat the National League squad in New York the previous evening.

The Allies were gaining ground in Europe and in the Pacific, but the Indians couldn't pick up an inch in the American League during the war years. Adhering to Landis' ban on southern travel, the Indians did their 1943 training in Purdue University's tremendous field house in West Lafayette, Ind. Peck traded Weatherly and Grimes to the Yankees for Roy Cullenbine and Warren "Buddy" Rosar. Bagby enjoyed his second straight seventeen-victory season, but the Yankees and Senators nosed out the Tribe.

The Boy Manager hit .327 and won the individual batting championship in 1944, but nothing could save the Indians by then, and they tied with the Athletics for fifth. Not only was Boudreau learning how to hit; he was learning how to manage. Some of his lessons were stiff and disagreeable. He had run-ins with Bagby, Heath, Cullenbine, Klieman, and Hockett. There were other individual cases. Collectively, the Indians confessed one major complaint about Boudreau. The kid pilot refused to associate with his players off the field. He was their teammate in uniform, but in street clothes he ate, talked, and traveled only with his coaches.

The 1945 Indians were probably the best of Boudreau's wartime teams. Late in April, between games of a double-header with Detroit, the Tribe traded Cullenbine for Dutch Meyer and Don Ross to afford new and needed protection at second and third bases. Mickey Rocco was more than adequate at first now that Les Fleming was in a shipyard. Paul O'Dea, whose promising career as a batter had been stopped by a serious eye injury, joined with Hockett, Heath, and Seerey in the outfield.

On May 29, Peckinpaugh swapped Rosar to the Athletics for Frank Hayes, even up. The sturdy Hayes was the top work horse of all catchers. He caught the final two games of the 1943 season for the Browns. Then the Browns sent him back to the Athletics, from whom they got him in the first place, and Hayes caught 155 games in a row for the Mackmen in 1944. He had caught 32 games consecutively at the time of the trade with Cleveland.

But before the full impact of Hayes' addition and other changes could be felt, Boudreau broke his right ankle. The Indians collapsed. Hayes tried his best to steady a wavering pitching staff (Frank caught 119 more games in a row and 4 more early in 1946 to achieve a total of 312 for an all-time record) but Boudreau's absence was too costly. The Tribe skidded, then fell apart. From a contender it became a sub-average wartime nine.

When the Japs quit on August 14, 1945, the Indians were in fifth place. Among the millions itching to peel off their uniforms was Feller. He was separated in Chicago almost immediately. The erstwhile boy wonder, now a man, had served forty-four months, and had earned eight battle stars as a gunnery specialist on the U.S.S. *Alabama.*

But could he still pitch?

That question was on a million tongues in Cleveland. Not that he was too old, for he was not yet twenty-seven. But the Army and Navy did strange things to athletes, especially boxers and baseball players.

Feller answered the question in person the night of August 24. A crowd of 46,477 wanted to see what the Navy had done to the strike-out king. It couldn't have hurt much. Bob struck out a dozen Tigers and won, 4 to 2, over his number-one mound rival, Hal Newhouser.

Feller won four more games before the close of the year, but not even his return was enough of an inspirational force to offset Boudreau's absence. The Boy Manager's ankle remained in a cast until almost the close of the campaign. Gromek won nineteen games and Reynolds eighteen. Heath hit .305 to set the pace for such wartime regulars as Ross, Meyer, Felix Mackiewicz, and Ed Carnett. Fleming returned late in the year to hit .329, but by then the Tribe was mired in fifth, four and a half games behind the fourth-place Yankees.

Peck and Boudreau put their opinions together in early October, and heads started to roll. The Boy Manager was not especially fond of Heath, Bagby, Hayes, and a few others. Heath went to Washington in exchange for George Case, the erstwhile base-stealing champion whose knee injury had become chronic. Bagby was swapped back to the Red Sox for a left-hander, Vic Johnson. Hayes didn't go until mid-1946, but his ticket was punched long before. Don Black was bought from the A's.

Prewar stars were coming back, and soon the brand of baseball would be improved. The big leagues would be the big leagues again, on the field and off. Gone were spring-training restrictions put into effect by Landis. Forgotten were intercity trips in open-window day coaches. No more lining up in front of smart-aleck hotel room clerks. Once more a fellow could ride to the ball-park entrance in a taxicab.

But best of all, to the wartime ballplayer, no more 4-F cracks! They dug deeper than spikes.

Happy days were ahead in 1946, happy days and fateful days.

No one, not even the wildest of the fanatics who lived and died with Cleveland teams in the prewar races, was brash enough to suggest a pennant for the Tribe in 1946. This was a departure from custom, to say the least, and a welcome one. It meant that Boudreau could start a season with the knowledge that no matter what he did, or how his team fared, there would be a minimum of criticism. He and the Indians had everything to gain and nothing to lose as they reported in Clearwater. After three years of training in field houses, or sweating out life and death in foxholes, the Indians greeted the Florida spring sun with open shirts.

But typical of Cleveland baseball, no spring could pass without a rhubarb. For once, Boudreau wasn't involved. The Boy Manager had broadened his viewpoints considerably since 1942. He'd learned how to meet situations, and neither his tongue nor the fines that tolled off it were as sharp or heavy as in his days as a neophyte boss. Black was the troublesome one. When Peck bought the good-looking right-hander from the A's, he was warned by Connie Mack.

"He should be a great pitcher, but he's a bad boy," advised Connie.

Peck talked to Black and exacted a promise.

"I won't drink," Don pledged.

Convinced, Peck advanced the pitcher fifteen hundred dollars on his 1946 salary. However, Don couldn't keep his word. He tried, but the disease, drunkenness, overpowered him.

Red-eyed and pugnacious, Black made his presence known in the hotel lobby one evening shortly after the Tribe arrived in Clearwater. He sought Peck, but the general manager was out with Boudreau for the evening. Don sounded off to all listeners, with the result the reporters were told of an impending fuss.

When Peck and Lou came in, Black retired to a corner with them.

"I want some money," he demanded. "My family needs help."

Peck balked, partly in stubbornness, partly in a realization that it was not good business operation to continue giving money to a pitcher he wasn't sure would return anything on the investment.

"Okay, then I'll have to quit and go home," threatened Don. There were hot words exchanged, and Boudreau threatened a fine. Finally Peck talked Don into going to bed.

After that uprising, Don gave the front office little trouble. But he didn't give them much pitching, either, and was shunted off to Milwaukee.

Boudreau juggled the holdovers, the newcomers, and the returning veterans in an attempt to fit the best man into each position. He needed, most of all, a center fielder. Not since Averill had there been a top-grade center fielder. Weatherly was brilliant, but short lived.

In a move of desperation, Lou turned to Bob Lemon, a returned Navy veteran. Lemon had done a spot of pitching in the service. But he was an infielder by trade and by inclination, the latter based on a desire to play daily and bat daily. Bob's case looked quite hopeless, though. He couldn't nudge Keltner off third or Boudreau out of short. And he wasn't a second baseman by training. Besides, Mack and Meyer were fighting it out for that assignment.

Boudreau put Lemon in center field because he had a strong arm, he was fast, and he was a good judge of fly balls. After the opening game in 1946, Boudreau thought his center-field problem was settled for the next ten years. Lemon made a brilliant, game-saving catch to give Feller a 1-to-0 triumph over the White Sox.

"If Lemon can only hit, we're in great shape," Boudreau told Peck. But he couldn't. He drifted to the bench, to pinch-hitting duty, and finally, because there was nothing else for him to do, to the bull pen to have a hitch as a pitcher. What a hitch that was to be!

Meanwhile, Feller was stumbling, and when the Tribe invaded New York late in the opening month, there was considerable talk to the effect that the Navy had ruined the strike-out king. He'd lost the intangible "it," went the stories.

But on April 30, he had "it." In the shadows of Yankee Stadium, twenty-seven-year-old Feller pitched his second no-hit game in the major leagues. His classic in Chicago had been hurled at the expense of a weak-hitting team. But this was Yankee Stadium, where pop flies fall into the stands for home runs, and where the mightiest of slugging teams, the Yankees, were trying desperately to lace out each pitch. Only one run was scored in the game. No one on either team let up for an instant.

One after another, the Yankees went back to the bench. Five of them walked. One was safe on an error. But the others became mere outs, and the great men of the Yankees were sorely griped. Di Maggio, Gordon, Dickey, Henrich, Keller, Stirnweiss, Etten, and Rizzuto were in the line-up and modern baseball hasn't offered a more dangerous list. No one thought of a no-hitter in the first inning when Boudreau, in one of his sensational acrobatic plays, made a miraculous pickup and throw of a deflected grounder. The scorer would have ruled a hit surely had Lou not completed the play.

Boudreau seems always to reserve his classical fielding performances for Yankee Stadium. In the war years when good baseball was at a premium, Lou would bring hardened Bronxites out of their seats time after time with spectacular stops or split-second throws.

But if Boudreau held something back for Yankee fans, so did Ray Mack. It was Mack who saved Bob's classic in Chicago in 1940 in making the last putout. And it was Mack who boxed a bounding ball for the last out again in 1946, recovered his equilibrium, and got the ball to first base ahead of the runner just as another Yankee was crossing the plate with what would have been the tying run. A homer by Frank Hayes was the only Cleveland tally off Floyd "Bill" Bevens.

The Indians settled into a groove in May. Feller was great and was piling up strike-outs by the dozens. But Gromek couldn't get postwar batters out. Neither could Red Embree. Reynolds, another wartime flash, had rough sailing. The club lacked power, and it lacked color.

There were rumblings of discontent among the fans, not at the manager as was usually the case with Clevelanders, but at the front office. The fans thought Bradley and Peck had been caught with their checkbooks down. Business was booming in many ball parks. But in Cleveland, with its two plants, business was terrible. Some of the stockholders in the Tribe were dropping remarks in such catch-alls as the regal Union Club, the Tavern Club, and other swank retreats—remarks that found their way to the sports pages of the *Cleveland Press* too frequently for the comfort of Alva Bradley.

"Mark our words," cried the *Press* time after time, "the Indians are on the market."

BILL VEECK ARRIVES

WHEN THE SPRING WIND whistles in Chicago, a big-league baseball game usually answers. So it was that the gusts roaring noisily around the corner of the Blackstone Hotel on Michigan Boulevard in mid-April of 1946 were harbingers of the opening of the National League season in North Side Wrigley Field, home of the Cubs.

Two men whose lives had been shaped by baseball were lunching in the hotel. One had come twenty-five hundred miles, mainly to watch a ball game. The other had come from Chicago's South Side, no great distance from Wrigley Field in miles but a lifetime away in loyalty.

Neither William Louis Veeck, Jr., nor Harry Grabiner was employed at the moment. Neither was job hunting, especially. But the mind of each was twisting and chafing in its restlessness. A baseball game was being played that afternoon, and they were not a part of it.

The thirty-two-year-old Veeck had come to Chicago from Tucson, Arizona, ostensibly to buy a new automobile and drive it back to his ranch. That ranch was his new home. It was purchased out of funds derived from the sale of the Milwaukee Brewers of the American Association. Veeck, ex-minor-league magnate, ex-Marine, ex-treasurer of the Chicago Cubs, ex-peanut hustler in Wrigley Field when his father was chief executive of the Bruins, was hemmed in by the great open spaces of Arizona.

Grabiner had spent forty years in the service of the White Sox. On the South Side, he had become an institution, nearly as powerful as the Comiskeys and certainly as well known in the baseball business. But he, too, had sold out and now at fifty-six, for the first time since his knee-pants days, Harry Grabiner had no stake in baseball or a baseball team.

Through the war years, Veeck and Grabiner had corresponded. Now, for one of the few times since young Bill had been invalided home with a crushed right foot—the mechanism of an antiaircraft gun had jammed during an operation on Bougainville—the spirited Veeck and the nervous, excitable Grabiner sat down to talk baseball and, also, to commiserate upon each other's idleness in the field he loved.

They dawdled over their food. Finally one of them made a statement. To this day Veeck swears he doesn't know which mouthed the words.

"Let's buy a ball club."

A sound suspicion is that the proposal was Veeck's. He was the younger of the pair, the more anxious to get into action again. Besides it was Veeck, not Grabiner, who had been born with a baseball in one hand and an idea in the other.

They went to the Cubs' opener and hurried back to the hotel. Half a dozen long-distance telephone calls were placed. One of them was to a source in Cleveland.

"I think we've got the key to the situation," enthused Veeck a few hours later. "That is, if we can do anything in Cleveland."

Three clubs were reported on the market at the time. Only two, Cleveland and Pittsburgh, were attractive to Veeck and Grabiner, though they had nothing to go on as yet except a fierce desire to swing back into the baseball whirl. "You pick the team," Grabiner conceded.

Veeck took off for Pittsburgh. En route, he stopped in Buffalo and sought the counsel of a wise, old, and loyal friend, Lou Jacobs, head of a nationally known concession company. Jacobs, then and now, is one of the great clearing houses of sports information. He knows, by means of contracts in ball parks, race tracks, and sports arenas, the financial standing and possibilities of nearly all famous promoters and franchise holders.

Jacobs was partial to the Cleveland deal, an understandable leaning inasmuch as his company had the concessions in the Pittsburgh park, but not in Cleveland. Veeck went further. He asked an expert and a friend, Charley Haines, to survey both cities and to recommend which team offered the greater potential earning power. Haines picked Cleveland.

In May, Veeck checked into the Hotel Cleveland—under his own name, a point to be remembered. For five days, Bill scoured the city. His sport shirt open at the throat, his limp pronounced, his pinkish, fuzzy hair cropped close, Veeck made a distinctive colorful figure as he purposely visited restaurants and cafés, hotels, gabbed with cab drivers, struck up conversations with strangers, drew, or tried to draw, talk about the Indians.

Yet not a Cleveland sports writer knew that Veeck was in their midst, working on the biggest baseball deal of his life and of the city's. A man who can't walk six feet now without returning a greeting, Bill Veeck was then merely a curious-looking, impish young giant who walked with a brace on his foot and wore Buster Brown garb.

Veeck learned two things from his five-day probe. One was that Clevelanders lacked information about their home team, the Indians. Surprisingly few knew the intimate or even statistical facts about the individual players. He found, too, that Clevelanders were much more apt to utter derogatory remarks about their players than they were to compliment them. And there were few expressions of love for the owners or the front office.

These findings were challenges to Bill Veeck. Here was a chance to educate fans, to create good will, to bring a civic unity out of a baseball chaos. All he had to do was buy the Indians. In truth, it was just about that simple.

Veeck and Grabiner moved quickly to the key to the Cleveland situation. They had heard that John Sherwin, Jr., one of the largest stockholders in the Tribe, wanted to unload his holdings. They had read, too, the denials by Alva Bradley that the Indians were for sale or could be sold. They knew the tales didn't jibe.

"Our man is Sherwin's attorney," Veeck told Grabiner. "Let's work through him."

Benjamin F. Fiery, the attorney, readily admitted that the Sherwins—John and his brother Francis—were anxious to get out of baseball. They were not baseball people by profession or inclination. They did not like the idea of being connected with a venture that was constantly in the public prints and nearly always, in Cleveland at least, in a defensive position.

Veeck and Grabiner organized their safari to find gold. They moved to Chicago, to New York, and then Veeck returned to Cleveland, incognito, or as nearly so as his appearance would permit. Veeck called on Fiery and made a bona-fide offer to purchase the Indians.

"Here's a check for ten per cent of the purchase price, just to prove that we mean business," Veeck told Fiery. "We have the money necessary to buy. Now we would like the promise, at least, of first refusal."

That granted, Veeck—registered in a hotel under the name of Edwards—holed up to await the decision of the Tribe stockholders. After a week, Veeck feared his identity would be learned. So he switched to the name "Lewis." But outside the hotel he was still Bill Veeck. He attended the National Open Golf Tournament at Cleveland's Canterbury Club and went unrecognized, limp, sports shirt, pink hair, and all.

But someone must have been doing some gossiping, because Alva Bradley was kept busy denying rumors that the Indians were to be sold.

The deal was arranged, and formal transfer was to take place the morning of June 21 in the National City Bank in downtown Cleveland. In its morning editions the *Cleveland Press* announced boldly that the Indians had been sold. The *Cleveland News* asked Bradley and other stockholders for verification. They denied the story and the sale.

There almost was no sale, at that. The price—1,600,000 dollars—had been agreed upon. One million was in cash, the remainder in securities and assets. The necessary money was on the desk. A loan had been promised by the bank. But there was one link missing. A man who was to put up one hundred thousand dollars hadn't arrived. He wasn't there by eleven fifty-five, and there was a noon deadline on the deal! Veeck paced the floor. Finally, in the last two minutes, the bearer of glad tidings stepped through the door.

The Cleveland Indians were Veeck's!

Now Alva Bradley couldn't deny that the team was for sale, though it was disclosed later that the executive's pose during all the negotiations had been by arrangement with John Sherwin.

234

A year previous, Bradley and Sherwin had discussed disposition of the Tribe. One of the reasons was the awkwardness of having five widows of former stockholders participating in club affairs. The husbands of Mrs. Tomlinson, Mrs. Martin, Mrs. Baker, Mrs. Crawford, and Mrs. C. L. Bradley had died. In the spring of 1946, Sherwin announced to Alva Bradley that he might step out.

"Well, John, that's your affair," said Bradley. "But we might have some good years coming up after the war. I'd like to take one stand if there is to be a sale. I don't want to know too much about it. I want to be able to say that I'm still the president of the team and let it go at that."

Yet Bradley couldn't surrender the Indians that easily after a nineteen-year association. When the stockholders gathered to consider Veeck's offer, Bradley resolved to make a bid for the team himself. He had formed a somewhat questionable opinion of Veeck from observations of the brash and flamboyant young executive when Bill represented the Milwaukee team at meetings of the major and minor leagues.

"I really wanted to save the Indians for Clevelanders and a sane operation," Bradley said later. "But negotiations had gone too far by the time I decided to act. I did think a lot about getting together new capital, but it was too late."

Alva Bradley retired from baseball with a wide smile on his face and with an open wound in his pride.

There were ten stockholders in the Indians on June 21. In a short time there were ten more. These latter were Clevelanders. Together they represented about 25 per cent of the stock "for local interest and good will."

Control of the Indians was vested almost entirely in Veeck. He owned 30 per cent of the stock. No other stockholder owned more than 6 per cent of the total. The next largest holding was around 6 per cent. Not even Grabiner owned more. The Indians were to be a Veeck operation, period.

Many of the first stockholders were Chicagoans who had been friends of young Bill, of his father, or of Grabiner. These included Lester Armour, Phillip R. Clark (with whom Veeck had once discussed purchase of the White Sox), T. Phillip

Swift, A. C. Allyn, Newton P. Frye, and Sidney K. Schiff, the latter an attorney who represented Veeck and Grabiner in their dealings.

When Veeck included New York in his May tour to raise money, he called upon an old friend, Bob Goldstein, Eastern representative for International-Universal Pictures and celebrated Broadway wit. Enthused, Goldstein plunged one hundred thousand dollars.

In the line-up of Cleveland stockholders, friendships played a major role. For example, Lou Jacobs of Buffalo knew a popular Cleveland lawyer, J. J. Klein, who was the legal representative of Bob Hope in many Middle Western activities. When Klein was offered the chance to buy stock, he telephoned Hope in New Orleans, and the comedian jumped at the opportunity not only to own stock in a big-league team but also to have a stake in his home town's club. As a youngster, Hope had clambered over the old League Park bleachers many times.

The list of "locals" was completed with the addition of George Creadon, Joseph H. Tyroler, Edward H. Blywise, Dave R. Jones, Ralph Perkins, Jack Harris, Richard Downing, W. Crozier Smith, and Fiery. One Detroiter, Herman Radner, a friend of Goldstein's, was included. Incidentally, Veeck made a special bid to John Sherwin to repurchase stock, but Sherwin declined.

"There's been too much talk already," he told Veeck. "I wouldn't want Alva Bradley to think that I had double-crossed him."

Veeck, Grabiner, and Boudreau sat down to dinner in a hotel suite the night of June 21. Headlines had screamed the sale of the club, the coming of Veeck, the last-minute attempts of Bradley to regain control of the Tribe.

These headlines had hinted, too, of a possible change in managers. One report insisted that Jimmy Dykes would move in immediately to replace Boudreau, with Lou being relegated to the player's ranks. Dykes had been one of Grabiner's managers at Chicago. Also, Dykes was currently "at liberty."

Even as the common fan, Boudreau had read every word in the day's reports. And he had noticed the references to

Gene Bearden

Largest crowd ever to see a major-league game—a part of the 86,288 fans in the Cleveland Stadium at the fifth 1948 World Series game.

Dykes and the seemingly positive statements that the new owners were determined to bring in a new manager.

"You probably want to know exactly where you stand, Lou," Veeck told Boudreau over steak. "Well, we're going to be very frank with you. We know about your ball playing. You're the best, and that's putting it mildly. But we have some doubts about your managerial ability. We have no plans to change managers immediately. We may never change. We're going to wait and see, Lou. Meanwhile, you're the manager and don't worry about anything else."

But Boudreau had other things on his mind. The Indians were in fifth place, the Red Sox were making a bid for their first championship since 1918 and, worse, were in Cleveland at the moment. They were to play the startled Tribe the next afternoon at League Park.

That day—June 22—never will be forgotten by Cleveland! It brought Bill Veeck, bizarre and boyish, into the full and uncluttered view of the sixth largest city in the nation. The most ambitious and resourceful showman in the history of baseball was on the loose. It is likely that the American League shivered just a little in its official boots. This was the same Willie Veeck who turned baseball in Milwaukee into a three-ring circus, who might have an elephant or a two-hundred-pound cake of ice delivered to a customer in the middle of a ball game.

Cleveland, one eyebrow cocked high, waited and wondered.

The old corporation's last gasp was emitted June 21. It got the receipts of that day's game. Beginning the next day, Saturday, the new owners would take such loot as was available, and at the time no extra help was needed to carry the box-office take to the vaults.

Veeck and Grabiner went to League Park Saturday shortly after noon. They were met by Frank Kohlbecker, the business manager.

"I suppose you would like to go upstairs to our offices and take over," Kohlbecker said. Grabiner nodded. Veeck shook his head.

"I'm going out in the stands," advised Bill.

Grabiner walked upstairs and greeted the entire office staff

—six people. He knew most of them—Mark Wanstall, the auditor who started to work for Charley Somers in 1910; Edna Jameson, the chief ticket dispenser, who joined the Somers forces in 1913; Byron Smith, a ticket seller; Ada Ireland, the telephone operator; Kohlbecker; and Roger Peckinpaugh, the assistant to Bradley.

These six—and the famous ground-keeping family of Emil Bossard and his stalwart sons, Harold and Marshall—comprised just about the only full-time, steady employees of the deposed clan. By way of leaping ahead, it should be reported that today's office force numbers a minimum of thirty people, with more certain to be added.

Veeck, coatless, his elbow-length, white sport shirt opened down to the third button, strolled around the lower deck of the old plant. He walked to the third-base side and started hippity-hopping down an aisle. It seemed that the three thousand pairs of eyes in the entire surroundings were on the figure of the new, fabulous president.

A grizzled fan, sitting half a dozen rows from the top section, yelled at Veeck.

"Welcome to Cleveland, Mr. Veeck," he greeted. Bill turned and flashed the grin that has melted a thousand service clubs since.

"Call me Bill," he requested.

Then he wandered into the bleachers and sat with the fifty-cent boys.

The Indians won for Bill that day, mainly because Hank Edwards hit a mighty home run over the right-field wall. But the scattered clients were not completely appeased because the Indians were still in fifth place, 17 games behind the leading Yankees, having won only 26 games while losing 33. A mere 297,000 spectators had paid their way into the home games.

Veeck looked at the figures and frowned. He looked at the standings and frowned. He looked over the roster and noted a horrifying lack of batting punch and pitching steadiness. He frowned again. Then he went to work.

Upstairs and on the field, Veeck's organization took form. On the field some rather insecure pitchers named Gassaway, Webber, and Berry were added. Heinz Becker was obtained for Micky Rocco. Frank Hayes was swapped to the White Sox for Tom Jordan. Johnny Price, a thoroughly entertaining acrobatic genius with a baseball, and Max Patkin, a toothpicky character who held the rather dubious title of a coach, came in. The customers roared at Price and Patkin. Boudreau growled. The fans wondered.

An orchestra made its appearance at each game. A tepee was thrown up in center field. Baseball was becoming a country-store business, with the hand-shaking Veeck literally meeting the customers at the ticket wickets, escorting them to their seats, and asking if they wanted mustard and pickle, both, on their hot dogs.

Upstairs, his office force was taking shape. No one was fired. Peckinpaugh and Kohlbecker quit. From Milwaukee came a slight, laughing man who wore rimless spectacles and answered to the rather typical Milwaukee name of Rudie Schaffer. He had been Veeck's general manager there. They had started out together as operators of the Brewers, and there had been many days of privation. Schaffer had shared Veeck's growing pains in baseball. They made an ideal combination, Veeck with his open-handed, public-spirited deals and promotions, Schaffer with his clever restraint on Veeck's spending.

Shortly thereafter, a dark-visaged young man made his appearance at League Park. His brother, Bob Goldstein, owned stock in the Indians. Once, in New York, Bill Veeck had said to Bob's kid brother Harold "Spud" Goldstein, "You were in Yankee Stadium today and saw this Cleveland nine murdered. Why don't you drop by in Cleveland, and maybe we can get you something better in the line of a victory?"

Spud, who had shepherded the cast of the *This Is the Army* show around the country, agreed. He stopped off in Cleveland one day and never got out. Veeck put him to work, first with temporary title of press agent, later with the more dignified cognomen of traveling secretary. Cleveland baseball writers will fight at the drop of a dinner check to uphold Spud's reputation as the best traveling secretary they ever knew.

Veeck reached for the moon from the beginning but, unfortunately, the Indians couldn't keep up with him in their daily exercises. Two things were mighty pleasing to Bill in that period. One was Feller's strike-out streak, the other was Boudreau's introduction, during a game in Boston, of the celebrated infield shift whenever Ted Williams went to bat.

Feller, picking up speed with each toss despite the miserable record of the Tribe as a team, surpassed his own personal strike-out record of 261 shortly after midseason. Rube Waddell's record of 349 victims was a long way off.

The "Williams shift" became the most controversial defense maneuver in the history of baseball. The idea was Boudreau's alone. For months he had sought a method of stopping the deadly Williams. He had devised a shift in his mind and on paper but never had tried it. Finally Williams forced the shift on himself.

Terrific Ted belted three home runs in the first game of a double-header in Boston, and the Indians retreated to the clubhouse, tails dragging, after losing a heartbreaker, 11 to 10. Boudreau was scorching.

"We'll stop that Williams," he barked in the privacy of the dressing rooms. "The first baseman will play right on the line. The second baseman will play closer to first than usual and back on the grass. I'll play to the right side of second base. The third baseman will be in my regular shortstop position. The left fielder will come in close. The other two will play in right field."

So was born the shift that provoked many of the most stirring arguments in modern baseball. That it bothered Williams was admitted by all, including Ted. Manager Eddie Dyer of the St. Louis Cardinals used a variation of the shift in the ensuing World Series with the Red Sox. Today the Indians still employ the shift, with frequent alterations.

Between the shift, Feller's strike-outs, and a new and astounding interest shown by Cleveland fans in the new operation, Veeck kept the Indians on the tip of the country's tongue. When Feller pitched against the Yankees on August 4, a mammoth turnout of 74,529—largest paid crowd in the city's history—nearly filled the stadium. A short time later trainer Lefty Weisman was honored for his twenty-five years of service to the Tribe, and 65,782 people cheered the portly muscle manipulator that evening.

240

Boudreau was omitted from the American League all-star squad through a twist in the voting for places, then done by the managers. So Veeck staged a night for the Boy Manager and called it "A Night for the Greatest Shortstop Ever Left Off the All-Star Team." He added fireworks and vaudeville to night games, strolling musical combinations to all games, and presents of nylon stockings to guests on Ladies' Days. To show his appreciation for Cleveland's response, Veeck threw a free game for the fans. No admission was charged. He also made a private deal with the White Sox about the visiting club's share of the gate receipts on the basis of five thousand paid admissions. More than double that number showed up.

Meanwhile, Feller was mowing 'em down. He was pitching out of turn, in relief, and whenever else it was possible. Bob was due to pitch against the Tigers on a Saturday, the day before the schedule's closing game. He had 343 strike-outs. Should he pitch on Saturday and take a chance on his tired arm, or wait until Sunday and pray that rain did not wash out the season's final? Bob and Boudreau waited. It was a wise move. Feller struck out five and finished with a total of 348 strike-outs, one above the accepted record of Waddell.

At season's end, Veeck looked over the attendance figures. The Indians had drawn 1,057,289 fans at home, more than any other Cleveland team! But the club was in sixth place. Veeck was not overjoyed. With all his theatrics, Veeck was a sound, trained baseball man, the result of a lifetime in the sport with his father and with the Cubs' organization.

Then, too, his foot was aching. The crushed member was getting out of medical control, partly because Veeck in his enthusiasm for his new work, refused to consider the physical penalty. He had spent two years in Naval hospitals. If he spent any more time in one—well, they could cut the damned thing off.

But first there was the World Series. While the Cards and Red Sox were batting in Boston, Bill sat on the concrete steps of the box occupied by Larry MacPhail, president of the Yankees. Here were two of the foremost talent gamblers the game ever knew. They talked trade. The Indians needed a second baseman, the Yankees a front-line pitcher.

Veeck wanted Joe Gordon, the famous Flash who was a part of Yankee tradition. MacPhail, who cared little for tradition, agreed to a swap if he could have Allie Reynolds, the roundish Indian right-hander. The deal was made within a few minutes, probably while one side was being retired.

"Boys, we'll be tough next year," Bill told Cleveland reporters as they walked back to the Hotel Kenmore after the game. "We've got Joe Gordon, a great second baseman. He'll give us power and can you imagine, too, Gordon and Boudreau working together! It'll be terrific."

There, for one of the few times in his recent life, Veeck was guilty of an understatement. Boudreau and Gordon were to be out of this baseball world in deed as well as in conversation.

On November 9, Bill Veeck went out of commission. In Cleveland Clinic Hospital, his right foot was amputated. Temporarily, the Veeck personalized sales campaign was frustrated. For the next four weeks, he would have to forego public speaking appearances—before the high school students in Mansfield or the Kiwanis Club in Coshocton or the Rotary Club in Erie or before a sewing circle in Lodi. He would have to forget, for a while, the art of grinning at people, telling corny jokes, and kidding about the Indians and Bob Feller and Lou Boudreau, and relating how Charley Grimm, in full baseball regalia, would stroll through the aisles of the Milwaukee ball yard, strumming his banjo and emitting folk songs.

But four weeks after the operation, Veeck was on crutches. Not sitting in Cleveland, but in Los Angeles, attending the annual winter baseball meetings. There he made one more deal. "A minor transaction," hooted the papers in Cleveland. Veeck traded Ray Mack and Sherman Lollar, neither of whom figured in Cleveland's future plans, to the Yankees for Hal Peck, an old Milwaukee favorite friend and outfielder; pitcher Al Gettel, and a left-handed pitcher very slightly known in minor-league circles and answering to the name of Gene Bearden.

"We beat the Yanks on that one," bragged Bill.

CHAPTER XXVIII

LARRY DOBY, NEGRO

THE NEW YEAR—1947—found Veeck under a full head of steam, though there was searing pain in the stump of his right leg. He traded Gene Woodling for Al Lopez and brought an old schoolmate statistical genius, Marshall Samuel, into the Wigwam as public-relations director. On his crutches he spurted from city to town to hamlet in northern Ohio, to dozens of luncheons and dinners in Cleveland, to spread the gospel of the Indians.

Around the ball-club offices a new face appeared. There was a new freshness to the features, a new snap in the stride. The red-haired young man was selling season tickets on a special plan. This was the streamlined, reformed drunk, Don Black. Alcoholics Anonymous, the marvelous organization that had brought Rollie Hemsley to his senses, had won another fight. Veeck helped, of course. Veeck doesn't take defeat in stride. When the bottle was beating Black, Veeck determined to help Don smash his tormentor.

With the arrival of February came Veeck's first artificial leg. To celebrate, he donned the cumbersome limb and threw a large-scale dance in a hotel ballroom. Bill foxtrotted awkwardly for four hours, a smile on his face. Then he retired to a room and lay for twenty-four hours while ripping pains tore at the flesh of his stump.

Back on crutches went Veeck to supervise the building of his own first, personal big-league ball club. Training quarters had been established at Tucson. The new deal in Cleveland baseball was to be complete, from roster to spring headquarters.

Boudreau remained. Whether Veeck was convinced that Lou was a satisfactory manager through the last half of the

1946 season is debated to this day. But Bill was visibly impressed by Boudreau's playing.

"He's the greatest competitor I ever saw," praised Veeck. "It's up to us to provide Lou with a good ball club before passing final judgment on him as a manager. But as a player —no one can touch that boy, no one ever!"

Veeck frequently expressed a desire to "surround" Boudreau with the best baseball brains available. Hence, Bill McKechnie came into the Wigwam. The sixty-year-old, silver-haired McKechnie had stepped out as manager of the Cincinnati Reds after a long and honorable career in the National League. In McKechnie Veeck envisioned an adviser to Boudreau who knew the value of pitchers, who could train and coach them. Too, Deacon Will, as McKechnie was informally known, was a calm operator who might be a fine counterbalance to the impulsive young Boudreau.

McKechnie joined Oscar Melillo and George Susce on the coaching staff. At the outset, Boudreau leaned more on Melillo, a long-time friend, than on McKechnie. But gradually Lou swung a share of his affection and confidence to Deacon Will. Unlike some of his predecessors, McKechnie was not backward in advising Lou or in expressing distaste with specific situations. No job hunter in the first place, McKechnie could afford to be honestly independent in expression, and he was, to the ultimate advantage of Boudreau.

The restlessness of Veeck and his disdain for losing clubs were emphasized in a size-up of the 1946 and 1947 rosters. More than twenty-five new players made their appearances at Tucson in 1947. Some stayed only overnight, but they were small particles in an over-all pattern Veeck hoped Boudreau would follow: give everyone a trial and keep everyone hustling for his job.

By mid-April, Boudreau had settled upon his first-line team, but he foresaw a lack of batting power in the outfield and shallowness in his pitching staff. The infield was set, and before an umpire's thumb had been jerked skyward the Tribe's inner cordon was being acclaimed the best outfit in the majors. Gordon, reliable, finished performer, was playing second base with a new relish. Next to him was Boudreau, the master shortstop. At third base was the steady Keltner, and on first base was the big and handsome naval veteran, Eddie Robinson, staging a comeback after a series of distressing personal and physical setbacks.

Jim Hegan and Lopez made up the best two-man catching staff in the business. A young outfielder up from Oklahoma City in the Texas League, Dale Mitchell, clinched one of the three garden jobs, but there was a scramble for the others. The long-hitting Seerey fought against strike-outs, and the speedy George Case against a chronic knee injury. Edwards was hurt. The weak-armed Peck, a good clutch hitter, won the right-field job.

But the pitching was too spotty, even in the spring, and the Indians were picked in the early polls to finish third or fourth. Such predictions did not deter the Cleveland fans from flocking to the box office. Right away the magic of Veeck's promotions was felt at the turnstiles. The largest opening-day crowd in the history of the major leagues, 55,014, turned out on April 15 to watch the Tribe meet the White Sox.

Two weeks later Veeck altered the geography of the stadium field. He installed a wire fence, five feet high, across the entire outfield from foul line to foul line. No longer would a batter be compelled to hit a baseball 420 feet to get a home run. No longer would 435-foot drives become simple outs as outfielders roamed at large in the biggest expanse in professional baseball.

Nearly four years before, Bradley and Peckinpaugh had scoffed at a suggestion by this writer that a fence be erected. Ballplayers charged that the Stadium was the most unfair park in the majors. A ball hit 350 feet in Yankee Stadium might be a cinch home run, but one hit 65 or 75 feet farther in the Cleveland Stadium and in the same direction would be caught with ease.

"The fence will stay permanently," Veeck decreed after the first trial. "Now our players will have a chance to hit some home runs at home like the Red Sox and Yankees."

Throughout April and May the Indians commuted between second and third places. By the time the first night game was to be played, with the colorless St. Louis Browns in late May, the Tribe's new legion of followers was about to get ecstatic.

Boudreau was hitting sensationally, Gordon was delivering the long ball, and it seemed that the team's main weakness in 1946 —lack of punch—had been eliminated. A stunning turnout of 61,227 for the night opener with the Browns was the answer to all this. Too, stockholder Bob Hope made an unannounced appearance, performed at home plate before the game, and put the gathering in a festive mood.

It was too good to last. By late June, the Indians were ten games out of first place. One week later, they were a dozen games behind the Yankees. The pennant race was just about over. But the Yankees were less fortunate with headlines. Most of those still belonged to Veeck.

On July 3, Bill told the baseball writers he had an announcement that "might interest them."

"We've signed a new ballplayer named Larry Doby," he said. There was a pause.

"He's a Negro."

There was a splitting silence in the room while Veeck let the words sink in.

"He'll be a great ballplayer," Bill went on. "He's a second baseman with the Newark Eagles in the Negro National League."

One reporter finally recovered his voice and asked when this new phenom was to report.

"In Chicago day after tomorrow," Veeck said.

A thousand thoughts raced through the minds of the scribes. Was this a publicity gag? What would the rest of the league owners say about the first Negro in their midst? What would the Indians say? Did Boudreau know? How would the Indians treat Doby? What would the Southerners in baseball say? How would Cleveland fans—and all fans—greet him?

Doby's last appearance in the Negro National League was to be the next afternoon in a double-header in Newark. This writer flew to Newark to get a first-hand impression of the dark-hued newcomer.

Mrs. Effie Manley, who owned the Newark team, was disconsolate before the final performance by the wiry twenty-two-year-old infielder for whom Veeck paid fifteen thousand dollars.

"I'm glad, of course, that Larry is getting the chance to be our first representative in the white major leagues," Mrs. Manley said. "But I'm afraid our team will be lost without him. He's a great ballplayer."

Doby didn't look it that day. He was so nervous he couldn't field a simple grounder. At the plate, he hit one home run, a tremendous drive over the left-field fence. Because of the speed with which the Negro league's rocket ball traveled when propelled by the lefthanded hitting Doby, the home run was pretty well discounted at the time.

He was excused from the second game to permit him to board a train for Chicago. There was a wait of an hour in the Pennsylvania station in Newark. Larry, sporty in a tieless, closed shirt, fidgeted on the hard bench as he held his pretty wife's hand.

"I feel—well, more than nervous," he confessed. "I feel almost like I was going into a new and strange world."

Contacts with white men wouldn't bother Larry. He'd played college basketball at Long Island University and professional basketball with mixed teams along the Atlantic seaboard. But the big leagues of baseball might be something else.

Doby was installed in a hotel on Chicago's South Side the next morning. Around noon, Veeck called for Larry and drove him to the White Sox park. In the offices of Leslie O'Connor, the Sox' general manager, Larry Doby inked his first major-league contract and was legally and officially ready to follow in the footsteps of Jackie Robinson of the Brooklyn Dodgers.

Veeck led the way to the Tribe's dressing room in Comiskey Park. Reporters and photographers trailed. Word of the approach of Larry had reached the room. When the door was thrown open, Doby stepped into the stuffy, steamy, and small clubhouse.

More than twenty-five ball players were in full uniform. Each sat in front of his locker. Most faces were turned to the floor. Not even the scuffle of a solitary spike on the bottom of a shoe broke the horrible, tomblike muteness. It was apparent that the team had been listening to a lecture by Boudreau. The topic had been Doby.

Larry walked past two or three rows of lockers and was guided into another by Lefty Weisman. Boudreau was there.

He shook hands with Doby and said, "Get dressed now, we'll be out on the field."

The Indians filed out of the room. Not a word was uttered. Larry Doby had been welcomed to the big leagues.

Throughout the first of two games scheduled that day, Doby sat at one end of the players' bench, silent and alone. Never a communicative man, Larry now was doubly self-conscious. A few Indians walked over to him, introduced themselves, and shook hands. Others chose to ignore the new arrival.

In the second game, Boudreau told Doby to play first base in place of Eddie Robinson. Larry had played several games at first in the Negro league, though second base was his normal position. Probably no one ever will know the tortures Larry endured in those nine innings. He fielded his position adequately, but he swung wildly at the plate, obviously "pressing."

Doby's debut had little effect on the Indians' status in the flag race. They were in third, fourth, or fifth place most of the time but still remained in the scramble for second place week after week. Not even a historic climax to a remarkable comeback by Don Black could alter their position.

The courageous right-hander who had beaten whisky turned in a magnificent no-hit game at the expense of his old teammates, the Athletics. What made Don's feat all the more sensational was a delay in an early inning because of rain. A twi-night double-header was scheduled, and Don was pitching in the first game with Bill McCahan as his opponent. Ironically, McCahan was to pitch a no-hit game later in the same season.

Black startled a crowd of 47,871 by blanking the A's, 3 to 0, in spite of six bases on balls. He struck out five. Black himself engineered the game's final putout on a toss to first base. As he started toward the dugout, Don was astonished to note that the first congratulatory handshake was given by the Philadelphia coach, Earle Mack, who had been instrumental in selling Don to Cleveland a year and a half before.

Cleveland's fans retained their loyalty even if the Indians were bogged down in the pennant chase. They staged two magnificent "nights," honoring the grand veteran, Mel Harder, and

248

later Black. Alcoholics Anonymous helped in the promotion of the Black festival.

Instead of letting the fans in free to the last game, Veeck turned over all receipts to the Cleveland Community Fund and rested upon one new laurel, another attendance record. Though they wound up fourth, the Indians drew 1,521,978 paid admissions.

Veeck's magic seemed more durable than the Indians, though there was a short-lived doubt about this a week or so after the season closed.

Then Veeck dared the wrath of the fans who had flocked to his shows, and no furor ever gave Cleveland a bigger or better civic headache.

Veeck was, and is, basically a dealer in baseball flesh. He likes new faces, new arrangements. Through much of the 1947 campaign he had talked to fellow operatives, including Bill DeWitt, then vice-president of the Browns, about assorted deals.

During the World Series between the Yankees and Dodgers, Veeck established social headquarters, along with most of the Cleveland writers, in Toots Shor's upper-case restaurant. Bill hauled the authors into a corner one by one.

"Now this must be off the record," he insisted. "What would you think about a trade of Boudreau to the Browns for Vern Stephens? There would be some others, but Boudreau for Stephens is the big part of the deal. Give me your honest opinion, but don't write anything about it."

Write anything about it? The authors couldn't even find their tongues to frame a reply. They had known, of course, of Veeck's stubborn refusal to accept Boudreau as the world's greatest manager. But in the eighteen months that Bill had surveyed Boudreau with great care, he had developed a wholesome regard for his manager, an opinion related closely to Lou's play in the field daily.

Veeck made one more point clear to the writers. He had not proposed the trade. The Browns had thought it up. They were unloading their high-salaried stars who had failed to lift the team out of last place. Veeck listened to the offer with interest because he had some misgivings about Boudreau's notorious aching ankles. These had collapsed before. Now that Lou was past thirty, they could fold up for keeps, Bill feared.

For a couple of days, the Cleveland reporters mulled the trade. Then a mere one-sentence mention of Boudreau's possible shift to the Browns appeared deep in a Chicago sports column. This eliminated the trade from the off-the-record class. The Cleveland writers caucused, agreed to spring the yarn the next day.

What happened in Cleveland never has been properly narrated, mainly because words do not fit the explosion. To say that the story broke is simply ducking the issue. The story broke through every front door in Cleveland. As an observer said at the time, "It smashed and splintered and shook the community by its civic heels until all hell popped loose."

Trade Boudreau? Peddle the idol of all bobby soxers, the handsome young Frenchman? Get rid of Boudreau and take those spectacular, superhuman plays at shortstop to another city? Exile Boudreau to St. Louis?

Cleveland kicked its heels over the Page Ones of all the newspapers. Veeck must be stark raving mad, fans howled. It seemed that in one grand swoop, Bill Veeck was bent upon undoing all the good he had compiled in more than a year of wooing the Ohio citizenry. Bill Veeck, the People's Choice, one day; Bill Veeck, the People's Target, the next. Scarcely had the day's first editions hit the streets than Veeck began receiving telephone calls in his New York hotel.

There was only one course open. He'd return to Cleveland and face the music. That night Veeck flew home. On his special, elbow-height crutches he visited dozens of bars and public meeting places. He stopped to talk to people on the street; or they stopped him. Women beseeched Bill to keep Boudreau. Men said he was completely crazy. Where would he find another shortstop like Boudreau?

The *Cleveland Press* observed humorously, "It is evident that Veeck didn't know Boudreau was immortal in Cleveland. ... Alva Bradley used to say that he hired the managers of the Indians and the public fired them. He's one Alva hired—and only an act of God can fire him, apparently."

Veeck is impetuous, but he is stubborn, too. Not even the

complaints and pleas of the fans could switch his view of the Boudreau-Stephens deal. But the Browns could and did. They withdrew their offer. The original trade involved Boudreau, George Metkovich, Byran Stephens, Dick Kokos, and an undisclosed amount of cash for Vern Stephens, Jack Kramer, Bob Muncrief, and either Paul Lehner or Walter Judnich.

The Browns may have retreated, but Boudreau's fans didn't. They signed petitions. They plagued the newspapers with letters. They threatened boycotts. They gathered in neighborhood bars and clubs and thrashed Veeck with sharp tongues. Even so, these fans couldn't bring themselves to a dislike of Veeck. Rather, they thought he had been contemplating a normal mistake. Bill had ingratiated himself too deeply in their affections by then.

He took some of the heat off himself by making a less pretentious swap with the Browns. He got Judnich and Muncrief for three untried players and twenty-five thousand dollars. During the December baseball meetings, Veeck did more business with the Browns. He paid fifty thousand dollars, plus Metkovich, for Johnny Berardino, who was obtained for the express purpose of a utility infielder. Of course, Johnny had the chance to run Joe Gordon off second base, but Joe had batted in ninety-three runs in 1947 and had matched thought for thought and instinct by instinct with Boudreau. It would take a mighty man to oust the Flash.

Two days later, Veeck peddled Red Embree to the Yankees for Allie Clark, a right-handed hitting outfielder. He gave the White Sox a catcher, Ralph Weigel, for the fleet center fielder, Thurman Tucker. He signed Elbie Fletcher, who had been the Pirates' regular first baseman in earlier years. He hounded President Clark Griffith of the Senators and Connie Mack of the Athletics, hopeful of dealing with one or both for pitchers.

Cleveland sports writers applauded such activity. Most of them wrote, too, that worse things might have happened to the Indians than a trade of Boudreau. Lou read the pieces and stormed privately. Certainly his position was far from secure. He didn't know whether he would be the Tribe's manager, or even the shortstop. Veeck, grim, refused to rush in and attempt to heal the breach.

For the breach was developing. Boudreau reasoned, understandably, that if Veeck had no confidence in him he could have little in Veeck. Lou made a trip to Cleveland. A few of the writers were greeted in cordiality. But most were frozen by Lou's manner. No, he didn't know what would happen. No, he hadn't agreed on terms for 1948. No, he had nothing more to say right then.

The Boy Manager was buffeted by winds of gossip. He remained close to his home in Harvey, getting almost daily reports on what was appearing in the Cleveland newspapers. Lou answered the long-distance telephone calls put in by writers. Yes, he'd be willing to play shortstop under another manager. Yes, he'd be willing to manage the Indians again, too. No, he didn't want to be traded especially.

The winter wore on. Veeck, never contrite, stuck to his grueling schedule of public appearances. There were more speeches than rumors about Boudreau. Bill was busy, driving one to two hundred miles nightly, talking to clubs and assemblies at noon, evening, night—any time, as he confessed, when more than six people gathered.

There had to be a showdown in the Veeck-Boudreau fuss with the start of spring training a matter of weeks away. Boudreau went to Cleveland for the all-important conference. It consumed an entire afternoon. Veeck emerged from his office at a late hour and threw the impatient reporters into spasms.

"Lou has signed a two-year contract," Bill said. "We have reached many agreements, and we're ready now to try to win the pennant."

A two-year contract! The manager Veeck didn't want—and said he didn't want—was more secure than ever, it seemed. Actually, though announcement never was made, there were two separate contracts signed. One considered Boudreau the ballplayer, the other Boudreau the manager. Each was for two years. The only difference was in a cancellation clause in the manager's contract. Lou could be fired as manager on short notice. Financial conditions never were revealed, though Boudreau undoubtedly was assured of an income of more than fifty thousand dollars.

There was a forced smile on Boudreau's face. He resembled

a performer going through with a distasteful drama. Veeck had insisted upon certain conditions, chief of these being that Bill be allowed to appoint the coaches. Melillo and Susce would be given other jobs in the Cleveland organization. McKechnie would stay, of course. Harder and the suave catcher-attorney, Herold "Muddy" Ruel, who had been deposed as manager of the Browns, became coaches.

"I wanted to surround Lou with the best baseball talent available," Veeck repeated an old statement of his.

THE 1948 PENNANT!

BOUDREAU WAS MORE INTENSE, more serious, more reserved than ever before when he greeted his squad at Tucson, March 1. A determination to force a good team out of the material provided was as apparent as the chips that Lou wore on each shoulder. His relations with Veeck became 100-per-cent commercial or economic. Social amenities were skipped. Boudreau had been a hero, an idol. He was determined to remain one even if it meant becoming a martyr to his employer's moods in the process.

Not all the new talent in the Cleveland organization was listed on the roster. There was a new vice-president, Hank Greenberg, the famed home-run slugger and former Tiger who played with the Pittsburgh Pirates in 1947. A new vice-president? The national baseball public asked a common question: Why?

Well, Veeck explained, Greenberg might possibly play some. He had bought stock in the ball club, of course. No, there was no idea of turning over the Indians to Greenberg.

"I chased Hank all winter," admitted Veeck. "We talked some about buying a minor-league club as partners. He wanted to get into the administrative end of baseball. When that deal fell through, I tried to think of something else. I wanted him with me. I didn't care whether he came along as a coach, a player, or a stockholder. Just so he came."

Greenberg was willing, but he demanded a financial share in any club he might join. Hence, it was announced that the handsome, tall, native Bronxite had become the "second largest stockholder" in the Indians. Veeck insisted that there was no special significance to that. "No one other than myself owns more than six per cent of the stock, and that goes for Greenberg," Bill pointed out.

Veeck was quick to foresee another advantage in the addition of Greenberg.

"He'll be able to help Pat Seerey," Bill said. Veeck had lavished money, patience, and reducing methods upon Seerey. Perhaps Greenberg could eliminate the flaws in the chunky slugger's swing that made him a frequent strike-out victim.

The Tribe chieftain made one more constructive move before turning over to Boudreau his talent for the first half of the 1948 race. He bought Russ Christopher, lanky pitcher, from the Athletics. Now the Indians were ready to settle down. In one of his first interviews of the spring, Boudreau sounded the tone of his club.

"They'll have to beat us to win the pennant," he said with confidence.

Lou knew that he needed only some more depth in his pitching staff to figure prominently in the race. His infield was established. Hegan, who had squabbled with Veeck throughout the winter over salary terms, talked his difficulties out with Bill in Tucson. Immediately he brushed aside all backstopping competition and became the strong man with the mask.

There was quantity among the outfielders, but the quality had to be determined. Mitchell was a sure thing in left. Edwards was running ahead of the pack in right. The newcomer Clark demonstrated early he was a good hitter. Judnich had been a long-ball hitter with the Browns, and there was a hope he would follow habit in his new surroundings. Yet Tucker was destined to open the season in center.

The key man was Larry Doby. The Negro had played outfield in the race circuits. He could throw, and he could run. There was every assurance he would hit. He needed training and experience. During the first day's practice, Veeck made a deadly serious remark to reporters. "Doby will be in our starting line-up," he predicted. The reporters scoffed.

The fate of the pitching staff rested with Lemon and Bearden. Lemon had made a final and definite switchover from the infield and outfield to pitching. During the winter Veeck had predicted a twenty-victory season for the righthander. About Bearden he was less positive, though the Arkansas southpaw had won sixteen games for Oakland and had posted an earned-run average of 2.86.

Boudreau, now openly hopeful, led the Indians home for the late April opener. Cleveland, accustomed to spring steamings over its ball club, let go with all valves this time. The hero, Boudreau, was safe at shortstop. The Negro, Doby, had proved during the long spring series with the New York Giants that he could hit big-league pitching.

A typical Veeck crowd of 73,163 sat in chilled glee at the opener with the Browns. It was a record opening-day attendance in the majors. And to climax the day, Feller toyed with the Browns, 4 to 0. The Tribe won its first six games. It was in first place until May 6 and bounced in and out of the lead three times in the next three weeks.

By June, not only Cleveland fans had the pennant fever. Veeck and Boudreau were seeing the tips of the rainbow, too. The Indians were back in first place, but it was apparent they would need bolstering to stay there. Boudreau had been an admirer of the throwing arm of Bob Kennedy of the White Sox. Veeck learned he could get Kennedy. The Sox took Seerey, who wasn't hitting enough home runs to offset his strike-outs, and Gettel. Bill and Lou felt that one more pitcher might be the clincher. Veeck went back to his favorite trading post, St. Louis.

He cast a few lines toward Cliff Fannin, but the Browns ignored the bait. They offered him Sam Zoldak—for another left-handed pitcher and one hundred thousand dollars in cash! Veeck huddled with Grabiner. Though it was only mid-June, the Indians had drawn a million people and were over the hill financially for the season. They could afford one hundred thousand dollars for a pitcher who had a meager record of two victories and four defeats. So the Browns took the hundred grand and left-handed Bill Kennedy.

If the Indians were chasing a pennant with their last-minute deals—Zoldak had been acquired just under the deadline for trades—so were the Athletics chasing the Redskins in the flag race. Hence, there was a solid advance sale for a double-header between the top rivals in the Stadium June 20. The reservations did not presage a record crowd, yet long before time for the first game, all seats were sold. The crowd spilled out of the stands and onto the ground in back of the fence ringing the out-field. By midafternoon, baseball's greatest attendance, 82,781, had been registered!

Cleveland, already daffy about its league-leading heroes, had something else to brag about after June 30. That night Lemon arrived at full major-league stature by pitching a no-hit game in Detroit. The fast-working right-hander struck out four and walked only three. The Tribe scored two runs off Art Houtteman in the first inning. They were all, and enough. In one hour and thirty-three minutes, the game was over and Lemon was in the record books for keeps.

But Veeck surrendered the headlines to Lemon only tem-porarily. The Ringling of the Wigwam precipitated a national controversy by advising Feller to refuse the invitation to par-ticipate in the annual all-star game. Baseball officials, reporters, and fans beat a country-wide assault on Feller. Bob had been having a little arm trouble. Besides, his record in early July—nine and nine was not too impressive. Feller made the decision to spurn the interleague contest, but Veeck stepped forward to take the blame.

There wasn't enough security in the Tribe's hold on first place to satisfy Boudreau. He talked daily with Veeck about the possibility of picking up another pitcher. Veeck, in turn, had his scouts combing the minors and even the semipro ranks. One of these scouts was Abe Saperstein, well-known booker of basketball teams and one of the best-informed men on Negro ballplayers.

Abe dropped into Cleveland about that time.

"What about Satchel Paige?" Saperstein asked Veeck.

"Well," returned Veck, "what about him?"

"You're looking for a pitcher. Paige can win in the majors," enthused Saperstein.

Veeck knew about Paige, of course. Exactly one year earlier, he had heard from Satchel direct. After Bill signed Doby, Paige dispatched a wire to the Cleveland owner.

"I can pitch and win for you," it read.

Veeck, not too certain how Doby would be accepted in the league, didn't want to plunge and sign two Negroes at the same time. Too, there was his fear that he would be charged with a publicity stunt if he signed Paige so soon after picking up Doby. So Paige was advised to wait.

Saperstein's assurances won over Veeck. Abe hurried to Chicago, picked up Paige, and returned to Cleveland with him. Satchel's arrival was guarded closely. So was his first appearance in the Stadium. It was in the afternoon of July 7. Satchel shuffled out to the pitching mound before 78,000 empty seats.

At the plate, swinging bats, were Boudreau and Greenberg. In turn, they faced the languid, lanky Negro right-hander. They were impressed, not only by his speed and assorted curves, but by his demeanor. This was just another job of pitching for Satchel but it earned him a place in the majors.

That night the ageless Alabaman, who walks as if it's too much effort to stop and sit down, won his lifelong fight to gain recognition in the major leagues. Whether Satch was forty-five or fifty-five no one knew except possibly Satch, and he wasn't telling. He drove bright-hued automobiles and wore flashy garments. He missed trains and was fined by Boudreau within a week after he joined the Tribe. Umpires questioned his delivery and opposing players tried every means to upset him. But Ol' Satch had been around too long to be bothered much. He just pitched, often hard, invariably with accuracy, always with confidence and courage.

The pennant race neared July's end, and the Indians were still in first place. Apparently they were not spring blooms. Boudreau was hitting a torrid .380. Keltner was on the grandest home-run spree of his career; Gordon was leading the club in driving in runs; Mitchell was batting well over .300. Doby had solved some of the mysteries of big-league pitching. He was striking out less and was improved in his fielding.

The knuckler that Gene Bearden threw began to take on a new importance. The willowy left-hander, the grab-bag prize the Tribe won from the Yankees, and Lemon were carrying the pitching staff. Those two and, of course, Paige. Feller was throwing home-run balls and losing games. And the blasts, even of Clevelanders, that followed his withdrawal from the all-star game continued.

After all, Feller was getting eighty thousand dollars, or

258

maybe more, for his work in 1948. The forty-dollar-a-week clerk sitting in the stands in Cleveland couldn't restrain himself. He booed whenever Feller had rough going on the mound. It was psychological booing, but it sounded like the same old inverted huzzah.

In and out of first place went the Tribe. The Red Sox, on their home grounds, spanked the Boudreau forces three straight times and tumbled them into third place, behind the A's and Red Sox. They fought their way back to the top, taking over and relinquishing the league lead three times in the month of August.

But there never was a question of the box-office championship. An exhibition game with the Dodgers for the benefit of the Cleveland Baseball Federation, parent body of amateur baseball, attracted 64,877. Veeck gave the receipts—more than seventy thousand dollars—to the sand-lot boys. A stunning turnout of 72,434 watched Paige pitch against Washington's colorless team. A record night-game throng numbering 78,382 packed the Stadium as Satch tamed the White Sox. In Chicago, the gates of Comiskey Park were literally battered and shattered by fans brawling to get inside and watch the sensational Negro hurler. Police reserves fought with ten thousand people outside the park to clear the streets.

The Indians never got more than spitting distance away from first place. Their first severe physical setback of the season occurred when Hank Edwards crashed into the fence in Cleveland and dislocated his shoulder. As August's hot days rolled in, Boudreau was rolled out of the line-up. He was dumped in a play at second base as Gil Coan, Washington outfielder, slid in. Lou's tender ankle was banged. His shoulder was so sore he couldn't lift his arm—his throwing arm—and his side was bruised. The Boy Manager went to the first-aid room, then to the hospital, and eventually to the bench.

The Yankees and 73,484 others—crowds of fewer than seventy thousand people weren't worth counting, it seemed—went to the stadium on Sunday, August 8, for a double-header. It was a bright, warm day. Only two percentage points separated the Indians, A's, and Yankees, the top three teams. The Red

Sox were in fourth place, a mere game and a half behind the three leaders.

With Boudreau hurt and aching, the Indians were fireless. In the seventh inning of the first game, the Yankees led, 6 to 4. But the Indians filled the bases and in came Joe Page, the big Yankee left-hander, to stem the rally. Thurman Tucker, a left-handed batter, was kneeling in the ring near home plate. He turned his head toward the dugout. There, pawing over the bats in the rack, was Boudreau. Tucker walked to the bench as every voice in the place cut loose with a cheer, a gasp, or possibly an epithet.

Boudreau, taped like a mummy, walked slowly to the plate. His right thumb, injured earlier, was so tender it could not be pressed against the bat handle. Lou was limping, and he favored his right side when walking. The public-address system announcement of "Boudreau batting for Tucker" was lost in the ovation to the young manager.

There were other right-handed pinch hitters on the bench. Why had Boudreau put himself squarely on the hottest spot imaginable? the startled spectators asked their neighbors. The answer was in Boudreau, in Lou's almost fanatical desire to win the pennant and, in the process, to show up Veeck just a little. Whatever the motive, Lou rose to the situation. He lashed a solid, line single to center. Two runners raced across the plate and the score was tied, 6 to 6. The Indians scored again in the eighth and won, 8 to 6. They also won the nightcap, 2 to 1. If Boudreau could do it, so could his men, it seemed.

Later in the month, the pitchers moved into the commanding positions in the Tribe's splurge. On August 15, Feller blanked the White Sox in the final three innings of the first game of a double-header. In the second game, Lemon twirled an 8 to 0 triumph. Facing the Browns next, Bearden turned in another 8-to-0 shutout. Zoldak, the hundred-thousand-dollar deadline purchase, hung a 3-to-0 setback on the Browns. And finally, in Cleveland, Paige froze out the White Sox, 1 to 0.

As of Saturday, August 21, Cleveland pitchers had not allowed a run in 39 consecutive innings. The American League record was 41 innings, established by the Cleveland Blues in 1903. It didn't take Lemon long to set a new mark. Facing the

White Sox on Saturday, Bob pitched eight scoreless innings to run the record to 47. The National League mark of 56 was within grasp. But Lemon walked Seerey, the lead-off batter in the ninth, and Aaron Robinson, the Sox catcher, blasted a home run over the fence. Dave Philley followed with another homer. The Indians were beaten, and their lead over the Red Sox had been cut to two games.

Yet there seemed to be little cause for worry by their fans. The Indians would regain their stride and gallop onward to their first championship in twenty-eight years, they felt. But their heroes dropped two more games to the White Sox the next day and, invading the East, promptly lost four out of six in Boston and New York. Cleveland fans stirred in anxiety. Were their beloved Redskins blowing up?

Another ten days passed and it seemed that the Tribe had shot its bolt beyond repair. At the windup of the traditional Labor Day double-headers, Cleveland was in third place, four and a half games behind the pace-setting Red Sox and three games behind the Yankees. Well, that was that, reasoned the fans. It had been a good try by the Indians, their best since 1940. Maybe next year...

Yet there was a singularly bright spot in the chaos. Bob Feller had regained his form. Many a wisecracking fan and writer had said, "When September comes, Feller will be carrying the Indians on his back." Such was the case, figuratively. The speed-ball king, regaining his confidence more and more with each start, knocked off six opponents in a row. Verily, Feller was carrying the Indians.

Boudreau's desire to win now became so overpowering he explored every opportunity to better his team's chances. During a final swing through the East, Lou called a meeting of reporters traveling with the club.

"We can win this pennant, gentlemen," he intoned. "I know we can, and so I don't want anything to interfere. I'd like to ask a favor of you. I wish that from now on—unless there are special circumstances—you'd agree to stay out of the dressing room after each game. I don't want anything said in anger or distress by a player or a writer that will create a situation. I'm asking you to help us all in this."

The reporters agreed to pass up the usual clubhouse interviews.

"I'll meet with you after each game," Lou promised, "and tell you all I can. But I'm afraid something might happen if any of you come in the clubhouse. We're all tense and excited, you as well as we. So I'd like to play it safe."

Day by day, Cleveland became more baseball crazy. The *Cleveland News* had several important games "covered" by old-time major-league stars, Cy Young, Elmer Smith, and Bill Wambsganss among them. Veeck turned author and "experted" one game. The Press added Tris Speaker to its writing staff. Speaker also was on the payroll of the ball club as a special adviser to outfielders. The *Plain Dealer* assigned three and four men to each game. Radio and television coverage blanketed northern Ohio and parts of Pennsylvania, Ontario, West Virginia, and New York.

Small wonder that three weeks before the end of the season, with the Indians four games off the pace, Rudie Schaffer, the business manager, crawled out from behind a mountain of mail and gasped, "We've got a million orders for World Series tickets already."

The hysteria was tempered sharply on September 13. That was an open date on the schedule, but the Indians and Browns had deadlocked in the second game of a double-header the previous day, and the Browns were held over in Cleveland to play off the tie. Don Black, the man who whipped the whisky bottle, pitched for the Tribe. He hurled two strong innings and in the lower half of the second frame became the fourth batter to step into the box against Bill Kennedy, a former teammate.

Black swung viciously at Kennedy's second pitch and fouled it back into the stands. He staggered slightly as he finished the swing, then walked away from the plate and turned in a small circle in back of Bill Summers, the plate umpire. A weird look was on Don's face. He spoke to Summers.

"My God, Bill, what happened?" he muttered, then sagged to a kneeling position. Summers bent over and asked, "What's wrong, Don?"

"It started—" Don started to explain, then hesitated, "on that last pitch to Pellagrini."

Ed Pellagrini, the Browns' shortstop, had taken a snapping curve ball for a third strike to close out the top half of the second inning. The physical effort expended in that pitch, plus the full-bodied swing at the plate a few minutes later, snapped an aneurysm. Blood flooded Don's brain and spinal chord.

The thirty-one-year-old pitcher was rushed to a hospital. Dr. Edward B. Castle, the Indians' physician, called Dr. Spencer Braden, noted brain specialist, into consultation. Surgery was considered and dismissed. Black's condition was too serious. Would he live?

"He has a fifty-fifty chance," said the doctors. Shades of Ray Chapman!

Black lived, but his career as a ballplayer seemed at an end. Veeck proposed a Don Black Night in the Stadium. The Red Sox were scheduled for one more appearance in Cleveland on September 22. They agreed to play at night when Veeck said he was giving the Cleveland club's share of the receipts to Don.

"I want the biggest crowd possible," Veeck told general manager Joe Cronin of the Red Sox. Joe McCarthy, the Boston club's field manager, wasn't too happy about the shift of the game. He was fighting with the Indians and Yankees for the pennant. One thing was sure about the Cleveland game, McCarthy reasoned correctly. Feller would pitch. McCarthy preferred Feller in daylight.

But he got him at night. Feller was magnificent. The Red Sox didn't get a hit until the sixth. They got only two singles and a double in total. Meanwhile, the veteran Keltner iced the game in the first inning with a tremendous home-run smash off Joe Dobson that sent 76,772 people into a spree of hysterics. The Indians breezed in, 5 to 2, and moved up into an exact tie with the Red Sox for the league lead, each having won ninety-one while losing fifty-five. It was the first time since August 25 that the Indians had been wholly or partly in first place.

Two days later the Indians lost to the Tigers, the Yankees thrashed the Red Sox, and there was a three-way deadlock among the Tribe, Sox, and Yankees. Only seven games remained on each team's schedule. Which one of the three, if any, would crack?

The schedule, said the baseball experts, favored the Indians.

They had their seven games with the injury-stricken Tigers and with the apathetic White Sox. Meanwhile, the Yankees and Red Sox had to play each other in four of their seven games.

Cleveland newspapers printed instructions to purchasers of World Series tickets. Police officials met to discuss handling of crowds and vehicular traffic. Hotel rooms had been booked months earlier. Through all this, Veeck wasn't too busy for gags. A fan with the catchy name of Joe Earley wrote a letter to the *Cleveland Press,* asking facetiously, "Why not a night for good old Joe Earley? They have nights for ballplayers who make much more money than I do."

Veeck gave Joe Earley a night on September 28. What probably would have been an ordinary attraction with the White Sox, good for a peak crowd of thirty-five thousand in the stands, was turned into a circus. Joe Earley and his wife got presents of toys, fowl, furniture, and finally a new automobile. The Indians promptly celebrated with Joe and 60,405 others by plastering the White Sox, 11 to 0, as Gene Bearden turned in a four-hitter for his eighteenth triumph.

Feller beat the Sox again the next day for his nineteenth. Now only three games remained to be played. The Indians were on top, two full games ahead of the deadlocked Yankees and Red Sox, and had only the Tigers to dispose of in Cleveland. One victory would insure a tie for the pennant, two would clinch it.

Cleveland rallied for the one hundredth time in the season. Mayor Thomas A. Burke proclaimed Sunday, October 3—date of the closing of the regular baseball schedule—as Bill Veeck day. The bubbling Veeck already had promised the gate receipts (which came to fifty-five thousand dollars) to the Community Fund for the second year in a row.

The Tigers refused to roll over and play dead, even with stars George Kell and Hoot Evers injured and side-lined for the year. They won the first game, 5 to 3. The Red Sox and Yankees, not scheduled that day, moved up in their tie within one full game of the pace-setting Tribe. Now all the Indians needed was one victory to clinch a tie for the title. Bearden provided that, his nineteenth, the next day with an 8-to-0 conquest of the Bengals. Meanwhile, the Red Sox were beating the Yankees.

Thus, with only one game apiece to play, the Indians held a full one-game edge on the Sox. The Yankees were out of the race, but could tie for second by beating Boston in the year's finale. The Indians were top-heavy favorites to come out on top. Rain in their game or in Boston could end the campaign in their favor. If they beat the Tigers, it didn't matter how the Boston–New York game turned out.

Only one combination of results could tie up the scramble and force the first play-off game in the history of the American League. The four teams upon whom the eyes of the entire nation were focused that Sunday brought about the deadlock.

The battle sites were jammed—32,000 in Fenway Park to watch the Yankees and Red Sox; 74,181 in the stadium in Cleveland. There it was Feller pitching against his old rival, the brilliant southpaw Hal Newhouser. In Boston McCarthy sent Dobson against the Yankees' raw recruit, young Bob Porterfield.

By the fourth inning in Cleveland and by the sixth inning in Boston, the pattern for the finish of the wildest American League race of them all had been traced in base hits and pitching failures. The Tigers rapped Feller hard and chased him in the fifth while assuming a 6-to-0 lead. The Red Sox chastised Porterfield by scoring nine runs in six innings. Not even a valiant performance by the peerless Joe Di Maggio could stop the Red Sox. On they raced and posted a 10-to-5 final score. Meanwhile, the Indians couldn't break through Newhouser with any sustained success, and Hal pitched his twenty-first victory of the year, 7 to 1.

There would be a play-off the next day in Boston, a site determined by the flip of a coin several days previous when there appeared the possibility not only of a double tie but of a triple deadlock, too.

Cleveland, emotionally weary from cheering, rooting, pleading, praying, hoping, and despairing, fought back its civic jitters and hoped for the best the next day.

As the game with the Tigers had worn on, Lou Boudreau began to think ahead of the current debacle. In the seventh inning, with all hope for the day gone, Boudreau and Gordon were talking as they trotted out from the dugout to their positions around second base.

"Well, it looks as if we'll have to go to Boston tomorrow for a play-off," Lou said.

Gordon agreed.

"What's your idea about our pitcher for that one, Joe?"

Gordon, who had grown through 155 games to be Lou's confidant as well as infield partner, ducked the direct question.

"Who's *your* man, Lou?" Joe parried.

"I was thinking about Bearden."

Gordon looked at his manager sharply. "You just took the words out of my mouth. So was I."

Right then Bearden was warming up in the bull pen, throwing softly. He was "keeping loose" in the event the Indians ever got back into the ball game or got close enough to the Tigers for Boudreau to use one of his best pitchers in a relief role. Lou sent the bat boy to the bull pen. "Tell Bearden to come into the bench and sit down," was Boudreau's message.

In the clubhouse after the game, the Indians were packing for the trip to Boston. Boudreau advanced to the center of the room.

"I've just been talking over our pitching setup for tomorrow with the coaches," he said. "We've decided on Bearden. Now, get this straight. That's only our opinion. It's not definite. We're all in this thing together. It's your money as well as mine. If you have any ideas of your own, speak up."

There was a spell of silence, broken by Gordon. The veteran second baseman had taken the place of Mel Harder as the players' representative.

"We've gone along with you for the season, Lou," Joe said. "That's been good enough for me. I think we'd be crazy not to go along with you for this big one."

Boudreau searched the faces of the others. Heads nodded.

"Then it'll be Bearden," Lou ordered. "But let's not talk about it. Let's not tell anyone who our pitcher will be. I don't want him bothered by people, and it's better this way for a number of reasons."

Speculation as to the identity of the play-off game pitcher

was widespread. Nearly everybody except Bearden was considered. The good-looking left-hander with the tantalizing knuckler and the Hollywood profile had pitched nine scoreless innings against the Tigers twenty-four hours before. Feller might come right back. Lemon had had two days of rest. Zoldak, Gromek, Paige—which would it be?

Ed McAuley of the *Cleveland News* either found out or guessed right. His story the next noon said Bearden would pitch, that the players had picked him during a team meeting. McAuley had the basic facts correct.

Half an hour before the start of the extra game, the choice of Cleveland's pitcher remained a mystery, even if not exactly a secret. Feller was eliminated. Lemon remained in the clubhouse later than the others. "It's Lemon sure," ran the gossip among reporters.

Meanwhile, Bearden was sitting atop the concrete wall next to the visiting team's dugout at third base. He might have been just a guy stopping in for a workout, judging from the interest he showed in the proceedings. He smiled when spoken to but gave no hint of his assignment.

Then he began to warm up and reporters dashed for their special leased wires to bulletin the stunning news. "It's Bearden!"

Equally surprising was McCarthy's choice of the veteran Denny Galehouse. Yet Marse Joe had sound reasoning in the background. In a game in Cleveland, Galehouse had choked off the wild Indians in the first inning after going in as a relief hurler. In the ensuing eight and two-third innings, the thirty-seven-year-old native Ohioan had restricted the Indians to only two hits.

Bearden was shaky at the barrier. He gave up a run in the first inning on a double and a single. In the second he jammed himself up by walking two men, including Galehouse, and allowing another single. Boudreau minced nervously at his shortstop position. Had he picked the wrong pitcher? Was the strain too much? Was Bearden's stomach failing him in this crucial hour?

Lou could have saved himself all that worry. After the second inning, the lean lefty with the whipping throw gave the Sox only two more hits. And a gathering of 33,957 moaned as Boudreau personally took over the mechanics of winning a pennant for himself and his pals.

In the first inning, the Boy Manager belted a home run over the left-field wall. In the fourth, after Lou and Gordon singled, Keltner rammed his thirty-first round-tripper of the year over the barrier. Boudreau poled another in the fifth, his eighteenth of the campaign. In the ninth, Lou rapped his fourth hit of the game, a single, and set up the scoring of the day's final run.

The result had been determined long before. The final score of 8 to 3 was basic arithmetic. Bearden had come through; Boudreau had been wonderful.

And Cleveland's Indians, ridiculed and romped over for twenty-eight years, were the American League's new champions!

Boudreau rushed toward Gordon, wrapped both arms around Joe. The Indians stormed from the dugout, picked up Bearden, and carried him off the field. In Cleveland, thousands poured out of offices and stores and celebrated in the streets. Business was suspended. Those rampant Redskins had done it.

As the Indians surged toward the runway leading to the dressing rooms on the first-base side of Fenway Park, a sport-jacketed, tieless young giant hobbled across the field. Bill Veeck and Hank Greenberg had been sitting in a box in back of third base. Over the infield hurried Veeck, half-dragging his artificial right leg. There was no pain there now, no memories of three trips to surgery in two years, no memory of those nights of aches and miseries in hospitals. Veeck tried to reach Boudreau before the manager started into the tunnel. He never quite made it. Lou was pushed forward by his back-pounding players. Bill had to delay his handshaking until the shouting Indians were locked in their clubhouse.

Half an hour later, the noise had abated sufficiently to permit Boudreau to address his squad.

"All rules off tonight...party at the hotel," Lou shouted. "Practice at Braves' Field tomorrow."

Boudreau turned to Veeck. "Anything you would like to say, Bill?" grinned Lou.

Bill shook his fuzz-topped head. "Just thanks, that's all."

UTOPIA

NOT SINCE THE HEYDAY of the great Yankee teams had an American League entry been such a favorite going into a World Series as were Boudreau's battle-weary Indians. Whatever leanings even the stanchest followers of the Braves had toward the National League representative were obliterated in Brooklyn four days before the close of the championship season.

The Braves had clinched the pennant, mainly on the stout pitching of Johnny Sain, the aggressive play of a rookie shortstop, Alvin Dark, the timely batting of Tommy Holmes, and the slugging of the one-time Tribe problem child, Jeff Heath, and of Bob Elliott. But Heath, sliding into the plate at Ebbets Field, had caught his spikes and fractured an ankle. The Braves' stock against whichever team won the American League's torrid race went down kerplunk.

The Indians were tired, to be sure, but they were still moving speedily on the momentum supplied by the wild finish of their own campaign. Then, too, a run down of their pitching and batting achievements made them all the more formidable.

Boudreau batted .355 to finish second to Ted Williams in the individual race. Mitchell compiled a fancy .336 average, while the rookie Doby, only a year and a half out of semipro ranks, surged over the .300 mark in the last few days to wind up with .301. Keltner just missed the charmed circle with .297.

The Tribe had power to burn. Gordon batted in 124 runs and added 32 home runs. Keltner drove in 119 and hit 31 circuit smashes. Boudreau batted in 106 runs and contributed 18 homers. Robinson had 16 home runs and 83 runs batted in. The regular infielders batted across 432 runs! Allie Clark, scourge of left-handed pitchers, stroked .310. Jim Hegan batted only .248 but caught 144 games and was far and away the best all-around backstop in his league.

There were two twenty-game pitchers, Bearden and Lemon. The great Feller had been stopped at nineteen, but he had come through at the right times. The Braves had no three pitchers to match the Cleveland trio.

"Power will win for the Indians," ran almost every prediction on the World Series.

Yet seldom has there been a World Series with less power revealed or with less animation by the players. The Indians were tired at the outset. After their triumph in the league race, anything else must be anticlimactic.

The tone of the Series was established in the first game when Feller tangled with Sain, the Braves' twenty-four-game star. They dueled in brilliance through seven innings. Feller did not allow a hit until the fifth and not another until the eighth. Sain gave up singles to Doby, Gordon, Keltner, and Hegan.

Neither team had had a runner as far as third base in the seven innings. Feller wavered at the start of the eighth and walked Bill Salkeld. Phil Masi ran for his fellow catcher. Mike McCormick's sacrifice moved Masi to second. Eddie Stanky was passed intentionally.

The stage was set for the most controversial play of the Series and one that will be discussed for generations. Ever since Boudreau had managed the Indians, he and Feller had collaborated on a pick-off play at second base. The throw is based on a count by the pitcher and the fielder that is started on a prearranged signal. The best base runners in the business had been trapped off second and retired on Bob's precisely timed throws.

Masi wandered off the cushion. Boudreau sneaked behind him and dashed for second. Feller wheeled and threw. Masi, startled, flung himself headlong at the bag. Boudreau tagged him on the shoulder.

Bill Stewart of the National League, umpiring at second base, flattened his palms over the ground. "Safe," he ruled. Boudreau charged him, yelling and objecting. Feller and Gordon joined in the complaining. The jockeys on the Cleveland bench went to work on Stewart. But Masi remained safe, naturally.

Feller retired Sain, but Holmes slapped a sizzling ground single into left, and Masi raced over the plate with the only run of the game. Feller's two-hit masterpiece had been wasted, and 40,135 Bostonians went away in high glee.

Lemon squared the Series the next day with a 4-to-1 victory before 39,633. Bob bobbed and weaved a little in the first inning but settled down to scatter the Braves' remaining six hits one to an inning. Manager Billy Southworth of the Braves nominated his ace southpaw, Warren Spahn, but the Redskins ran him off the hill in the fifth. Boudreau and Doby, each with a double and single, were the big guns in the Cleveland attack. A sensational double play by Boudreau and Gordon lifted the game above the routine.

In the first two games, no murderous clouting had been registered. But those who had predicted that the Tribe's power would decide the Series took new hope as the teams entrained for Cleveland and the next three games. The players of both teams were overjoyed in their pocketbooks. No matter how the Series ended, their individual shares of receipts would be close to record size.

There were many ticket snafus before the opener in Cleveland's sprawling stadium, and instead of a jam-packed park, the third game was started before only 70,306 customers. Rested three days since his sensational victory in the play-off classic, Bearden was in rare form as he floated his knuckler through the stiff breeze blowing off Lake Erie. Gene gave up five hits, two of which were followed by double plays. The Indians could get only five hits, two by Bearden himself. Gene doubled in the third and scored on an error. In the fourth, a walk and singles by Robinson and Hegan made the score 2 to 0, and there it remained.

Boudreau came up with a surprise starter in the fourth game. Steve Gromek, sidearming right-hander, had shown flashes of his old skill late in the season and Lou rewarded him with a World Series assignment before 81,897. For the second time, Southworth's pitcher was Sain, and for the second time Sain pitched beautifully. But this time he was not so fortunate as he was in Boston.

Mitchell's single and Boudreau's double netted a run in the first. In the third, Doby peeled off the first home run of the Series, a smash over the fence in right center. With those runs, Gromek outlasted Sain in a 2-to-1 game that was one of the best pitched and best played of the entire set.

Cleveland was running its highest baseball fever of a hectic season. The Indians were leading in the series, three games to one. It could all be over Sunday, October 10. Feller would try again. Lemon, Bearden, and Gromek had won World Series games. The king of the moderns, Feller, was due for his just reward.

The largest mass of humanity in the history of the game descended on the stadium. Close to eight thousand stood behind the outfield fence. Others stood in the stands or squatted on steps. The official count was 86,288!

Ironically, the biggest crowd saw the worst ball game. Obviously far off form, Feller lasted until the seventh. He managed to maintain a 5-5 tie until then, mainly because Nelson Potter, the Boston starter, had been chased in the fourth by Hegan's home run with two on. Mitchell had tagged Potter for a homer on the game's second pitch.

The Braves decided in the seventh to manhandle Feller and whoever followed him. Elliott had slammed two homers off Feller earlier. In a wild inning high-lighted by five singles, two walks, one error, and a balk by Satchel Paige, the fourth Cleveland pitcher of the day, the Braves scored six times, sewed up an 11-to-5 crushing conquest, and sent the Series back to Boston for conclusion.

The sixth and final game was the best of the entire Series. Lemon started after his second triumph and outpitched Voiselle for seven innings while 40,103 loyal New Englanders groaned. Mitchell and Boudreau doubled for one run in the third inning, but the Braves came back, with the equalizer in the fourth on Elliott's single, a walk, and Mike McCormick's single. Gordon opened the sixth with a home run, a mighty drive over the left-field fence. Then a walk, Robinson's single, and an infield out produced one more run. In the eighth, after Spahn had replaced

Voiselle, the Tribe increased the lead to 4-1 on successive singles by Keltner, Tucker, and Robinson.

The World Series seemed to be all over right then, but the Braves promptly showed they were still in the ball game. Holmes singled. Torgeson scored him with a solid double to right. Lemon, unnerved, walked Elliott. Boudreau trotted to the pitching rubber, took the ball from Lemon, and signaled to the bull pen. In strolled the long, lean left-hander, Bearden, hero of many Boston incidents. But this wasn't the terrifying Bearden of before. Clint Conatser greeted Gene with a liner that rattled the glove of Tucker in center. Masi doubled, and Boudreau's jitters tripled. But Bearden himself tossed out the next batter and the pay-off battle moved into the ninth with the Tribe guarding a 4-to-3 lead.

Bearden walked the first Brave, Stanky, and Connie Ryan ran for him. Then Sibi Sisti, batting for Spahn, attempted to sacrifice. He popped a fifteen-footer in front of the plate. Hegan made a spectacular grab of the ball and then doubled the astonished Ryan off first base.

The Series was over; Cleveland had won!

But Bearden wasn't carried off the field this time. It had been a drab, wearisome World Series. The Indians had fought their big battles in the American League. These fusses with the National League were almost boring except for the money. The Indians collected 6,772 dollars each, a record pay-off, while the losing Braves were rewarded with 4,651 dollars apiece, a little under the highest previous total for a loser's share.

HEROES ALL

CLEVELAND MADE PLANS TO worship at the spikes of its heroes, the all-conquering Indians. Immediately after the decisive game in Boston, the new World Champions boarded their special train for the return to their home base.

On the train, where fizzing and bubbling liquids drowned out the metalic clicking of the wheels, the Indians and many of their wives were in the dining car.

Joe Gordon, the team's titleless leader, called for quiet. He raised his glass and fixed his eyes on Boudreau.

"To the greatest leatherman I ever saw, to the damndest clutch hitter that ever lived, to a doggone good manager, Lou."

The Indians drank. A young, grinning guy at the far end of the diner lifted his glass, too, and there was a glaze of tears over his eyes.

Bill Veeck, 34, had hit the jackpot so early in life.

The city of Cleveland was prepared for the arrival of its heroes that next morning. Shortly after dawn, multitudes assembled the length of Euclid Avenue, the city's chief business artery. Thousands forced their way into the Union Terminal.

The Indians walked through police-guarded lanes of humanity to the street levels. There they climbed into top-down convertibles. The morning was warm, the sun bright. School officials had not dismissed classes officially.

"If you want to go downtown to see the Indians come home, you will not be marked absent," teachers were instructed to say.

How many people cheered, applauded, slapped, touched, and idolized the Indians on a five-mile, slow-motion cruise from Public Square to University Circle never will be known. Police guesses were a minimum of three hundred thousand. Never in the city's history had a returning hero or band of heroes, home from war or conquest, ever received such a welcome.

"I never knew the real Cleveland until today," gasped Bill Veeck. "This is impossible to believe."

Of all the men who wanted to sit in on a World Series, Harry Grabiner possessed the strongest urge. He was not only vice-president of the Indians. He was their most rabid fan. Too rabid. As the Tribe made its pennant bid late in the summer, Grabiner collapsed. He was removed to his summer home in Michigan.

Two weeks after the World Series was over, Grabiner died. The small, intense executive who lived and suffered with each pop fly and each simple grounder through forty-five years in baseball did not get to share in the power and the glory.

Grabiner played a major role in setting up the organization that astounded the world in 1948. The Indians broke all records for attendances. They drew 2,620,627 fans at home and established new world records for largest crowds at a single, doubleheader, night game, opening-day game, and for the season.

They contributed the American League's Most Valuable Player, Boudreau; the major leagues' executive of the year, Veeck; one of the rookies of the year, Bearden; the pitcher of the year, Lemon; and, probably, the sensation of the year, Satchel Paige.

Veeck was not only the top executive in baseball; he was also the busiest at the major leagues' meetings in December of 1948. Most operators of world champions have been content to sit tight with their teams. Not Veeck. He sold Muncrief to the Pirates and engineered a series of trades with the White Sox that transferred catcher Joe Tipton and pitchers Bob Kuzava and Ernie Groth for pitchers Joe Haynes and Frank Papish.

He swapped Robinson, Klieman, and Haynes to the Washington Senators for first baseman Mickey Vernon and pitcher Early Wynn. Within a few weeks after Steve O'Neill had been fired as manager of the Detroit Tigers, Veeck added the rotund Irishman to the Cleveland coaching staff. He moved up Muddy

Ruel to a farm system executive post to make room for O'Neill.

Professional baseball in Cleveland was introduced in 1869, according to the initial pages of this book. But the average Ohioan will argue that baseball in Cleveland started in 1946 when the common people's beloved burr head—William Louis Veeck, Jr.—arrived.

It may have started earlier, but it never really got going good until then.

INDEX

by Robert M. Boynton of the Society of American Baseball Research

Boudreau, Lou, 204, 207, 215–16, 220 (photo opposite), 226–28, 236–37, 242–44, 246, 249–53, 254–68; appointed manager, 218–20; biographical information, 220–22; debut, 205; exempt from military service, 223; fielding saves no-hitter for Feller, 229–30; lectures team about Doby, 247; most valuable player, 275; and players, 225; "Williams shift," 240; wins 1944 batting championship, 225

Bradley, Alva, 149 (photo opposite), 153–56, 158–61, 167, 175, 179, 182, 203, 208, 217, 219–20; Allen torn shirt incident, 188–89; bans 1933 radio broadcasts, 174; "cry babies" incident, 210; Feller "cover-up" case, 196; financial difficulties, 177, 230; fires O'Neill, hires Vitt, 199–200; fires Vitt, rehires Peckinpaugh, 214; introduces Boudreau as new manager, 218; retires from baseball, 235; sale of Indians, 233–34; threatens to sue Evans, 197

Bradley, Bill, 36, 39, 43, 45, 48, 53, 59–60, 62, 69

Bradley, Charles "Chuck," 153, 155–56

Brenzel, Bill, 181

Broca, Johnny, 203, 207, 217

Brooklyn Dodgers, 120–34

Brotherhood, 21, 25

Brown, Clint, 161, 165, 180–81

Brown, Lloyd, 180–81

Buckeye, Garland, 138, 142, 143, 161

Burkett, Jesse, 27, 29

Burnett, Johnny, 164, 171

Burns, George, 107–8, 124–25, 135, 139, 142, 161

Burns, John, 78

Bush, Donnie, 168

Cadore, Leon, 128

Caldwell, Ray "Slim,"103–4, 105, 107–8, 110, 115, 122, 130; 1920 World Series loss, 126–27; drinking regimen, 104–6;

Campbell, Bruce, 180, 181, 183, 184, 192, 207

Campbell, Clarence "Soup," 215

Carrigan, Bill, 82, 83

Case, George Washington, 245

Castle, Dr. Edward B., 263

Chadwick, Henry, 11

Chapman, Ben, 203, 207

Chapman, Ray, 72, 84 (photo opposite), 90, 92, 99, 107; fatal beaning by Carl Mays, 110–12; posthumous World Series share, 136

Chase, Hal, 118

Chicago "Black" Sox, 108, 117–19, 137

Christopher, Russ, 255

Cicell, Chalmers "Bill," 169–70

Cicotte, Eddie, 117, 119

Clapp, J. E., 15

Clark, Allie, 251

Clarke, Justin "Nig," 49, 57

Clarkson, John G., 27, 28

Cleveland ballparks: Brookside Park, 74; Case Commons, 4; Kennard (E. 46th) at Cedar, 13; Payne and 39th Ballpark, 17; Willson and Garden Streets, 8. *See also* Cleveland Stadium; League Park

Cleveland baseball teams (first mentioned): Blues (Bluebirds), 35; Bronchos, 39; Forest Cities, 2; Indians, 75; Napoleons (Naps), 43; Spiders, 19

Cleveland newspapers, 181, 262; *Leader,* 13, 27; *News,* 56, 79, 83, 199, 234, 262, 267; *Plain Dealer,* 30, 39, 61, 79, 157, 210, 214, 223, 262; *Press,* 24, 36–37, 43–44, 52, 65, 91, 111, 117, 157, 178, 208, 214, 230, 234, 250

Cleveland Stadium, 166–73; center field background, 194; construc-